Social Fabric

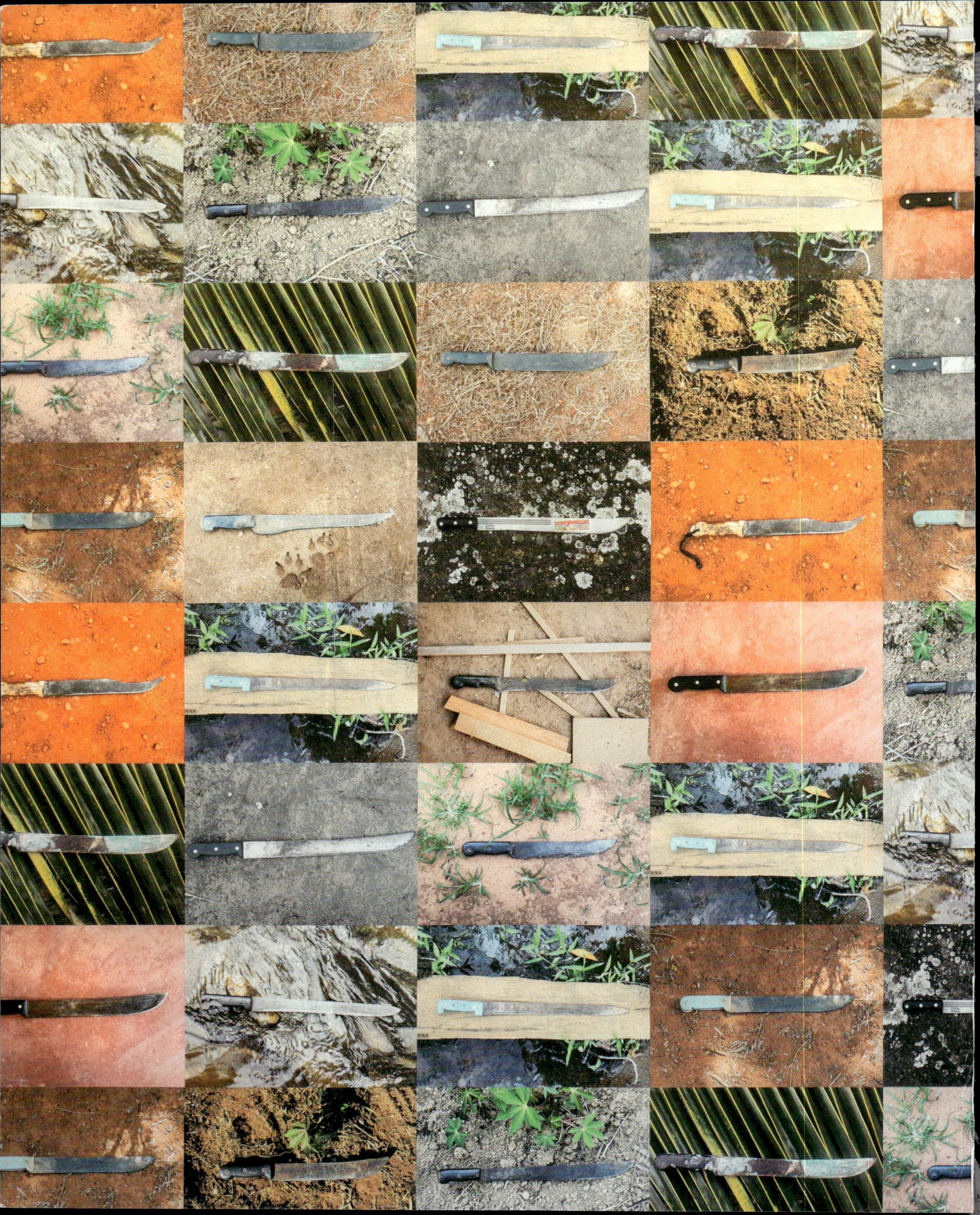

Social Fabric

Art and Activism in Contemporary Brazil

Edited by Maria Emilia Fernandez,
Adele Nelson, and MacKenzie Stevens

Visual Arts Center | The University of Texas at Austin

Distributed by Tower Books, an Imprint of the University of Texas Press

Published on the occasion of the exhibition *Social Fabric: Art and Activism in Contemporary Brazil*, organized by the Visual Arts Center at the University of Texas at Austin, September 23, 2022–March 10, 2023. Curated by Adele Nelson, Associate Professor of Art History, UT Austin, and MacKenzie Stevens, Director and Curator, Visual Arts Center, with Maria Emilia Fernandez, Assistant Curator, Visual Arts Center.

A complete Portuguese translation of this catalogue is available as a free ebook online: https://utvac.org.

Visual Arts Center
The University of Texas at Austin
2300 Trinity Street
Austin, TX 78712

Printed in Canada
First edition, 2023

Distributed by Tower Books, an imprint of the University of Texas Press

The paper used in this book meets the minimum requirements of ANSI/NISO Z39.48-1992 (R1997) (Permanence of Paper).

Cataloging in Publication Data is available from the Library of Congress
ISBN: 978-1-4773-2846-0 (paperback)
ISBN: 978-1-4773-2853-8 (PDF e-book)
LCCN: 2023942851

Cover image: Rosana Paulino, *Tecido social* (Social Fabric), 2010 (detail). Monotype and sewn thread on fabric. 90 9/16 × 114 15/16 in. (230 × 292 cm.). Courtesy of Mendes Wood DM, São Paulo, Brussels, New York.

Frontispiece: Sallisa Rosa, *Resistência* (Resistance), 2017–present (detail). Inkjet prints on paper, wheat paste. Dimensions variable. Courtesy of the artist.

Packaged by Motto Publishing Services

Designed by M. Wright

Contents

vii Preface: Brazilian Art at the Visual Arts Center | *MacKenzie Stevens*

1 **Introduction** | *Adele Nelson and MacKenzie Stevens*

Artist Interviews

7 Stitching Memory: Interview with Rosana Paulino | *Lorraine Leu*

11 Quotidian Transmutations: Interview with Castiel Vitorino Brasileiro | *Maria Emilia Fernandez*

17 Listening to the Collective Voice: Interview with Aline Motta | *Maria Emilia Fernandez*

23 **Plates**

Artist Texts

68 Carta aos indígenas do planeta Marte com códigos de reconhecimento do planeta Terra / Letter to the Indigenous Peoples of Planet Mars with Recognition Codes from Planet Earth | *Denilson Baniwa*

74 Jupiter is Here. Celestial is Everything. | *Castiel Vitorino Brasileiro*

78 Fundamento / Foundation | *Maré de Matos*

81 **Installation Views**

Artist Entries

105 Denilson Baniwa | *Thiago Ferreira*

107 Castiel Vitorino Brasileiro | *Maysa Martins*

109 Guerreiro do Divino Amor | *Jana La Brasca*

112 Jaime Lauriano | *Lucy Quezada*

115 Maré de Matos | *Chasitie Brown*

117 Aline Motta | *Jennifer Sales*

120 Lais Myrrha | *Pilar Dirickson Garrett*

122 Antonio Obá | *Thiago Ferreira*

125 Rosana Paulino | *Martha Scott Burton*

130 Sallisa Rosa | *Eva Caston*

On Exhibitions and Pedagogy

133 Memories, Histories, and Fictions: The Sociogram as Method | *Catalina Cherñavvsky Sequeira*

137 Citation, Translation, and Representation: US Exhibitions of Brazilian Art | *Adele Nelson*

141 Artist Biographies

145 Contributors

148 Exhibition Checklist

155 Acknowledgments

159 Credits

Preface
Brazilian Art at the Visual Arts Center

MacKenzie Stevens

Since the Visual Arts Center (VAC) at the University of Texas at Austin opened a little over a decade ago in 2010, we have centered artists. This act of centering has taken many forms over the last thirteen years—from installations to performances, from exhibitions to artist residencies, publications, and other forms of creative production. The VAC's programs benefit from our connection to the Department of Art and Art History in the College of Fine Arts, and we have flourished because of the community of artist practitioners, scholars, and educators who have helped us cultivate an environment of learning, dialogue, critical inquiry, and experimentation through creative expression. The VAC has built a reputation for engaging in interdisciplinary exchange, fostering programming that draws from a range of fields and disciplines. This commitment to interdisciplinary work was essential to the realization of *Social Fabric: Art and Activism in Contemporary Brazil*, which benefited from the collaboration of scholars and artists working across disciplines and media within the sphere of UT Austin and at institutions across the United States, Brazil, and Europe. It was an honor to be part of the curatorial team for this exhibition, and I am indebted to the incredible tenacity and passion of Adele Nelson (associate professor of art history and associate director of the Center for Latin American Visual Studies) and Maria Emilia Fernandez (assistant curator, Visual Arts Center). This exhibition truly exemplifies the VAC's mission: to provide a platform for artists to experiment, take risks, and spark dialogue for social change.

Social Fabric began with an idea forwarded by Adele Nelson and Sônia Roncador (associate professor of Portuguese studies) in 2019 to showcase Brazilian special collections from the world-renowned Benson Latin American Collection alongside works by contemporary Brazilian artists in the VAC. This proposition expanded into an extensive multiyear collaborative project foregrounding contemporary art in Brazil, with a specific focus on the intersection of art and activism.

How are artists reflecting on and responding to the far-right turn we have been experiencing on a global scale, and what forms do these responses take? These questions motivated and informed the curatorial framework for *Social Fabric*, and the answers are as varied as the communities who live in the territory now known as Brazil. Incorporating a range of media, from large-scale sculptural installations to intimate watercolor paintings, from photographs to video, *Social Fabric* aimed to illuminate the heterogeneity of activist art in Brazil while also demonstrating a shared concern—how the country's colonial past shapes the present. Over a three-year research period—the bulk of which took place during the COVID-19 pandemic—the exhibition grew into an expansive show, featuring sixty-seven artworks by ten artists and occupying more than half of the VAC's galleries. The role of activism in visual art has garnered much attention across disciplines, and the artists in *Social Fabric* contribute to these conversations, questioning the forms activist art can take.

This catalogue furthers the discussions sparked by Denilson Baniwa, Castiel Vitorino Brasileiro, Guerreiro do Divino Amor, Jaime Lauriano, Maré de Matos, Aline Motta, Lais Myrrha, Antonio Obá, Rosana Paulino, and Sallisa Rosa in the VAC's galleries, foregrounding their shared critique of the narratives and histories once considered (and perhaps still considered, by some) to be foundational to Brazilian identity and to the social fabric of Brazilian society. Through artist interviews, artist-produced texts, and essays on each artist, these nationalized histories and narratives are revivified and disassembled, the spatial construction of memory and the possibility of recovery is tested, and the formation and fluidity of identity is addressed.

Social Fabric came to fruition through the guidance, expertise, and participation of many people. Colleagues at other universities and arts institutions within the United States, Brazil, and Europe lent their ideas, their time, and their expertise. Students from UT Austin played a fundamental role in the exhibition's development, and their involvement was catalyzed during three of Nelson's graduate seminars in art history. A number of these students also contributed entries and texts to this catalogue. Likewise, the staff in the Department of Art and Art History and the incredible team of art preparators who work with the VAC were an invaluable part of the process of planning the exhibition, lending their exceptional skills and insights to the realization of complex commissions. The VAC is proud to have organized this exhibition and to publish this catalogue distributed by our colleagues at Tower Books. A complete Portuguese translation will be published and made available as a free ebook on the VAC's website.

Introduction

Adele Nelson and MacKenzie Stevens

As Brazilian artist Denilson Baniwa tells us, "Every territory is invention."[1] So how does a nation demonstrate what defines it: who are its citizens, what are its histories and its cultures, what does it believe in? *Social Fabric: Art and Activism in Contemporary Brazil* explores these questions, interrogating the "social fabric" of Brazil through the work of ten contemporary artists. Assembling works made over two decades, from 2003 to 2022, *Social Fabric* asks us to consider what makes a society and how this is articulated through visual culture. Blurring the line between art and activism and spanning drawing, installation, painting, performance, photography, printmaking, sculpture, textiles, and video, the works included contribute to both local and global conversations about the state of democracy, racial injustice, and the violence inflicted by the nation-state. The artists compel us to question how the agendas and policies of those in power are visually articulated in public space and inscribed in official narratives. They encourage us to reflect on the function of art as a platform for critical engagement with the historical, political, and cultural configurations of a particular place.

Activism is understood as vigorous, direct action in support of a political cause, and many discussions of art and activism focus on physically activated, participatory works. The limits of such an approach are evident when looking at the work of artist Rosana Paulino, who is a touchstone for the exhibition and many of its artists. Her artistic practice, composed largely of two-dimensional and three-dimensional works conceptually shaped by the iterative and suturing operations of both printmaking and embroidering, forcefully reveals and counters the racist and misogynistic ideological underpinnings of systems of social organization and representation. More useful for understanding Paulino's methods, and those of the other artists included here, is South African photographer Zanele Muholi's articulation of "visual activism." Writing in 2012, Muholi noted the absence of LGBTQIA+ people from mainstream histories of South Africa, stating, "In the face of all the challenges our community encounters daily, I embarked on a journey of visual activism to ensure that there is black queer visibility."[2] Julia Bryan-Wilson, Jennifer González, and Dominic Willsdon highlight the flexibility of Muholi's term and focus on how it offers another mode for understanding the relationship between art and politics beyond an assessment based on effectiveness, describing visual activism as "the abandonment of neutrality."[3]

Social Fabric assembles the work of ten early- to midcareer Brazilian artists—Denilson Baniwa, Castiel Vitorino Brasileiro, Guerreiro do Divino Amor, Jaime Lauriano, Maré de Matos, Aline Motta, Lais Myrrha, Antonio Obá, Rosana Paulino, and Sallisa Rosa—who refuse to remain neutral about the terms of the "social contract" in Brazil, the Americas, and beyond.[4] In so doing, they shed light on myriad forms of gendered and racialized violence and create spaces for community reevaluation and self-construction. The exhibition is not a historical survey but an investigation, combining works by artists, the majority of them Black, Indigenous, LGBTQIA+, and women, who critique the idea of "Brazilianness" as a social construct based on colonial legacies bolstered through state-sanctioned narratives and histories. Care was taken to include a range of works by each artist in order to show the scope of their production. Likewise, visitors encounter works by the same artists throughout the exhibition, allowing for a sort of visual refrain. This open-ended approach foregrounds the variety of strategies of the artists featured here while advancing new ways of interpreting their work through particular pairings and groupings.

Artistic networks of exchange and intergenerational dialogues, thematic congruencies, and explorations in varied media informed the placement of works in the galleries. Works are juxtaposed and grouped into clusters in an effort to illuminate connections between artists. Paulino's *Atlântico vermelho* (Red Atlantic, 2017), for example, was positioned in proximity to works by Lauriano and Baniwa that address the exploitation of land, people, and resources, visualizing these histories in maps and historical documentation. Together, they form a poignant and powerful critique of systems of oppression and the legitimization of extractivism by the nation-state. The earliest works in the exhibition, *Tecelãs* (Weavers, 2003) by Paulino and *Bestiário* (Bestiary, 2005) by Myrrha, suggest the expansiveness of these artists' visual activism, encompassing, on the one hand, an animate and haunting reimagining of female fecundity and self-protection/self-annihilation and, on the other hand, a biting scrutiny of the role of the mainstream media in the rise of fake news. The placement of these works enhances their visual intensity: Paulino's *Tecelãs* is positioned opposite her *Tecido social* (Social Fabric, 2010), a multipanel monotype-printed textile filled with images that address current and long-standing violence and with a repetition that matches the magnitude of the figures in *Tecelãs*. Myrrha's video, presented on a Sony Trinitron monitor, occupies a window box overlooking a busy path on the University of Texas at Austin campus, calling to mind a television in a store display and the role of televised media in the public sphere. The most recent works in the exhibition (from 2021 and 2022) are by Brasileiro, Divino Amor, Matos, Myrrha, Paulino, and Rosa and utilize materials as varied as earth bricks, embroidery, ink, fiber optics, limestone, and watercolor, further amplifying the scope of visualities and histories evoked.

Brasileiro and Divino Amor created works on-site for the exhibition; Brasileiro came to Austin for a research-focused site visit in March 2022, and both were in residence in Austin for four weeks in fall 2022 to produce their projects in collaboration with the Visual Arts Center's preparators. Brasileiro centers Afro-diasporic cosmologies and evokes prehuman planetary histories and celestial realms in *Jupiter is Here. Celestial is Everything.* (2022), which is composed of materials local to Texas, including limestone rocks, mesquite wood, soil, and a large ammonite fossil borrowed from UT Austin's Non-vertebrate Paleontology Laboratory at the Jackson School Museum of Earth History. She resets the historical register to create what she describes as an anticolonial space within the colonial institution of the art gallery, a temporary and contingent site for solace and learning. The work's ephemerality is reinforced by her requirement that the installation's materials be recycled at the exhibition's close. Divino Amor's large red-painted room adjacent to Brasileiro's installation is comprised of videos and light boxes—engrossing, humorous works that mash up high and low culture to reveal the contemporary ubiquity of cultural narratives that mask and buttress white supremacy.

Most of the sixty-seven works in the exhibition were produced in the last decade, during a period of tense political turmoil in Brazil. The rise of far-right political and social movements drove not only the impeachment of Dilma Rousseff, Brazil's first female president, in 2016 and the election of fringe politician Jair Bolsonaro in 2018, but also the attempted censorship and suppression of cultural expression—with institutions, exhibitions, artists, and curators targeted. The nation has also experienced economic and legal upheavals, including massive public protests—notably in June 2013 in response to a proposed increase in public transportation fares—an economic recession, and multiple corruption inquiries. The assassinations of Marielle Franco, a Black gay politician and activist, in 2018 and Paulo Paulino Guajajara, an Indigenous environmental activist, in 2019 fueled further social justice movements. The murder of George Floyd in 2020 in the United States was also a global flashpoint. These events, along with the COVID-19 pandemic, have led to wide-ranging societal debates, reckonings with long histories of injustice, and the recent democratic rejection of Bolsonaro's bid for a second term.

The artists included in this exhibition illuminate Brazil's recent history and its relationship to the past while participating in the resistance to democratic erosion. Above all, they reveal that the social fabric of a nation is an elusive fiction without acknowledgment of the powerful narratives that erase, conceal, and reject the persistence of colonialism.

NOTES

1 Baniwa so titles his series *Todo território é invenção*, including *A Amazônia é uma invenção* (The Amazon Is an Invention, 2019), a pen-and-ink work on paper included in the exhibition (see plate 2).

2 Zanele Muholi, "Faces and Phases," *Transition*, no. 107 (2012): 113.

3 Julia Bryan-Wilson, Jennifer González, and Dominic Willsdon, "Editors' Introduction: Themed Issue on Visual Activism," *Journal of Visual Culture* 15, no. 1 (2016): 8.

4 For a discussion of race in Brazil and the United States, including the social contract and tenets of exclusion and universality within liberal political theory, see Denise Ferreira da Silva, *The Global Idea of Race* (Minneapolis: University of Minnesota Press, 2007), 261–67.

Rosana Paulino, *Assentamento no. 2* (Settlement no. 2), 2012–2013 (detail).

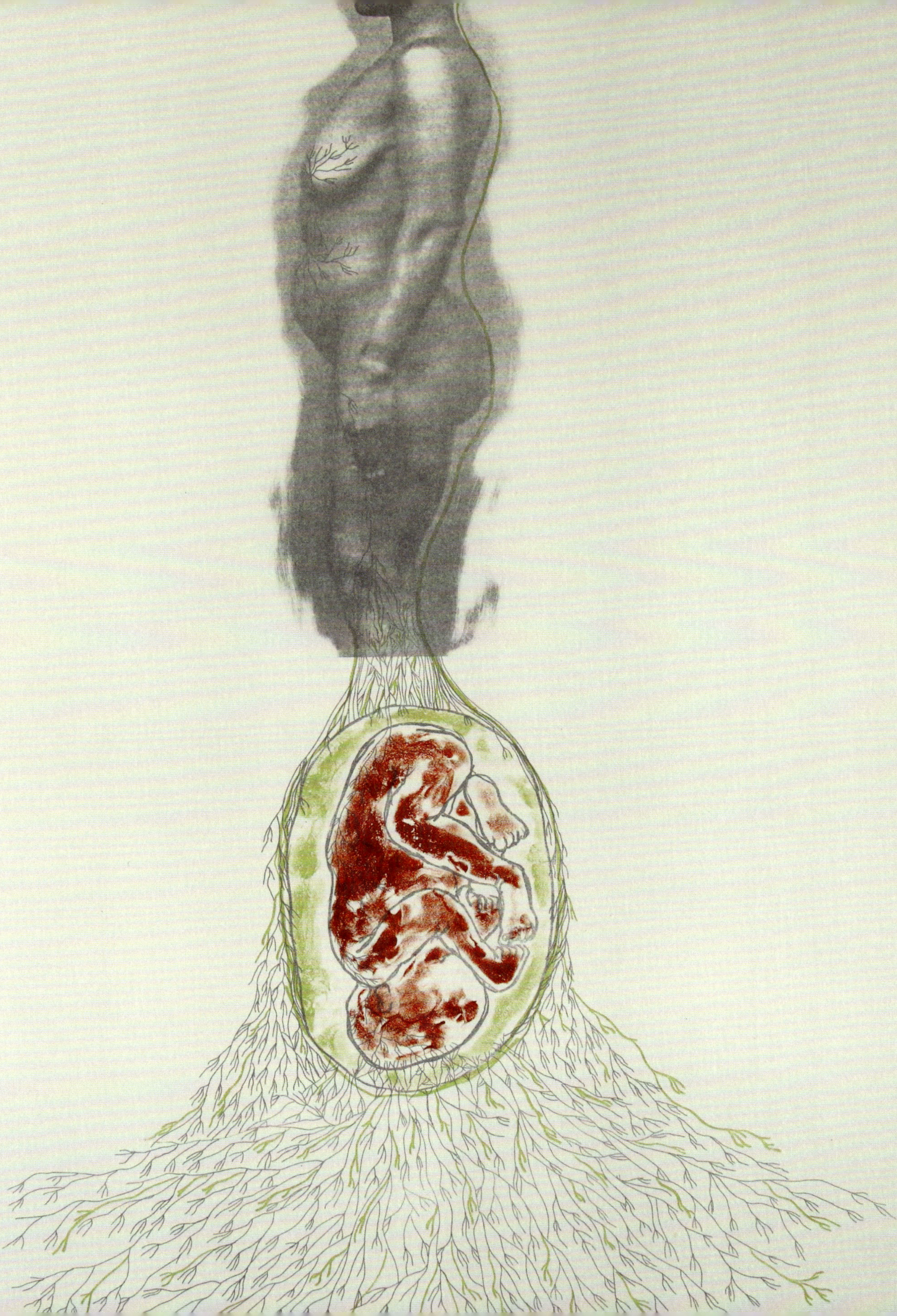

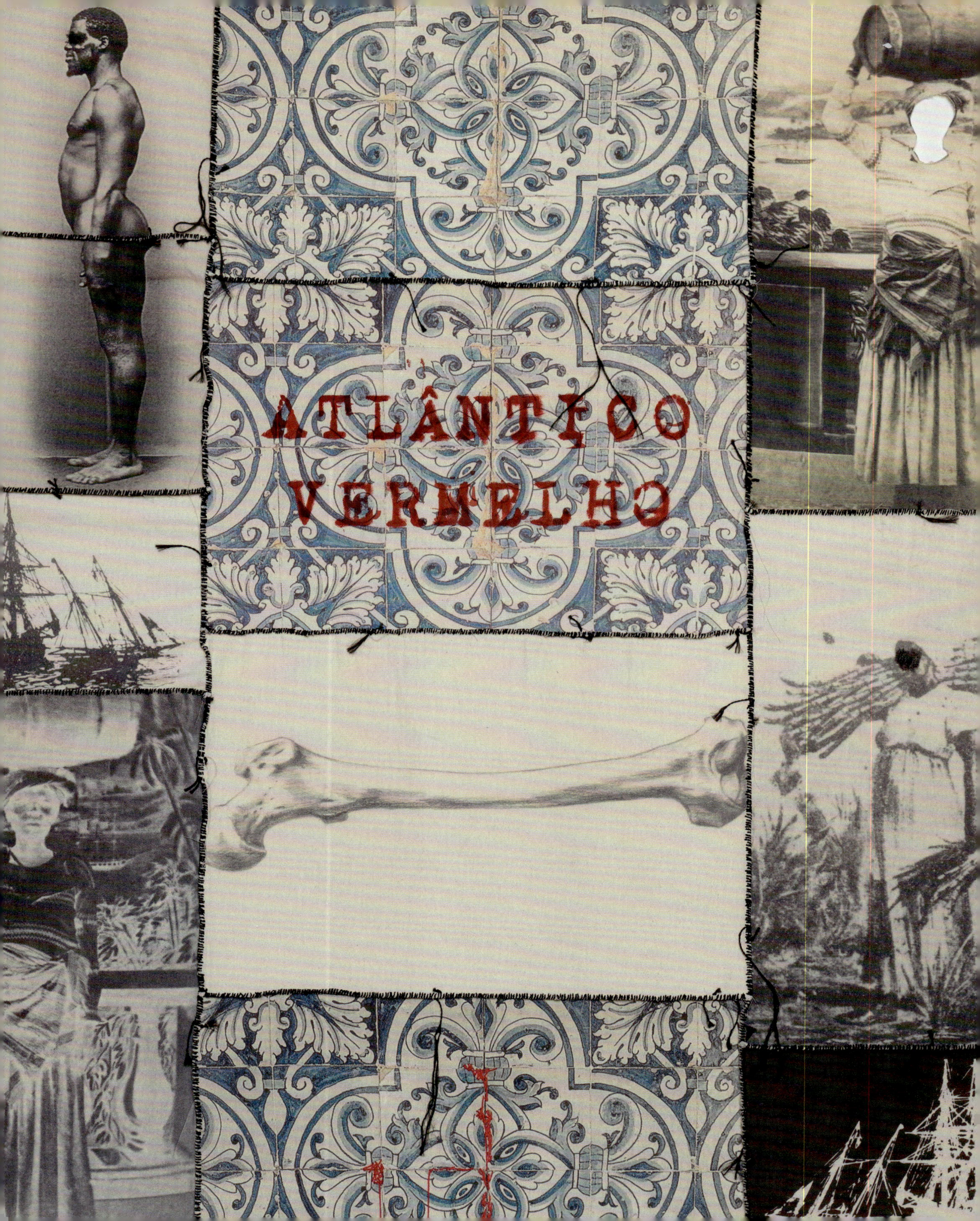
ATLÂNTICO
VERMELHO

Stitching Memory

INTERVIEW WITH ROSANA PAULINO

Lorraine Leu

Interview conducted in Austin, Texas, on February 22, 2020

Lorraine Leu: I am wondering if you could comment on the experience of being a Black woman in contemporary Brazil.

Rosana Paulino: Economic indicators reveal that Black women occupy the bottom of the bottom of the social pyramid in Brazil. Even when we have a high level of education, we continue to be seen as being without aptitude, not capable. And those of mixed race are seen as that woman who is all body, good in bed, hot. When we talk about the Black female psyche, what are the models we turn to? If you delve into psychology, the myths and archetypes are all European. You have Venus, Athena, Demeter. Where does the Black woman fit in? Physically and psychologically we have no mooring. This is the discussion among Black women, Black feminists, because we have no real role models of success, of Black women who reach higher rungs in society; nor do we have physical role models, or the possibility of thinking about the Black psyche. We are adrift.

LL: Brazil is the largest Black diaspora in the world, but what is its role in the diasporic conversation? Because in Brazil there is not merely the legacy of slavery, there is the living presence of slavery. For a long time, you were the only voice in the arts scene researching and talking about that presence in everyday society. I think that Brazil often remains sidelined from that more diasporic conversation.

RP: Yes. Brazil has remained sidelined from the conversation. It is absurd. Brazil has traditionally turned its back on that discussion. But with new and younger artists and art historians on the scene, Brazil is finally positioning itself in the area of visual arts as a major voice, and a particularly important voice, coming as it does from the largest Black population outside of Africa

Rosana Paulino, *Atlântico vermelho* (Red Atlantic), 2017 (detail).

and also because the quality of this new artistic production is garnering attention outside the country—from critics and curators—because it is powerful work. The visual arts [had previously] been dominated by the upper middle class, the elite, elites who have always made a point of not seeing themselves as Brazilian, not seeing themselves as descending from Black people, even when they are.

LL: There was no questioning of the basis of social relations in Brazil, not just in art but in general public discourse.

RP: No, there wasn't. I think the great role that Black artists have played, not just in the visual arts but in dance, theater, and literature, is to revise that history, to challenge and question that history. There was a white, European hegemonic narrative that made use of the story of racial democracy to justify the exclusion of many. That was always the main narrative in Brazil. [Since] about ten or fifteen years ago, this really has been strongly challenged, pushed back on, by Black people in the most diverse cultural areas.

LL: It is such a strong narrative, because it has kept Black people and Afro-descendants "in their place." What will be the impact of this challenge, this frontal attack on that narrative?

RP: I think it will lead to significant protagonism on the part of the Black population, of Black people seeking things they've not had. Of Black people demanding a place at universities, demanding an end to police violence; of the LGBTQI population demanding their rights. In that sense, it is a boiling point. I believe that in the medium to long term—I don't believe that change occurs quickly—those on the periphery of the big cities can see this movement growing among young Black people, among Black women. This change is coming; of that I have no doubt. The problem is what we will have to endure until we manage to change the picture.

LL: What is the role of your art in that movement, in making those demands, in challenging the dehumanization of Black Brazilians that is the basis of police violence and genocide?

RP: All artists whose work engages with the political in this way are always balanced on a knife-edge. While I don't like to see my work as militant, my work comes from inside me and from the unease that I feel in this society. And in that sense, sure, that discomfort is widespread, because other people are also in this situation. I think my work can be a lit fuse, a catalyst, so that people start having conversations that have usually been silenced. I don't like the idea of militant art, because I think of illustrative work like social realism or the so-called heroic works of Nazism, so I will always think of that when I think of art in the service of politics, which mine is not.

LL: It's a personal, intellectual engagement as well?

RP: I'd say personal more than intellectual; it's emotional. This discomfort is so big, the lump in my throat so big, that I have to speak. And obviously, I will express myself through the visual. That is my language—the one I speak with fluency. Those who also identify with that discomfort and feel that pain will be drawn to my work and see themselves there.

NOTE

The interview was conducted during Paulino's visit to the University of Texas at Austin as a keynote speaker at the 2020 Lozano Long Conference, "Black Women's Intellectual Contributions to the Americas: Perspectives from the Global South," held February 20–21, 2020. The conference was a groundbreaking gathering of Black women scholars, activists, intellectuals, and artists from a wide swath of the Americas and the Caribbean. Faculty organizers Lorraine Leu (LLILAS/Spanish and Portuguese) and Christen A. Smith (Anthropology/African and African Diaspora Studies) recorded interviews with Afro-Brazilian keynote speakers Rosana Paulino and Sueli Carneiro. A slightly modified version of the Paulino interview was published in *Portal: Web Magazine of LLILAS Benson Latin American Studies and Collections* on October 28, 2020, with editing and translating from the original Portuguese by Susanna Sharpe. This version is at https://sites.utexas.edu/llilas-benson-magazine/2020/10/28/voices-of-black-brazilian-feminism-conversations-with-rosana-paulino-and-sueli-carneiro/. The full interview, "A função da arte no Brasil contemporâneo: Uma conversa com Rosana Paulino e Lorraine Leu," is available on the Cite Black Woman podcast at https://soundcloud.com/user-211649525.

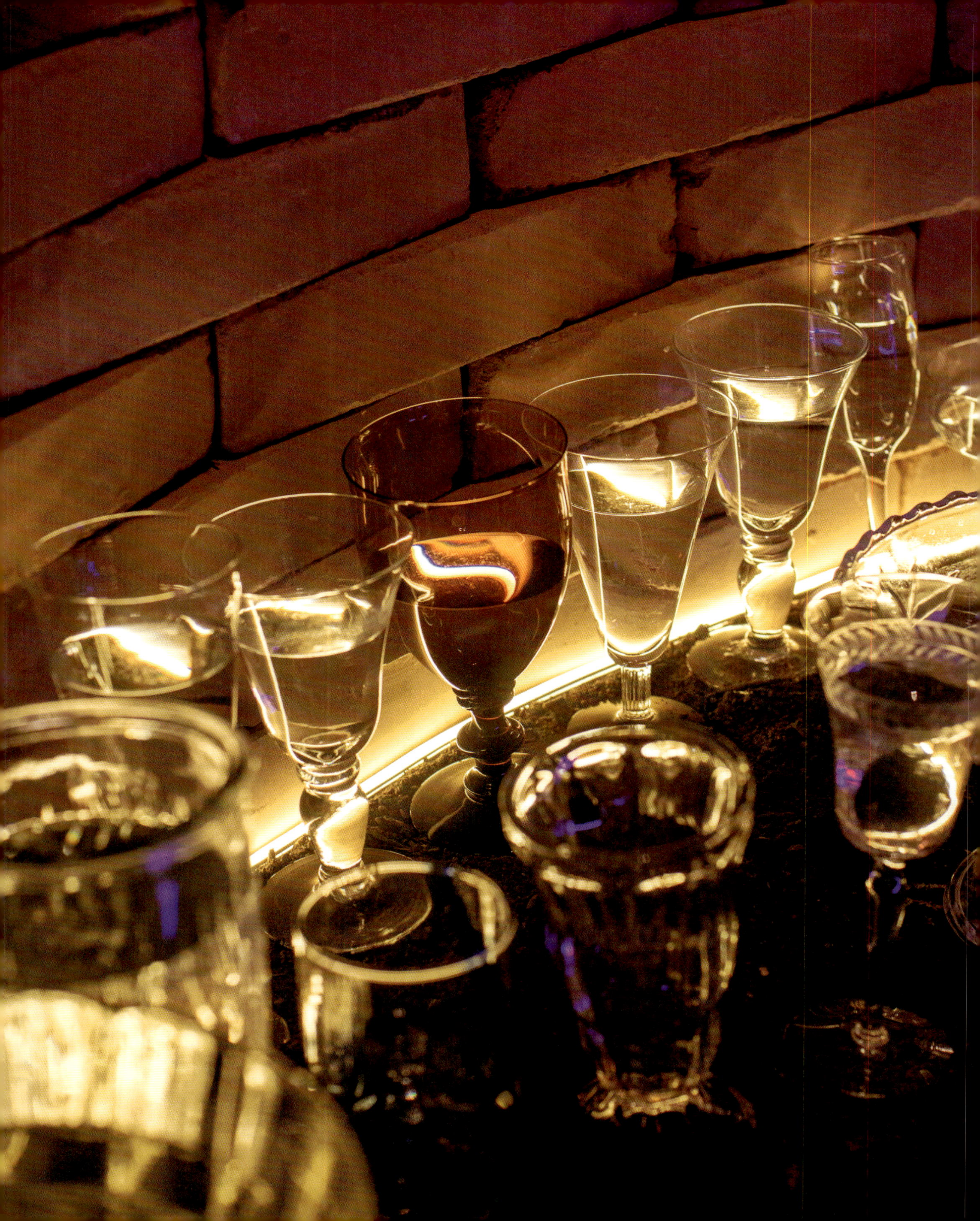

Quotidian Transmutations

INTERVIEW WITH CASTIEL VITORINO BRASILEIRO

Maria Emilia Fernandez

Interview conducted in Austin, Texas, on March 24, 2022

Maria Emilia Fernandez: As a starting point, I would like to quote a statement you made in a previous interview, where you say that "no origin is discovered, all origins are created."[1] Thinking about this notion of origins and your work around healing, I would like to ask how archival research—whether it be a familial archive or a historical archive—in which Black and Indigenous peoples have been silenced or made invisible can become a form of reparation and a way to think about the future?

Castiel Vitorino Brasileiro: The first thing that's important to say is that I consider Brazilianness a trauma. Trauma is Brazilian, and for me, trauma is to have been born in Brazil. Trauma is living together in this nation, so I don't celebrate Brazilianness. Even if there exists a decision—if there has been and continues to be a decision on the part of Black Brazilian movements, especially in the last fifty years—to reclaim the status of the construction of the nation. This is true; it's a fact—we participate in the construction of this nation, but to say that Brazil is Black is not a path I follow.

What I do isn't a formula; it's another path, another direction, because I consider Brazil a giant cemetery. We coexist with murder in every instant—murder brought about by police violence and other contemporary genocides. Epistemological murder and psychic and emotional murder. With this in mind, I abandon the Brazilian idea of death. I relate to the fact of death, with the word "death," and with the experience of dying through other cosmologies, especially those systematized by cultures of Bantu origin.[2] I consider all practices of violence from the point of view of annihilation, and not that of death, because I see a difference between death and annihilation.

Castiel Vitorino Brasileiro, *Jupiter is Here. Celestial is Everything.*, 2022 (detail).

MEF: Death is the death of the body? What's the difference between death and annihilation?

CVB: Annihilation is the colonial control of life. And death is the fact that makes life possible. Death is transfiguration. Trauma is Brazilian, *O trauma é brasileiro*, which was the title of my first exhibition, the trauma of forgetting.[3] When Brazil kills Black people, Indigenous people, it kills in hopes that those lives will cease to exist, and this is also the Brazilian form of miscegenation: you mix, mix until one stops existing; this is the process of whitening.[4] But that's where it gets super complex, because Brazil holds within it three centuries of Africa—the sixteenth, seventeenth, and eighteenth centuries—but at the same time it is stuck in these three centuries. Brazil has a museological relationship with Africa. Brazil doesn't redistribute. It keeps, but it doesn't return. Brazil doesn't know contemporary Africa; it knows the Africa it has decided to believe is real.

MEF: This idea of a museological relationship is very interesting. It means that Brazil also controls the narrative regarding the origins of the country.

CVB: There is a phrase by Beatriz Nascimento that serves as an opening quote in my book: "The history of Brazil is schizophrenic."[5] Schizophrenia is a distortion of reality, but before being a distortion, it's the creation of a reality from delirium. There are many deliriums of Brazil: on the one hand, there are white, Brazilian, Latin American people that desire and live a hierarchy and yearn for a white European and American ascendence; and on the other hand, a fetishization of the African presence in Brazil exists. And, at the same time, Brazil really does possess very important African content and histories. The condition of mixing at the expense of misogyny, hygienism,[6] and racism makes us believe originary deliriums with delirious origins.

It doesn't make sense to me to say that we don't have historiographic materials—yes, we do. Obviously, coloniality exists, and it erased an immense number of documents. It was a great and lamentable loss; that's unquestionable. However, today, I ask myself what do we have, and what are the choices we make—we Black communities—in relation to what we have. I have various critiques of us.

In my city there is a public archive on the same street as my house, so my research is born in great part from that proximity. The state of Espírito Santo is still an Italian and German colony. Italian and German families were brought to Espírito Santo at the beginning of the twentieth century in the postslavery context; they received financial subsidies, land, [and] jobs from the Brazilian government. These families immigrated in the context of quotas created by the government. In 2019, when I visited the Arquivo Público do Estado de Espírito Santo (Public Archive of the State of Espírito Santo) in Vitória, there was a form we had to fill out, something simple but very intense. There was only one question, something like, "What did you come here to study?" There were only two options to answer this question, which speaks to what the institution presumes about your research. One of the two options was "Italian and German immigrations," and the other was "others." What "other" histories are these?

I feel as though I'm at a crossroads because I keep thinking about the institutionalization of memory. I want memory to be stored in the public archive. However, I ask myself how long will I have to wait for memory to be stored in this archive? How long until I am able to venerate it? An origin, it's constructed with memories, isn't it? That's why Brazilian trauma is forgetting. If you forget where you're going, you become hostage to a memory that coloniality will create for you. And this is what my research is about, as I titled my 2020 documentary: *Lembrar daquilo que esqueci* (Remembering What I Forgot).[7] What does coloniality make me forget? That I have another origin that isn't Black; the word *negro* is *necro*. My origin isn't rottenness—it's transmutation.

MEF: Brazilian trauma, as you lucidly identified, is a trauma of forgetting. Is remembering that which you have forgotten a collective process or an individual process? Is it a process that depends on others?

CVB: It's totally collective. My work can't be thought of within identitary limits. If you grab a rock today, you can see time within it. In a little piece of rock, you have an immense notion of thousands of years, so, that's what it's about. That's my life, my existence. It's my ecological process. Memory is ecology—it's not identitary. If I say, "Ah, memories as a Black travesti, as a trans person, as a Black trans woman." These memories are already given. There are no surprises; identity is a formula. Now, if you perceive me as a dark person, as an animal, as a hybrid of animal, mineral, vegetable, or extraterrestrial forces . . . If I describe myself in this Bantu complexity and abandon the modern descriptions of who I am for the fields of psychiatry and anthropology . . . If I describe myself as a terrestrial Being, an earthling, as matter ordained, ordered and controlled by the moon, a life in liberty, a person in transfiguration, a Black trans woman that can feel the moon while they breathe under the sea, everything becomes more complicated.

MEF: Yes, we don't have histories for these existences because they don't fit into a category, into a box.

CVB: Exactly, exactly. I think that's the challenge. I have opted to transfigure or transmute many, many lives, many matters, and I believe that's the challenge against coloniality. That's the challenge that we who live coloniality need to take on. I feel this—the challenge of constructing collective forms of transmuting histories that coexist here. This is a challenge related to the conditions of mixing, but not the mixture of miscegenation. That's what Denise Ferreira da Silva says in her text "On Difference without Separability."[8] How can we live cultural difference without reinforcing a cultural hierarchy? How to circumvent this idea of the Other, how to confront this desire to say to the supposed Other that their life is less than ours? So, that's how I feel Denise's words in me, that's how I use her thoughts in my life.

Transmutation is special, but it's quotidian. The question is not when it begins, but how we manage to sustain it when it occurs. It happens all the time. We breathe, we transmute. Time itself changes constantly. The weather, time passes, so it's transfiguration that characterizes life on planet Earth. When you say, "No, only men and women exist and that's it," this is a way to deal with transmutation, because . . .

MEF: You are not dealing with it.

CVB: Not dealing with it, distancing oneself from it, and separating oneself from transfiguration. That's racialization. There are whites, Blacks, Latinos, Arabs, Jews. We go about creating new racial categories, and those categories are constantly limiting, constraining, making it impossible to deal with people in other ways. That's why I question the issues of identity. I question them because there are other people developing their work about the importance of identitary processes, and they're fundamental to my work, just as my work is fundamental to theirs. But I'm not going to do the work of defending identity. I've done it before, but that moment has passed. I'm not better than anyone; it's not a hierarchy.

MEF: I understand. It's just a path.

CVB: Now I'm forging another path.

NOTES

The interview was conducted in Portuguese and edited for concision and clarity. Sean McPherson translated the interview from Portuguese to English.

1 Rizzia Rocha and Luís Thiago Dantas, "Interview with the artist Castiel Vitorino, author of the work 'Body-Flower,'" *ARTEFILOSOFIA* 15, no. 28 (April 2020): 237.

2 The Bantu peoples are constituted by a large linguistic, historical, and cultural group, and today are located in a vast area across the countries of Central, Eastern, and Southern Africa speaking several hundred Bantu languages. On Bantu cosmologies, see Kimbwandende Kia Bunseki Fu-Kiau, *African Cosmology of the Bântu-Kôngo: Tying the Spiritual Knot, Principles of Life and Living* (Brooklyn: Athelia Henrietta Press, 2001).

3 Castiel Vitorino Brasileiro's first solo exhibition, *O trauma é brasileiro*, took place at Galeria Homero Massena in Vitória, Espírito Santo, Brazil, from June 11 to August 24, 2019.

4 The logics of *branqueamento* (whitening) were a foundational aspect of Brazilian identity at the end of the nineteenth and beginning of the twentieth century but persist in the twenty-first century. Whitening was attempted mainly through policies promoting European immigration in the face of the abolition of slavery. The theory, as well as the desire, on the part of the Brazilian white elites was that the Brazilian population would become whiter as mixing between races continued. See, for example, Thomas E. Skidmore, *Black into White: Race and Nationality in Brazilian Thought* (New York: Oxford University Press, 1974).

5 Historian, poet, theorist, and organizer Beatriz Nascimento made the statement in a 1988 interview. "CULTNE - Beatriz Nascimento - Entrevista exclusiva," 1988, video, 43:34, 29:53–29:56, https://www.youtube.com/watch?v=6VmPjhOTozI. See Castiel Vitorino Brasileiro, *Quando o sol aqui não mais brilhar: A falência da negritude* (São Paulo: Editora N-1, 2022), 11.

6 During the first decades of the twentieth century, in Brazil, hygienics was often coupled with eugenics, and the virtues of strength and health were associated with whiteness. See Maria Lúcia Boarini and Oswaldo H. Yamamoto, "Higienismo e eugenia: Discursos que não envelhecem," *Psicologia Revista* 13, no. 1 (2004): 59–72.

7 Castiel Vitorino Brasileiro, *Lembrar daquilo que esqueci*, 2020, documentary, video, 20:13, available on the artist's website at https://castielvitorinobrasileiro.com/vid_lembrar daquiloqueesqueci.

8 Denise Ferreira da Silva, "On Difference without Separability," in *32a Bienal de Artes de São Paulo: Incerteza viva* (São Paulo: Fundação Bienal de São Paulo, 2016), 57–65.

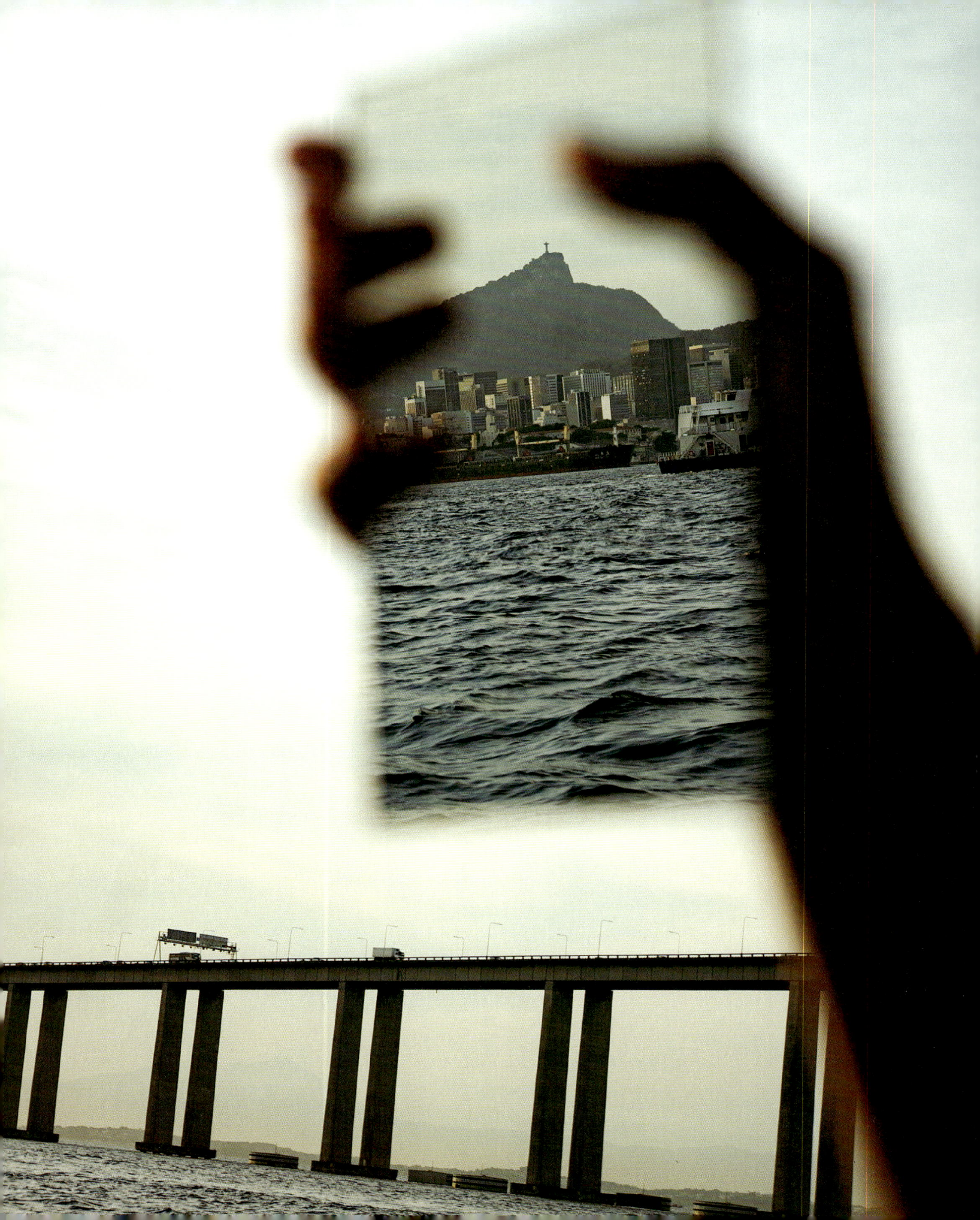

Listening to the Collective Voice

INTERVIEW WITH ALINE MOTTA

Maria Emilia Fernandez

Interview conducted in São Paulo, Brazil, on April 22, 2022

Maria Emilia Fernandez: I would like to focus on *Pontes sobre abismos* (Bridges over the Abyss, 2017), the first video in your trilogy, specifically on the affectionate quest to retell or rewrite the genealogy of your family while also addressing the forms of class, gender, and racial violence that continue to exist in Brazil.[1] Let's begin by talking about the possibilities of reparation in your practice, and whether you see your work as a form of practicing redress, of remedying colonial traumas and engaging in a different kind of activism.[2]

Aline Motta: I don't think I'm an activist in the sense that my work has a clear and straightforward message. The work is not hermetic but it's not that direct either. There are many entry points and people connect with it in different ways, and it's made to be like that. This redress you describe is a form of reparation, but when you repair something, it's never going to look like it was. An act of reparation is an articulation of this loss, one that provides a way to reengage with pain so that it can travel different neuropaths.

In *Pontes sobre abismos*, the story ends with the fable of the leopard and it throws people off.[3] What's happening with this leopard story? Scholar Kênia Freitas, who wrote about this, was so precise to connect this last scene to the rest of the video. As Freitas explains, that's how the leopard knows who he is, by his scars.[4] That's what makes a leopard a leopard. Otherwise, it would be another animal. You put yourself out there, and you can get bruised. But by getting bruised, and by sharing your story, you become who you are. I hadn't made that connection at all; I was just looking for a way to end the film.

Aline Motta, *(Outros) Fundamentos #2* ([Other] Foundations #2), 2017-2019 (detail).

MEF: The closing fable is also a sign of who you choose to bring closest to you, who you allow to touch those scars and learn the stories behind them. How did the fable of the leopard come about, or where did you first encounter it?

AM: I did some of the research trips for the films [of the trilogy] with my father in Minas Gerais. And then, I went with my boyfriend at the time to Vassouras, a rural area in the state of Rio de Janeiro, and then we went to Portugal, and the last trip was to Sierra Leone. These trips were such a small affair, with no specialized film crew, so to speak. I guess it contributed to the seemingly simple framing of the footage, all of it handheld shots, and mostly static ones. I thought to myself, *This trip to Sierra Leone, I can't mess this up, I have to organize this in the best way possible*. So, I hired a travel agency, and the guide that accompanied us told me so many stories, because we were together 24-7 in the car going places. He was the loveliest person, and he told me stories from the civil war in Sierra Leone, when he was a kid. He told me the story about the leopard, and it stuck with me. The day after [that] he asked me, "Do you remember the story of the leopard?" I said that I remembered, but he still repeated the story. Repetition is a value, and of course it's an Afro-Brazilian value and it's an African value. There are so many things ingrained in the work that are actually values; there's the repetition but also a sense of respect and consideration in honoring older people and how they survived in a way that now this collective voice can emerge.

There's all of this call and response, because you say something, and then the other person or people repeat what you just said, or a slightly different version of it. You see this in African American churches all the time. You hear it once; the second time you are already repeating it. The question is, though, who is responding? It is a collective response. You ask it as an individual, but you are asking for the response of the collective, and the work was built like that.

MEF: How did you arrive at the ritual performances we see in your video trilogy? For example, when did you decide that you would print the photographs on textiles and submerge them in different bodies of water, such as rivers and oceans?

AM: I was a script supervisor for fifteen years and I worked on film sets for twelve hours a day, starting very early in the morning, and I only had one day off a week. My schedule was totally off, and I was very tired and burnt out. Then I got that first grant, the Rumos Itaú Cultural grant. I could finally stop working as a script supervisor, and I started sleeping! It was magic. I was back in that dream world, where everything is possible, where you can fly, where you can talk to people that have passed, where you can project the future and you can go back into the past and make something different. I had been missing that for a long time. I just needed that time of solitude, of being in touch with this spiritual realm. Every day, I would begin to wake up, and in those moments, that's when these images started coming. The water just started flowing, really flowing. For hours I would just be in that sort of dream state. It was so quiet that sometimes I didn't even know if I was still sleeping. And I think the work reflects that gentleness of waking up and not having to rush to go to a film set.

MEF: It sounds like you were working toward a very particular way of thinking about the passage of time, and how memory and repetition play a role in your practice. Perhaps all those thoughts and reflections needed to slowly simmer for as long as they did.

I also wanted to ask you about the figure of your grandmother and the role she plays in *Pontes sobre abismos*. Two years before she passed away, she shared a missing piece of the family tree with you—a name that would send you on a long research journey that continues to unfold today. Why is it that the work of remembering stories and telling them, of passing knowledge to future generations, often falls on grandmothers?

AM: Grandmothers sometimes are not men and are not women, and sometimes they're not old. Some people—they have these roles in their societies or at some point in their lives—they are grandparents to someone. Although I don't have children, sometimes I have to put on my grandmother's clothes, literally. Because a grandmother is not a person, it's an entity. It's an elder. It's the mediator of this world; that's what I write in my text, *Water Is a Time Machine*.[5] I think it's gendered, but it's gendered in a way that anyone can wear those clothes—provided that they have the skills, or if they hone their skills.

It's true that in my case, it was really my grandmother and that she was in my family biologically, but it could have been somebody else. She really put me back on track. I was veering, turning into somebody, someplace else, and she put me back on track through her story, through fiction. It's fictionalized—not meaning that it didn't happen or that it's not true; it's just that by making it a fiction, it becomes accessible to everyone. It's true that I found out who Enzo[6] was, but even if I didn't have that specific address of the house, or the name of the family, still, it could be imagined; it could be perceived as true, or as real, making it real again. That's the magic that you do by creating art. There's a transmutation.

MEF: Why is it important to you that this story be accessible to everyone? What is it about that shared experience and collective understanding that might help fight back against injustice and racism, even if it goes about it very slowly?

AM: People now are creating a verb that doesn't exist. It's the verb "to hope," but it's *esperançar*, which means to build hope, to instill hope. If you can't *esperançar* and you were born in Brazil, if you can't believe that things will get better eventually—get better in the sense of reparation of these terrible things that have happened—then you can't make it another year, another day, if you can't hope. I feel that a lot, by having been born here in Brazil, and by having lived in so many places, and speaking so many languages. When you get hold of a language, you can handle so much more. That is something I also say in the text, that "lineage is language."[7] You get hold of all this knowledge that's been shared centuries before. But really, I know that being born here gives you an extra responsibility, more than in some other countries. Everybody, of course, has responsibility in everything. But I don't know—when I was in Sweden, the responsibility seemed to fall in other priorities.

I have this responsibility as an artist. That's why I always make sure that I speak to everyone, and I hope that the word will spread. When you are born in this country you see so much inequality and so much racial stigma, prejudice, and racism; you have to do something about it. My way is through art. Some people are going to become politicians, some people are going into education, which I love. I feel I'm an educator more than an artist, in the sense that I have to educate through my means, through the way that I know best, which is by creating these works that can communicate. The work is so much more. Making works of art is like creating a shared learning device.

NOTES

1 Motta conceived of these films as a trilogy and often presents them together as a six-channel video installation. The trilogy includes *Pontes sobre abismos* (Bridges over the Abyss), 2017, 8:28; *Se o mar tivesse varandas* (If the Sea Had Balconies), 2017, 9:11; and *(Outros) Fundamentos* ([Other] Foundations), 2017–2019, 15:48 (see plates 20a–c).

2 According to Black feminist historian Saidiya Hartman, "Redress is itself an articulation of loss and a longing for remedy and reparation," an impossible form of compensation in the face of the violence and erasure of slavery. *Scenes of Subjection: Terror, Slavery, and Self-Making in Nineteenth-Century America* (New York: Oxford University Press, 1997), 77.

3 From Motta's narration in *Pontes sobre abismos* (2017), we learn that in ancient times, the Leopard was very good friends with Fire and would visit him regularly. One day, the Woman Leopard asked if she too could meet Fire and suggested he bring his friend home. Fire eventually accepted the invitation and asked the Leopard to build him a trail of dry leaves so that he could make his way there. "Upon seeing her house in flames, the Woman Leopard asked, 'Is this your friend?' And that is how, all scorched, the Leopard acquired his rosettes."

4 Kênia Freitas, "Afrofabulações e opacidade: As estratégias de criação do documentário negro brasileiro contemporâneo," in *Pensar o documentário, textos para um debate*, ed. Laecio Ricardo (Recife: Editora UFPE, 2020), 201–28.

5 "Grandmothers are healing forces in our community. Grandmothers mediate conflicts while knowing that conflict is rootwork, that the mediation of conflict is rootwork too. . . . One grandmother's performance is the collective performance of all grandmothers. It is the performance of a whole lineage of women, and it manifests through multiple means and across multiple dimensions, acting and coming up against various affective layers that can sometimes be traumatic. They are ancestral plurivoices." Aline Motta, *An Essay: Water Is a Time Machine* (São Paulo: ybytu, 2020), 22. Also see the artist's book *A água é uma máquina do*

tempo (São Paulo: Fósforo Editora/Luna Parque Edições, 2022); *Water Is a Time Machine*, trans. Sophie Lewis and Julia Sanches, special edition for the Sharjah Biennial 15 (Sharjah, UAE: Sharjah Art Foundation, 2023). "Water Is a Time Machine," *Latin American and Latinx Visual Culture* 5, no. 2 (2023): 140–44.

6 Enzo Pereira de Souza, the white son of the family who employed Motta's Black great-grandmother, Mariana. His full name emerges in the artist's research, featured in the headlines of old newspaper social columns, but with each mention of his name in the archive comes the haunting absence of Mariana and the child that he disowned, a baby who would grow up to be Motta's grandmother, Doralice.

7 Motta, *An Essay*, 22.

Plates

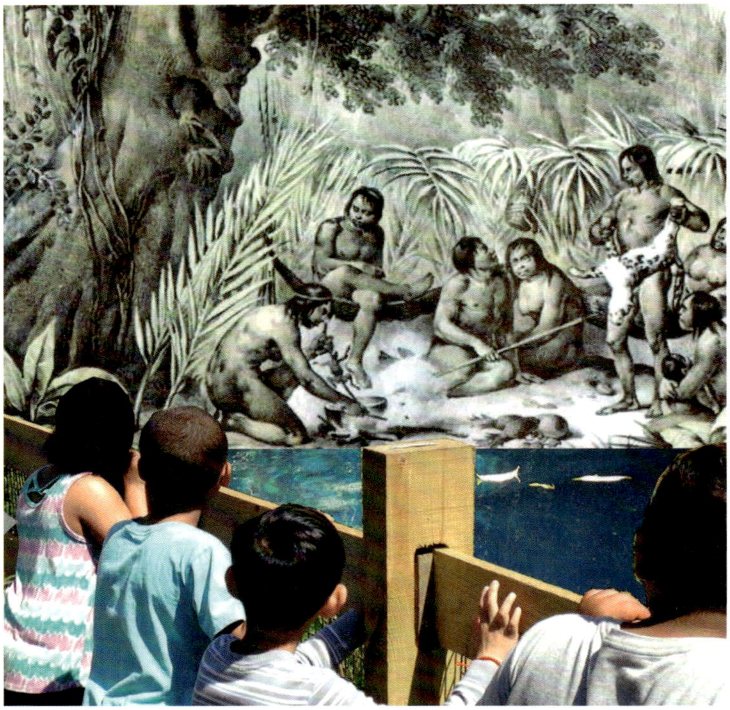

1 Denilson Baniwa
Zoo terra indígena
Indigenous Land Zoo
2018

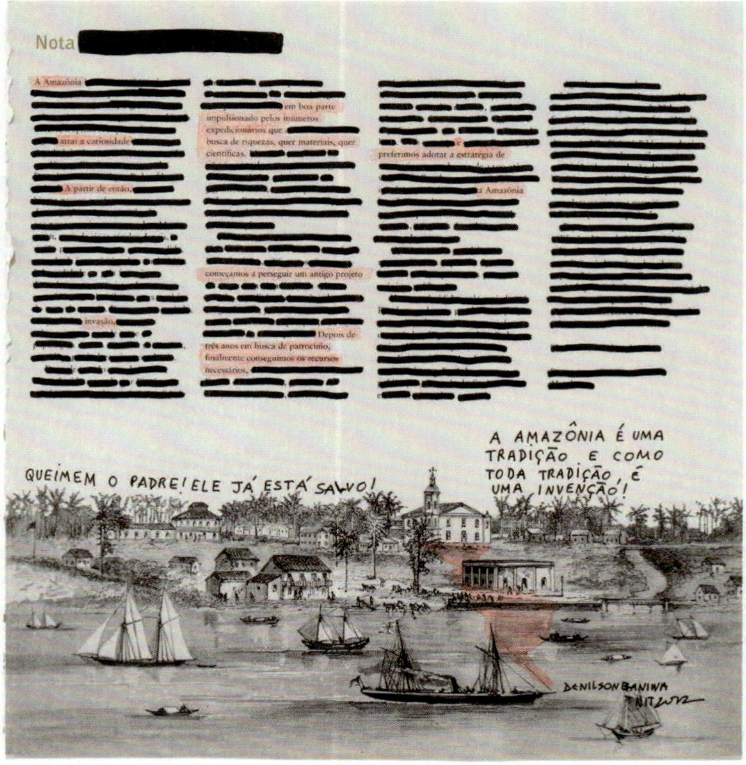

2 Denilson Baniwa
A Amazônia é *uma invenção*, da série
Todo território é invenção
The Amazon Is an Invention, from the series Every Territory Is Invention
2019

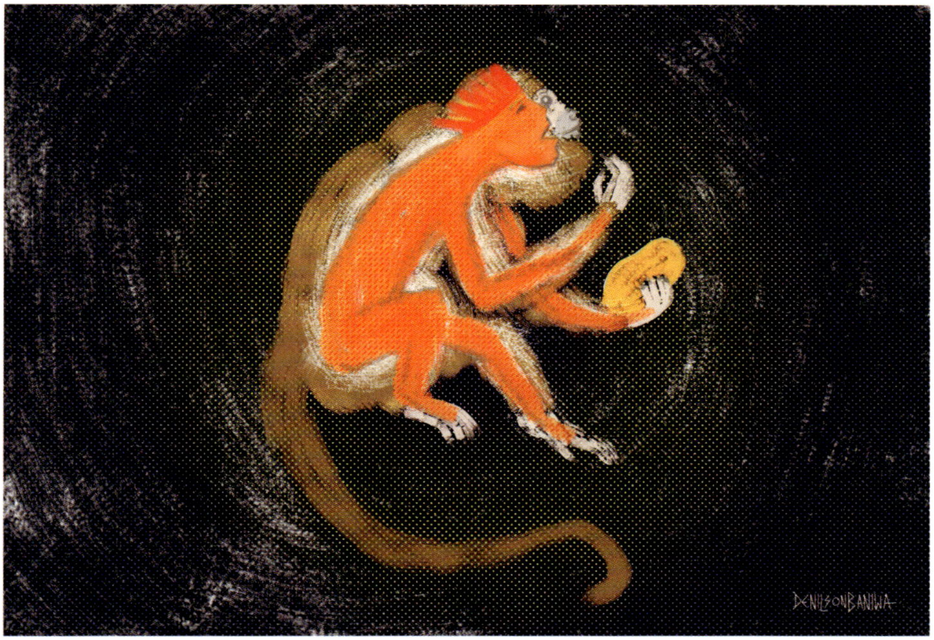

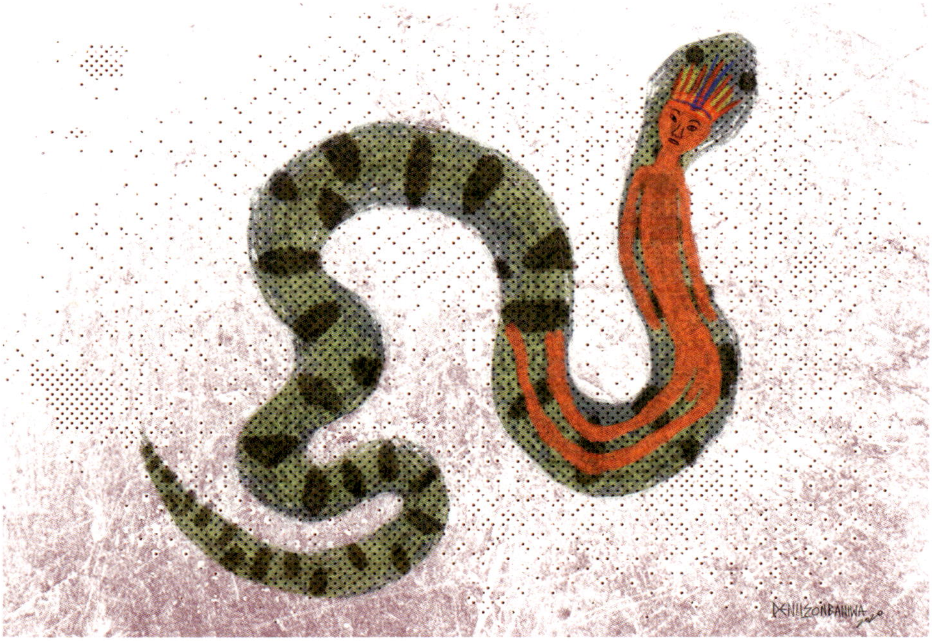

3 Denilson Baniwa
Kwatá-tapuya, da série *Perspectivismo ameríndio*
Kwatá-tapuya, from the series Amerindian Perspectivism
2019

4 Denilson Baniwa
Sukuryu-tapuya, da série *Perspectivismo ameríndio*
Sukuryu-tapuya, from the series Amerindian Perspectivism
2019

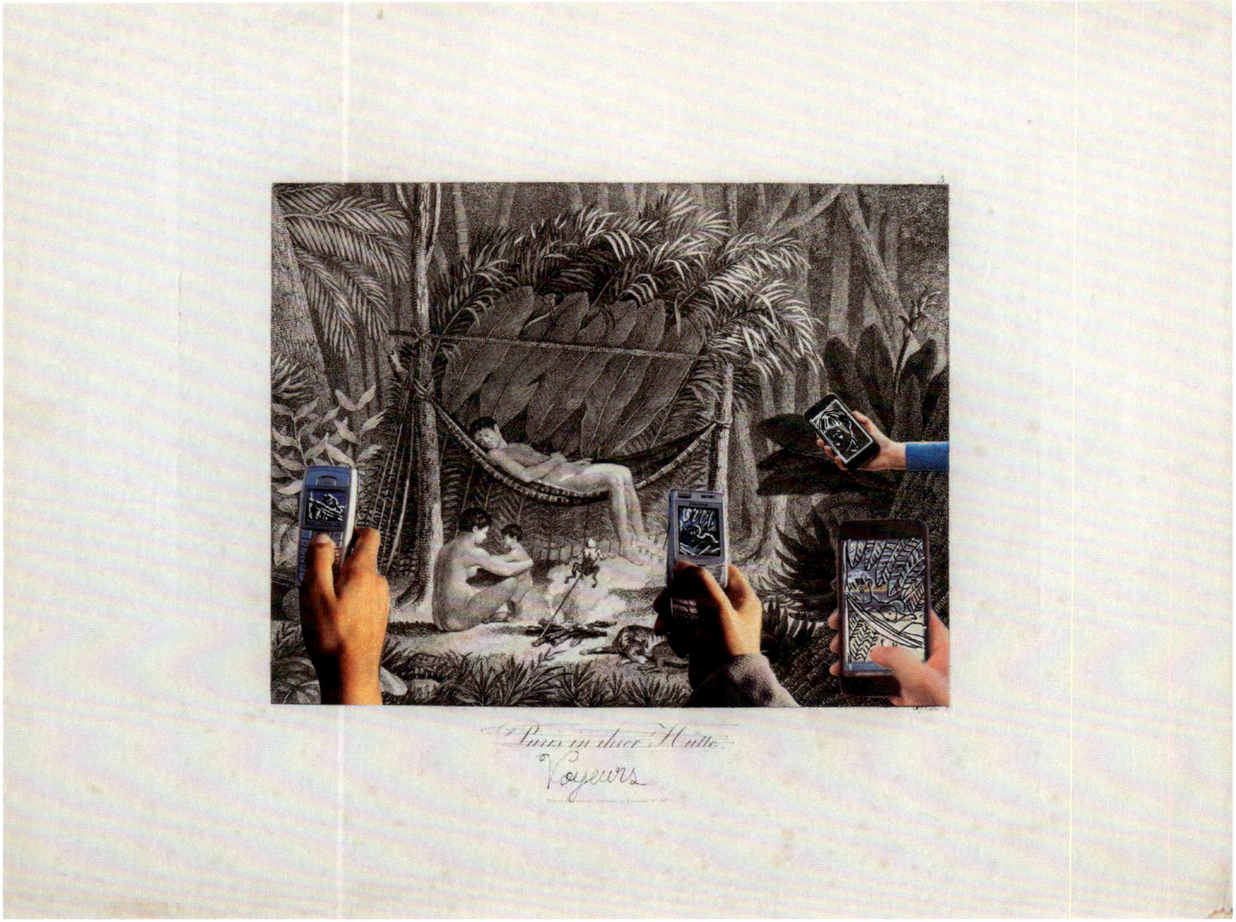

5 Denilson Baniwa
Voyeurs
2019

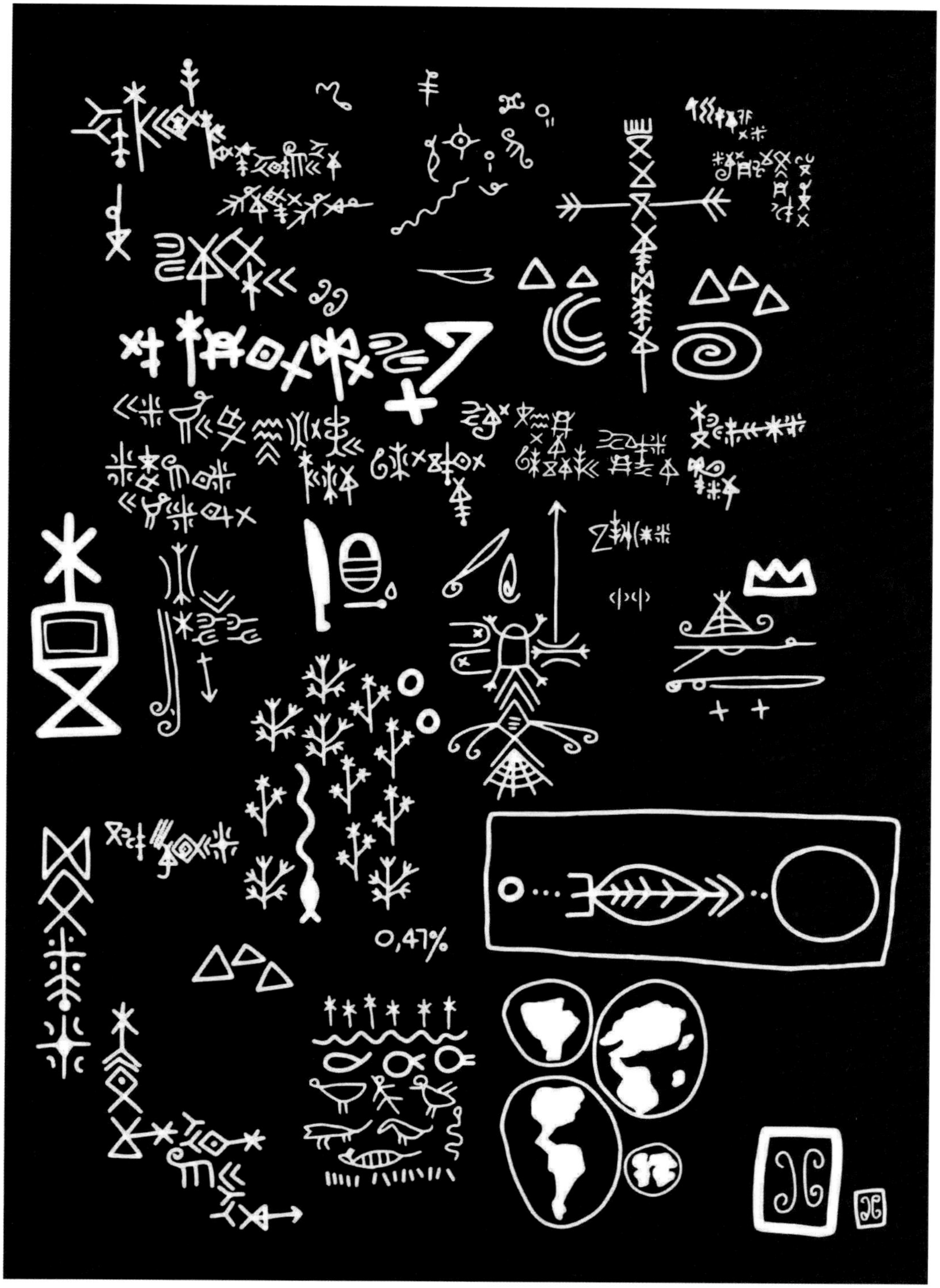

6 Denilson Baniwa
Carta aos indígenas do planeta Marte com códigos de reconhecimento do planeta Terra
Letter to the Indigenous Peoples of the Planet Mars with Recognition Codes of the Planet Earth
2020/2022

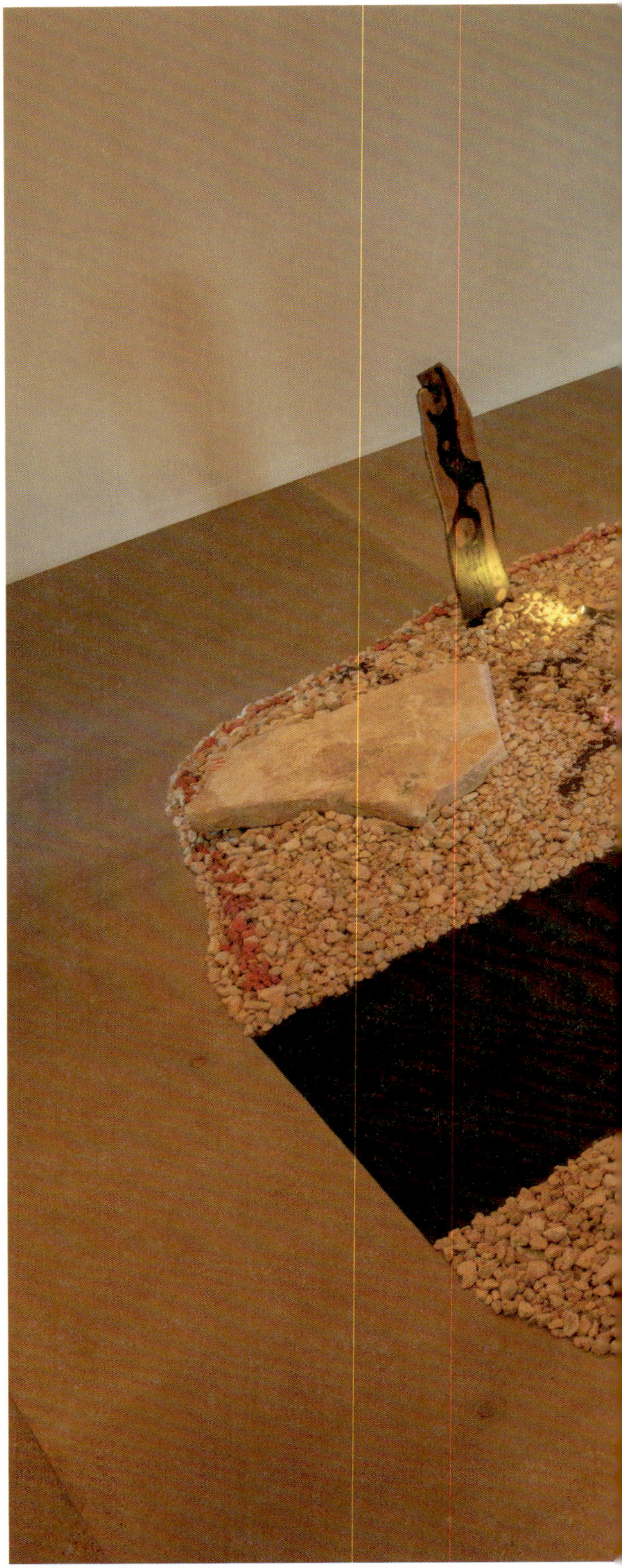

7 Castiel Vitorino Brasileiro
Jupiter is Here. Celestial is Everything.
2022

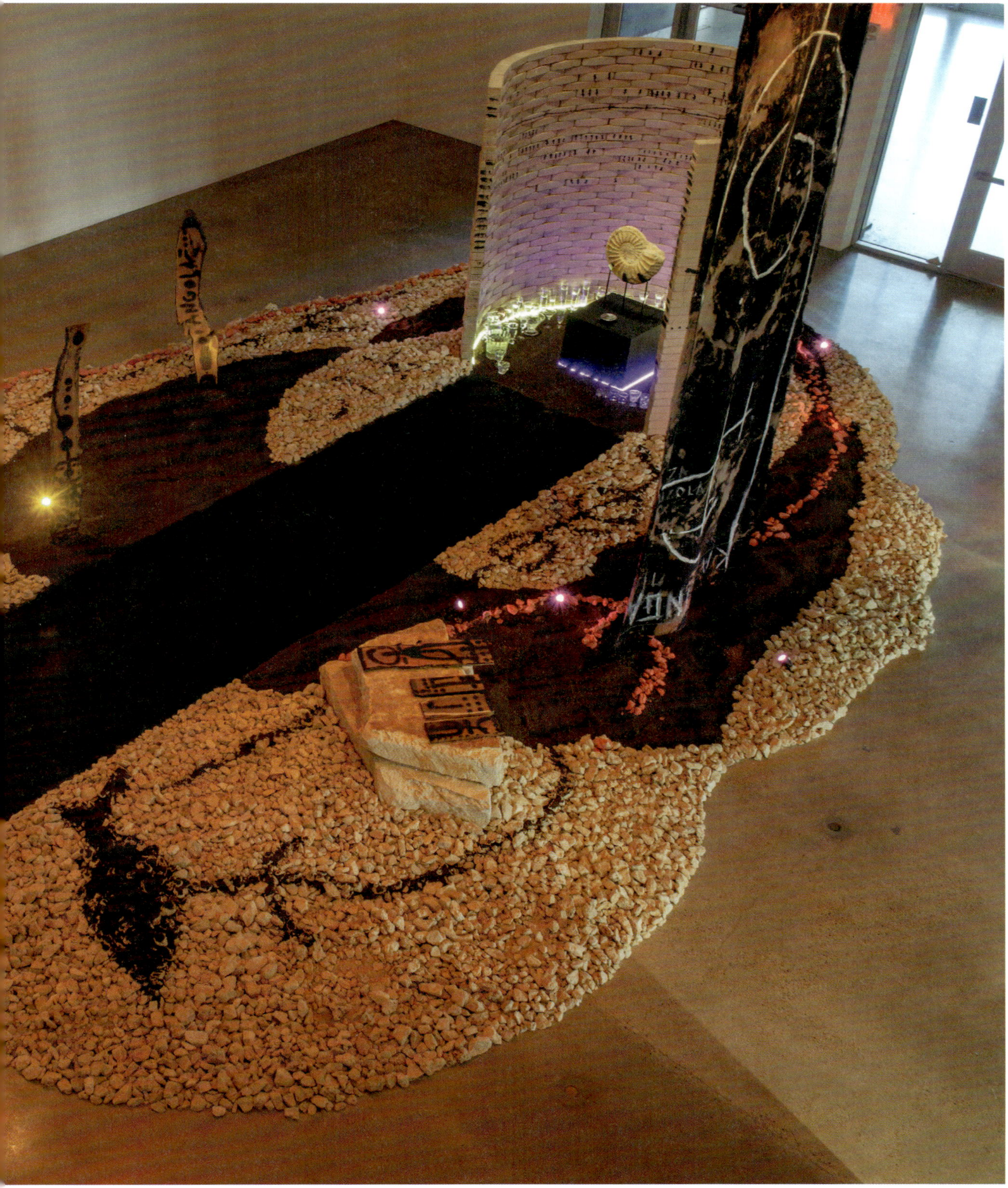

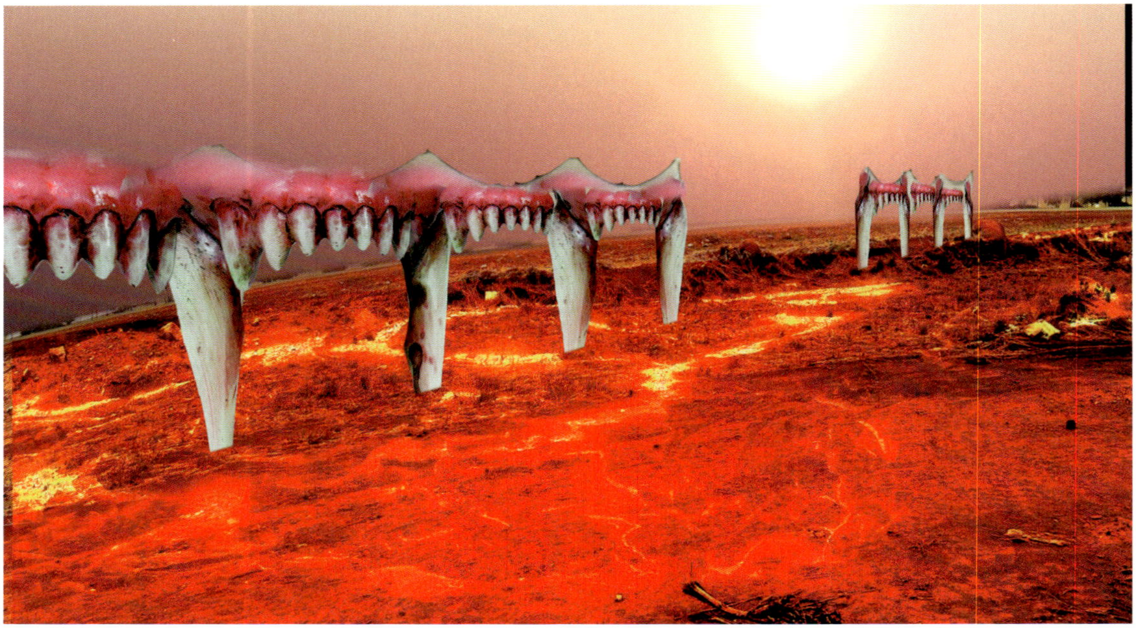

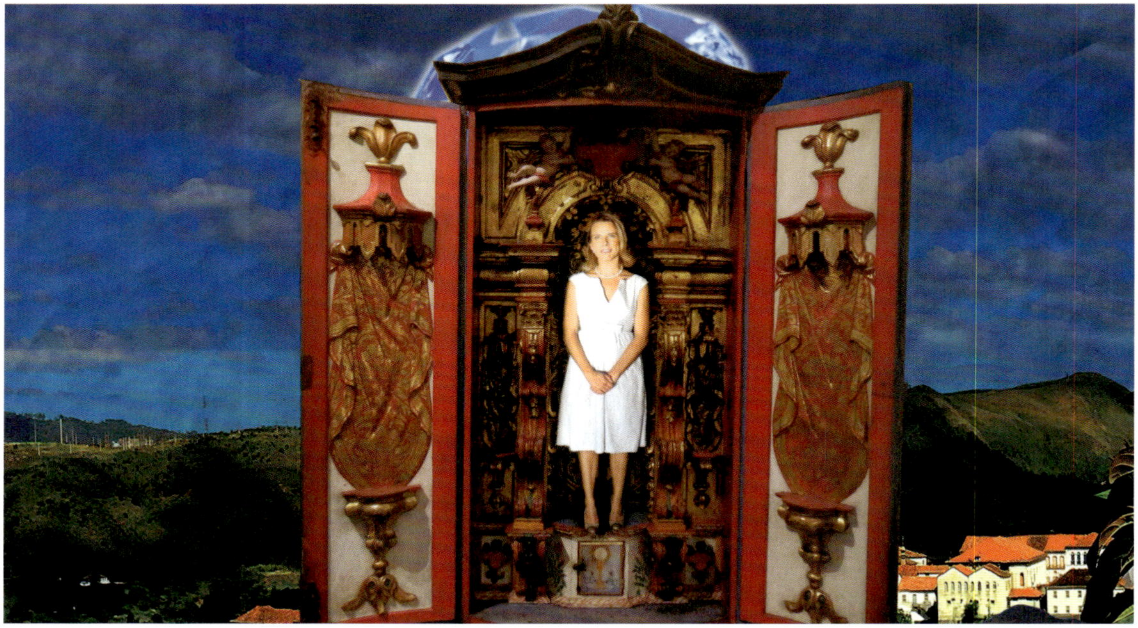

8 Guerreiro do Divino Amor
Still from *A cristalização de Brasília*, da série *Atlas superficcional mundial*
Still from Crystallization of Brasília, from the series Superfictional World Atlas
2019

9 Guerreiro do Divino Amor
Still from *O mundo mineral*, da série *Atlas superficcional mundial*
Still from The Mineral World, from the series Superfictional World Atlas
2019

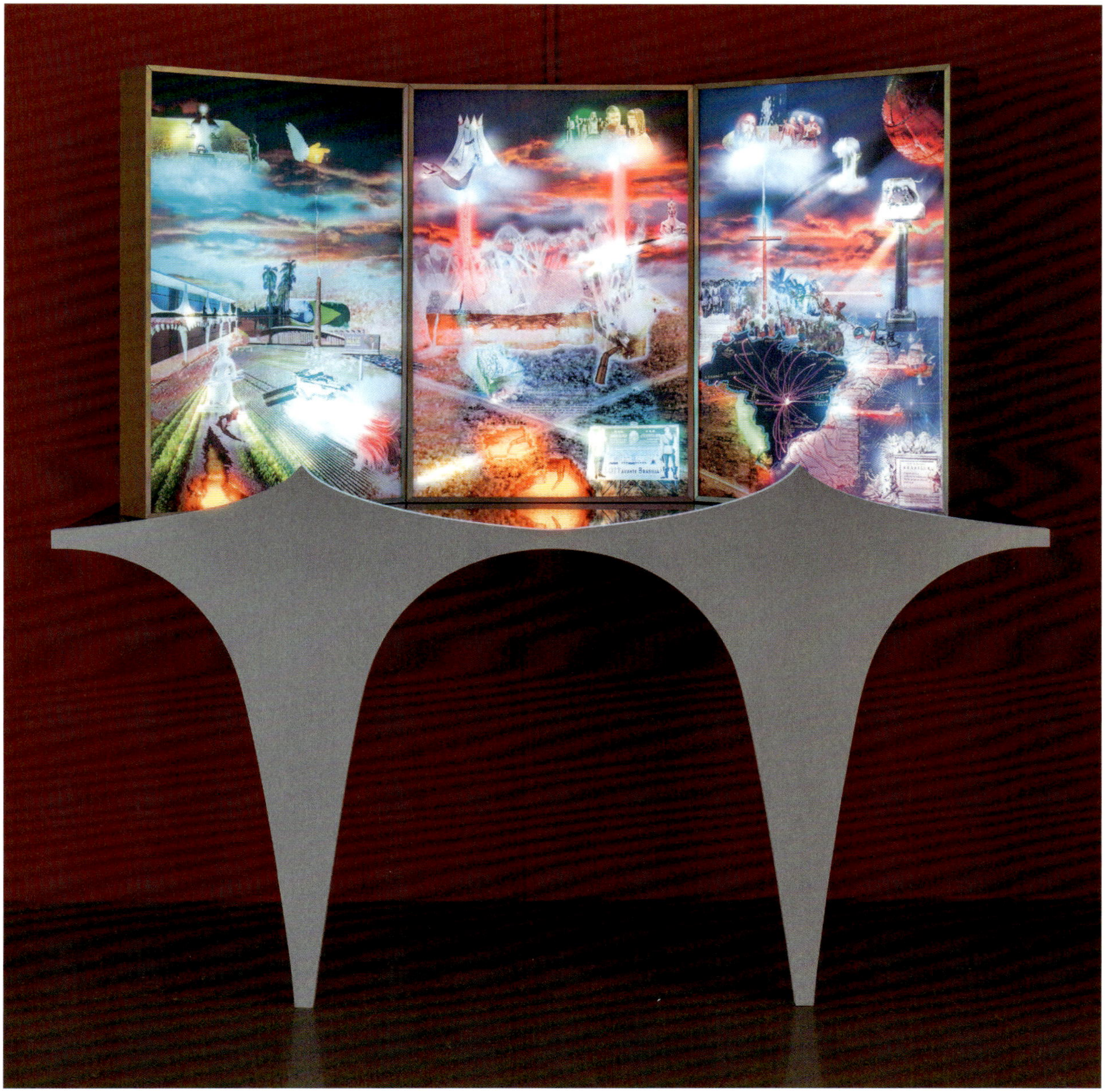

10 Guerreiro do Divino Amor
Trilogia cristalizada de Brasília: Formação, cristalização e desabrochar de uma nova Alvorada
Crystallized Trilogy of Brasília: Formation, Crystallization, and Breaking of a New Dawn
2022

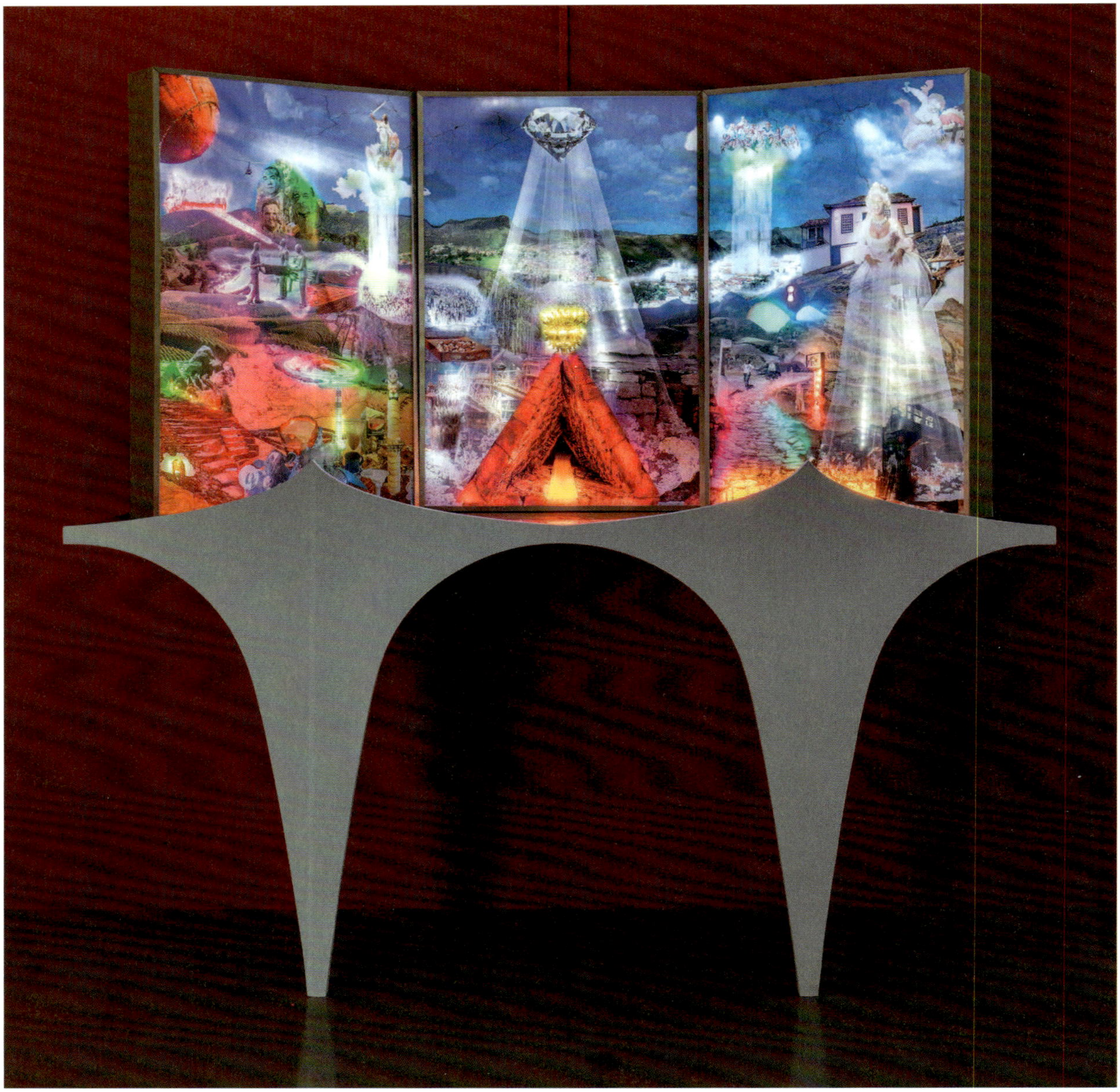

11 Guerreiro do Divino Amor
Trilogia mineral
Mineral Trilogy
2022

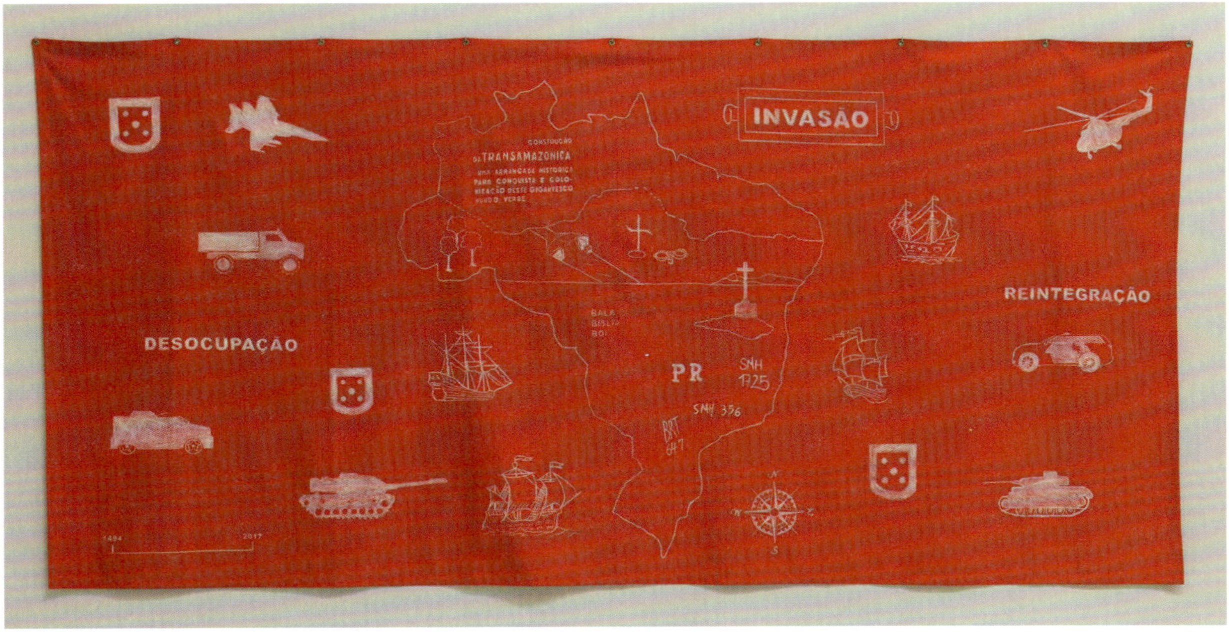

12 Jaime Lauriano
Invasão
Invasion
2017

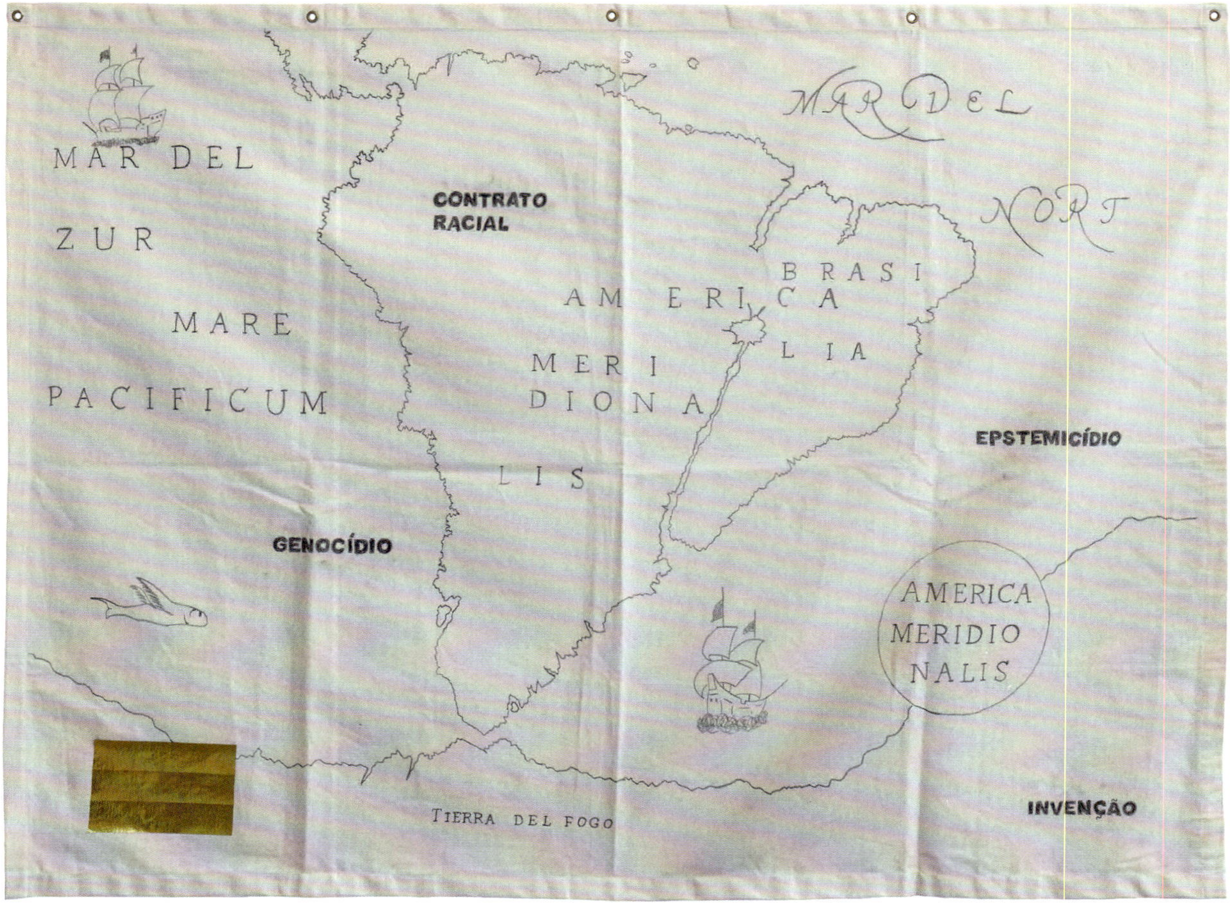

13 Jaime Lauriano
America meridionalis: invenção, epistemicídio, contrato racial e genocídio
America meridionalis: invention, epistemicide, racial contract, and genocide
2019

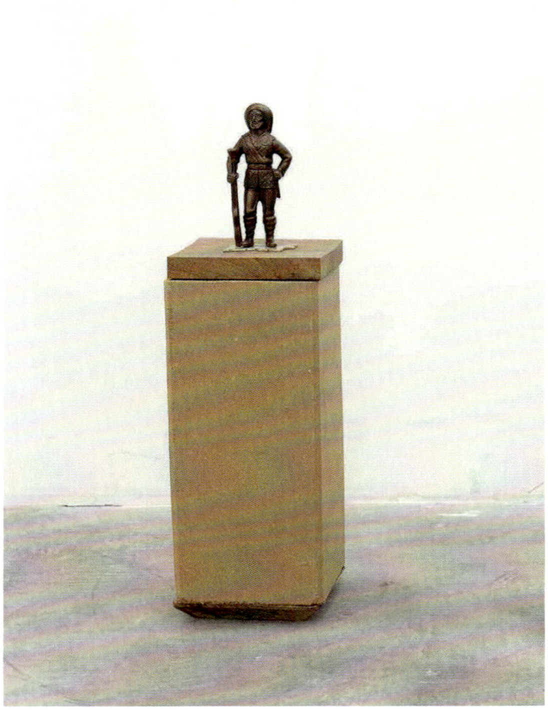

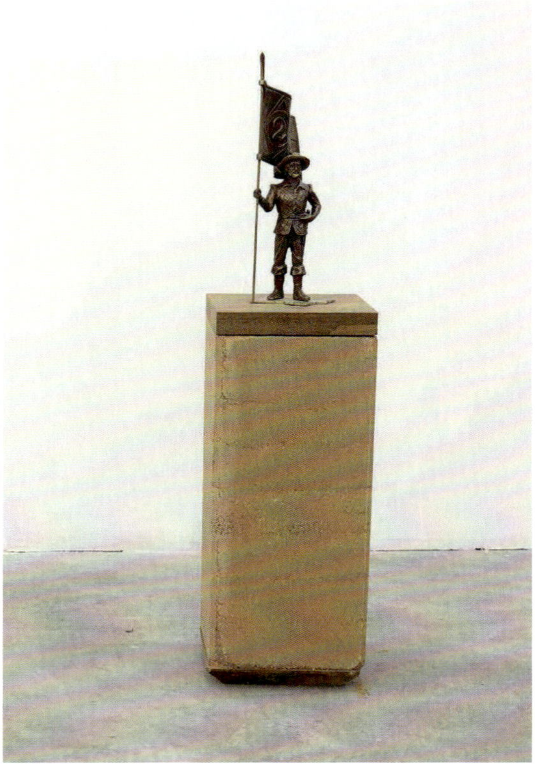

14 Jaime Lauriano
Bandeirante #1
2019

15 Jaime Lauriano
Bandeirante #2
2019

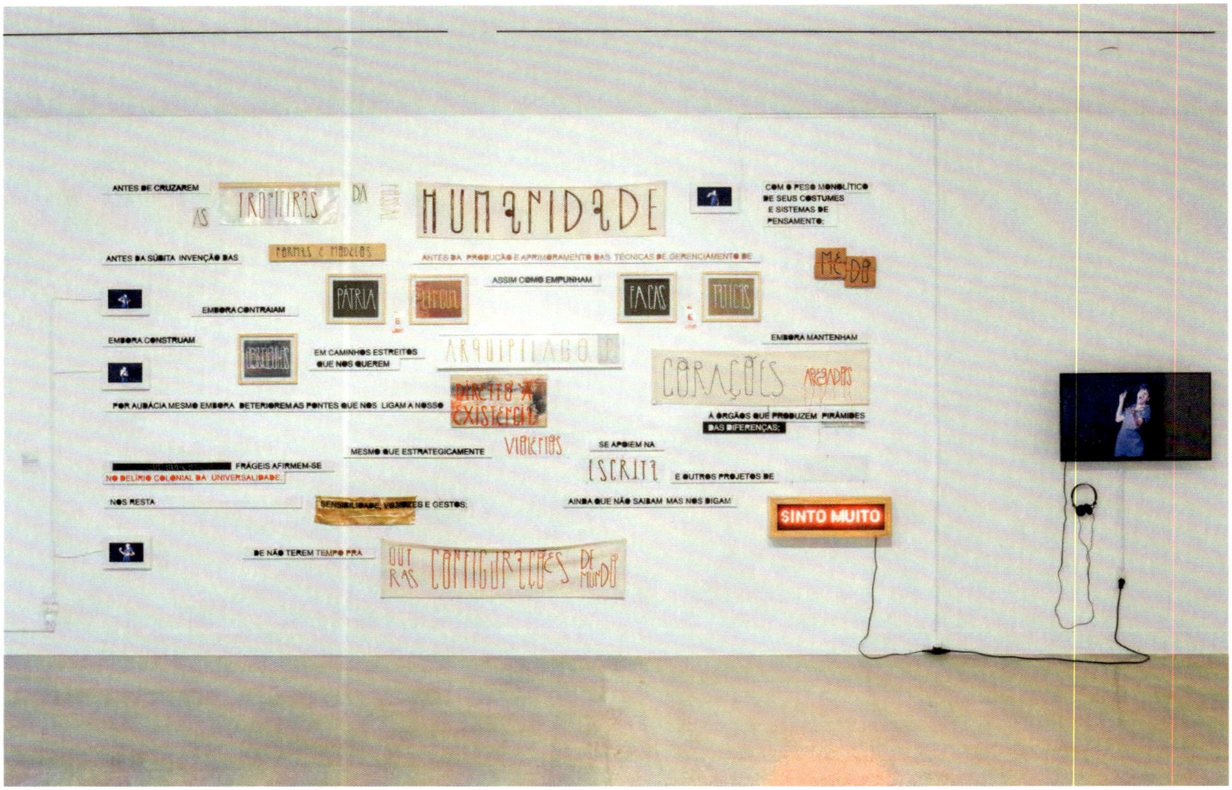

16 Maré de Matos
Fundamento
Foundation
2019

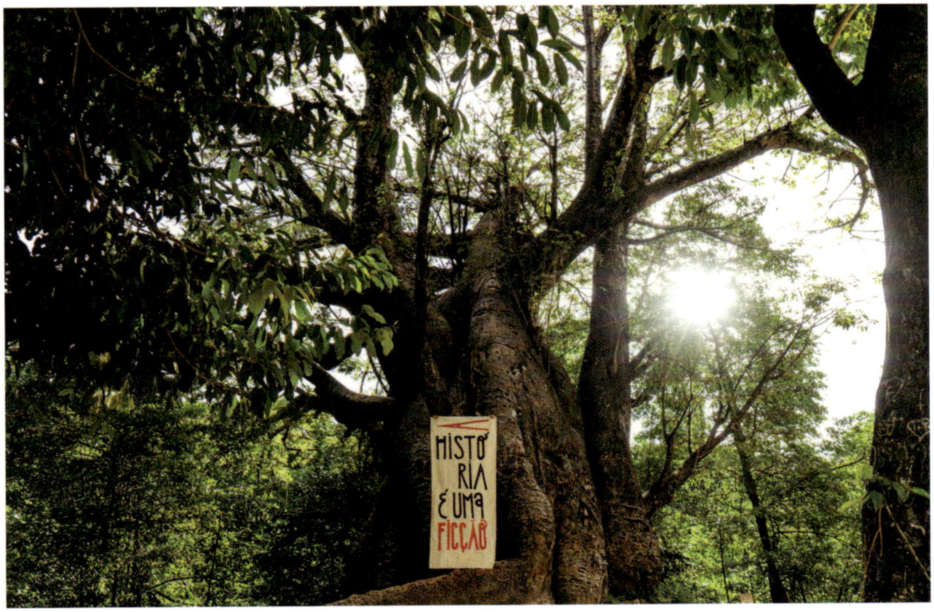

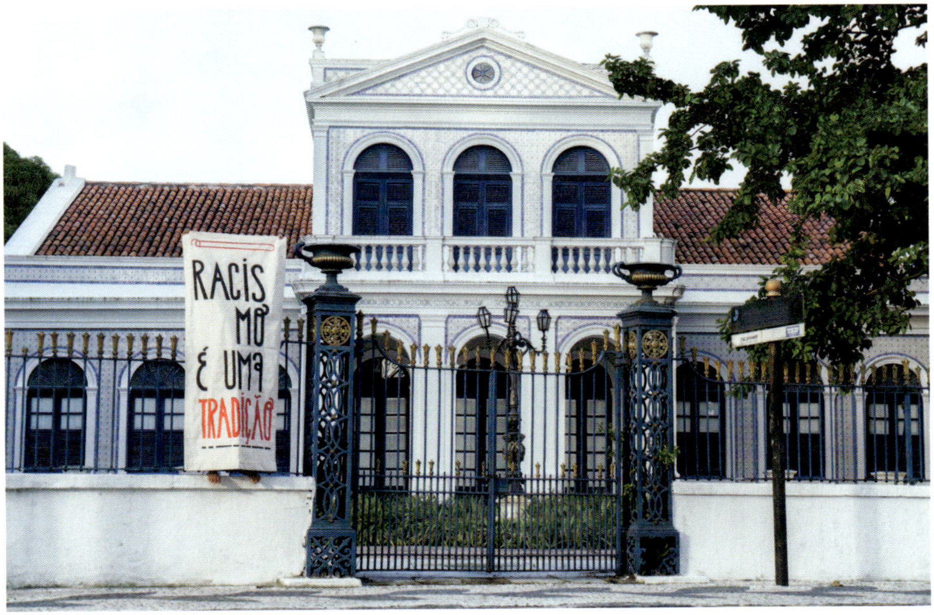

17 Maré de Matos
História
History
2019–present

18 Maré de Matos
Racismo
Racism
2019–present

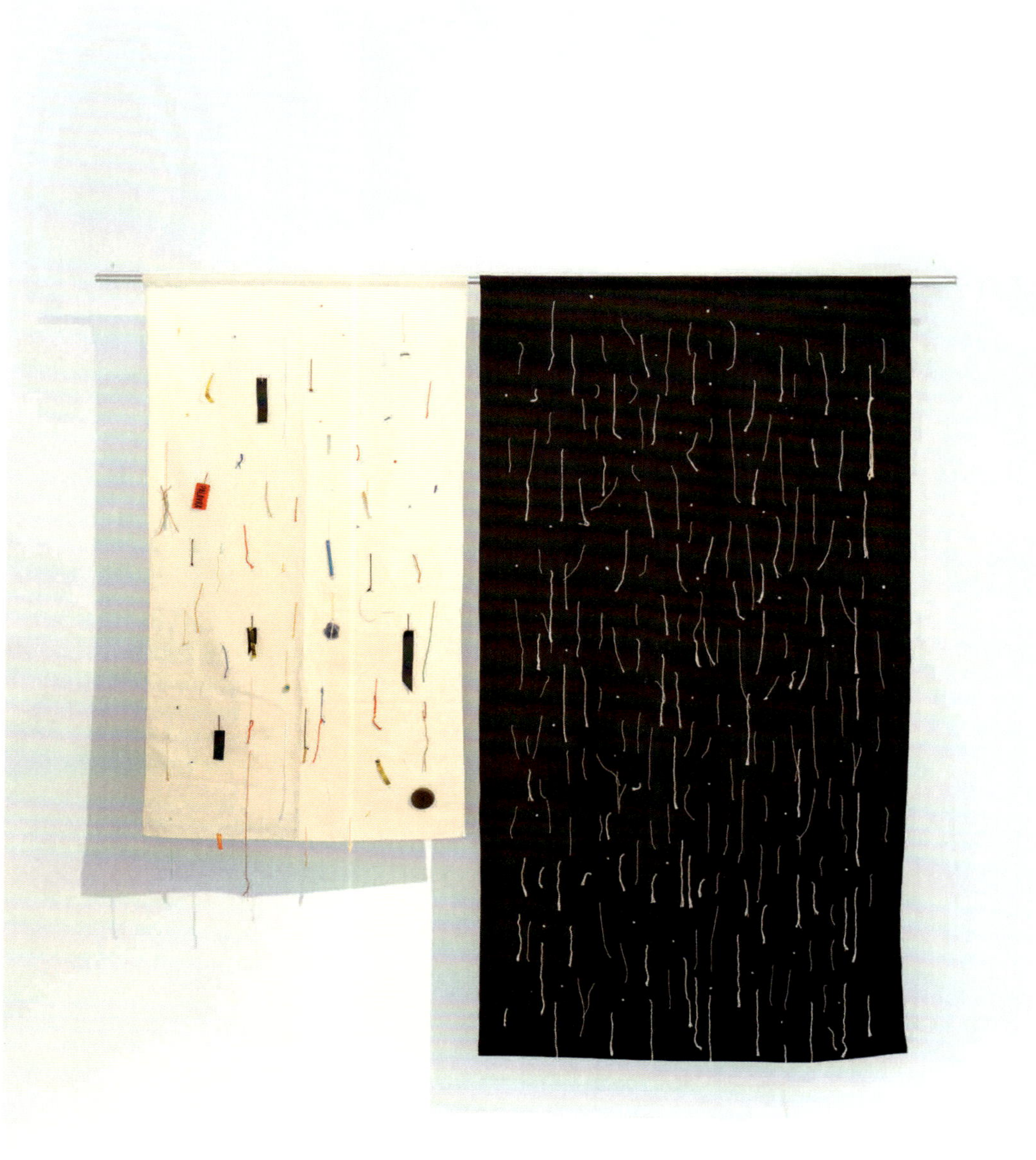

19 Maré de Matos
Mais nascimento que morte
More Birth than Death
2021–2022

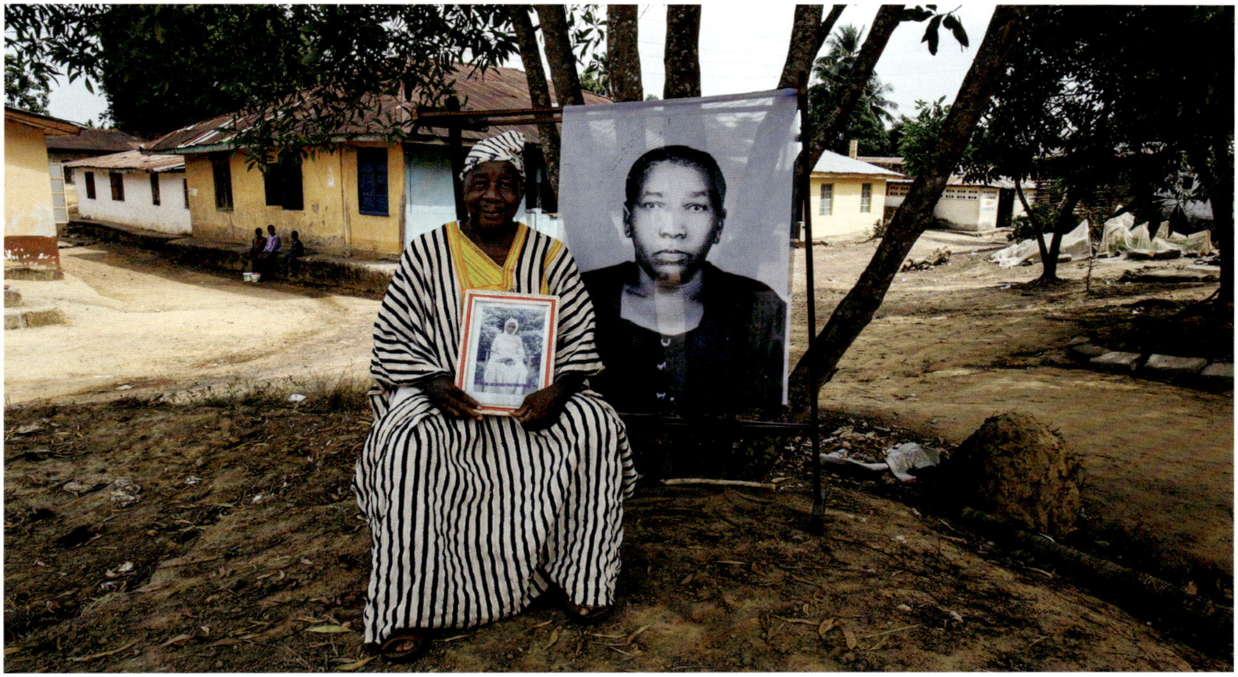

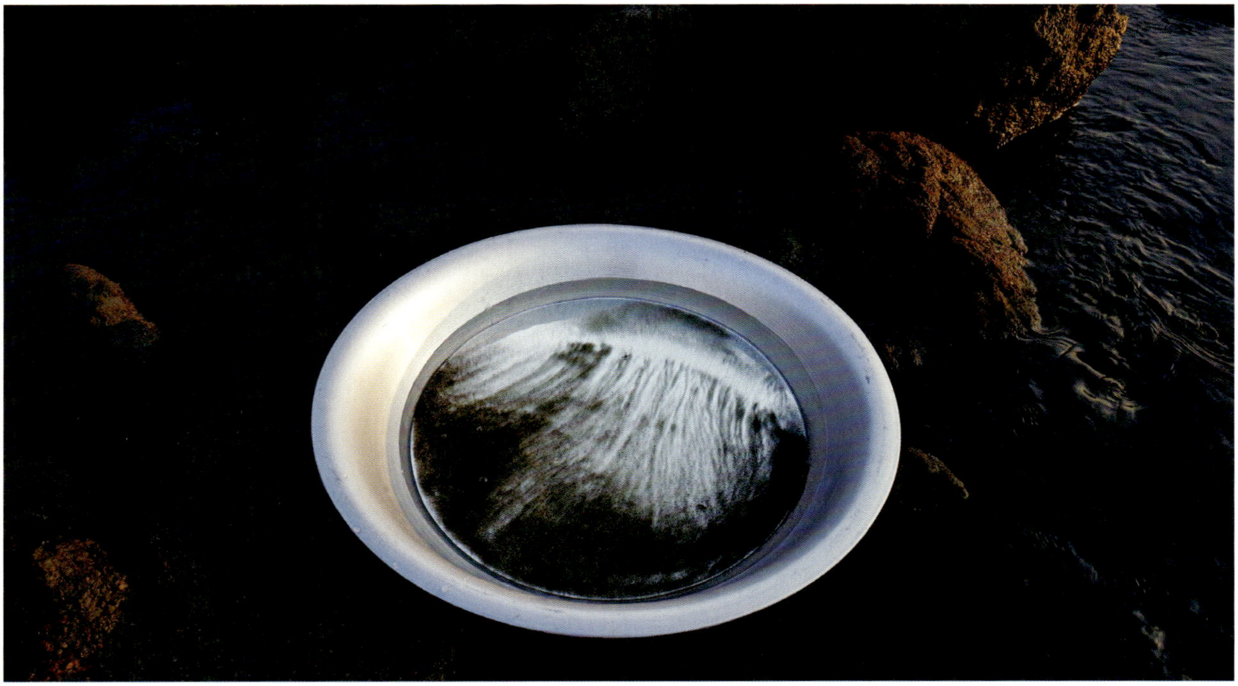

20a Aline Motta
Still from *Pontes sobre abismos*
Still from Bridges over the Abyss
2017

20b Aline Motta
Still from *Se o mar tivesse varandas*
Still from If the Sea Had Balconies
2017

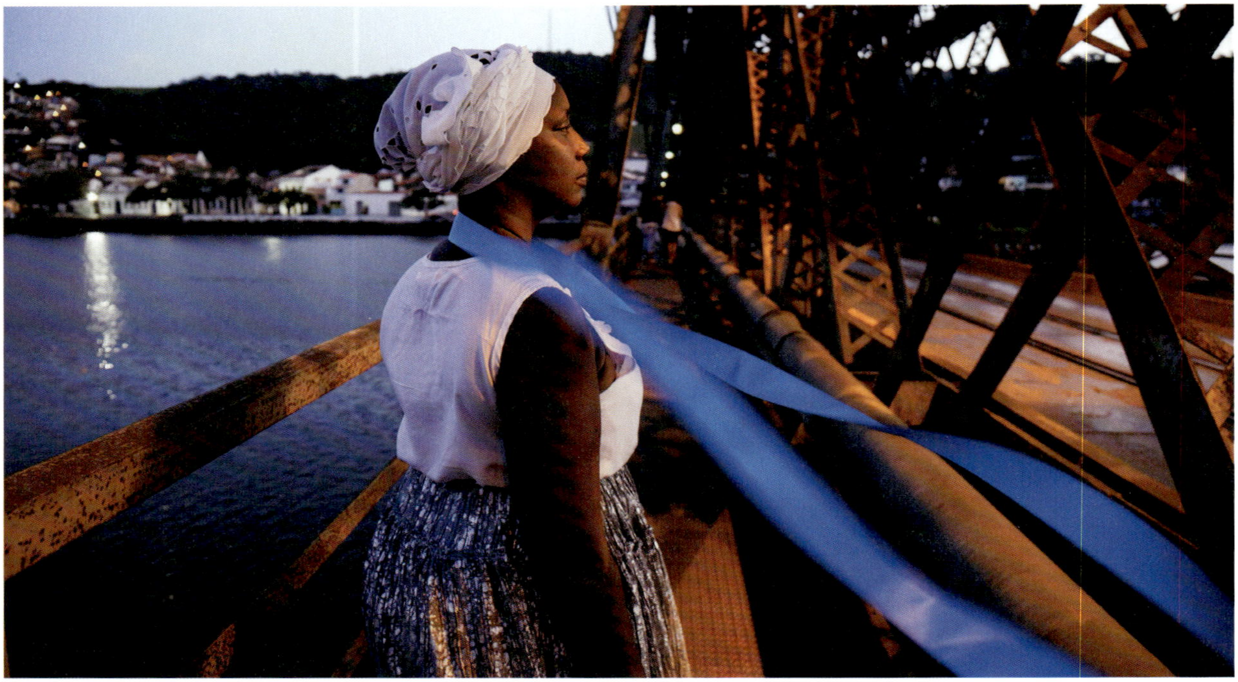

20c Aline Motta
Still from *(Outros) Fundamentos*
Still from (Other) Foundations
2017–2019

21 Aline Motta
Pontes sobre abismos #2
Bridges over the Abyss #2
2017

22 Aline Motta
Pontes sobre abismos #24
Bridges over the Abyss #24
2017

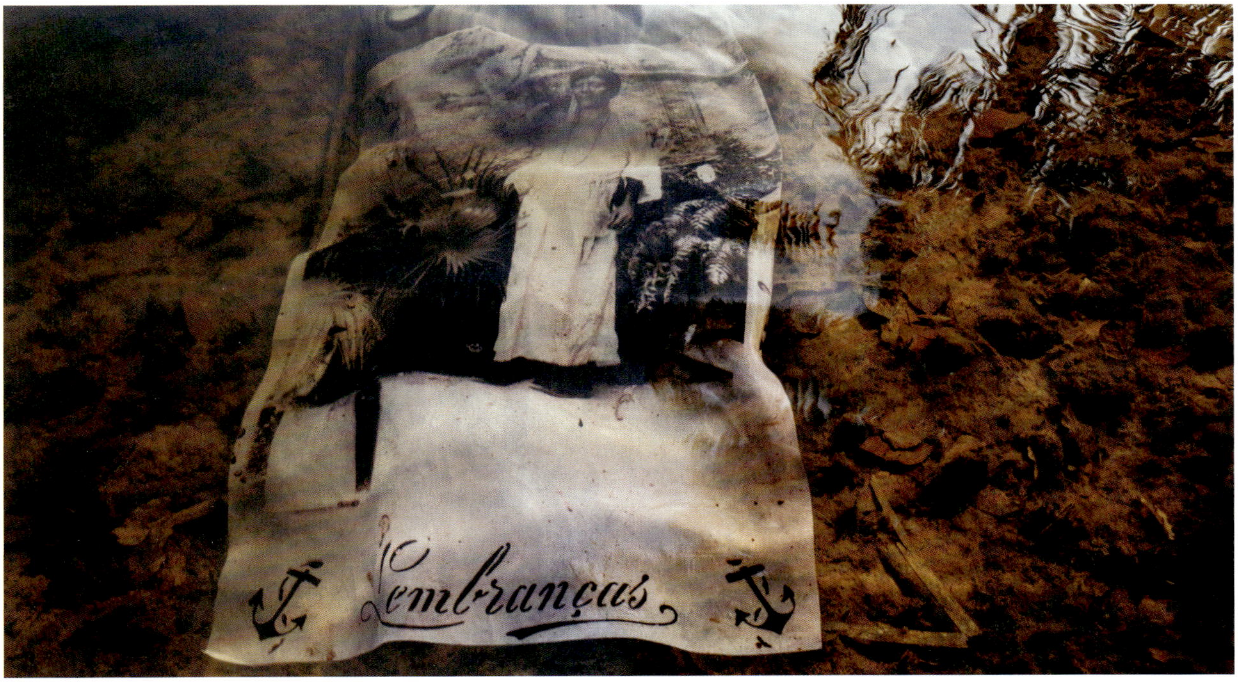
Lembranças

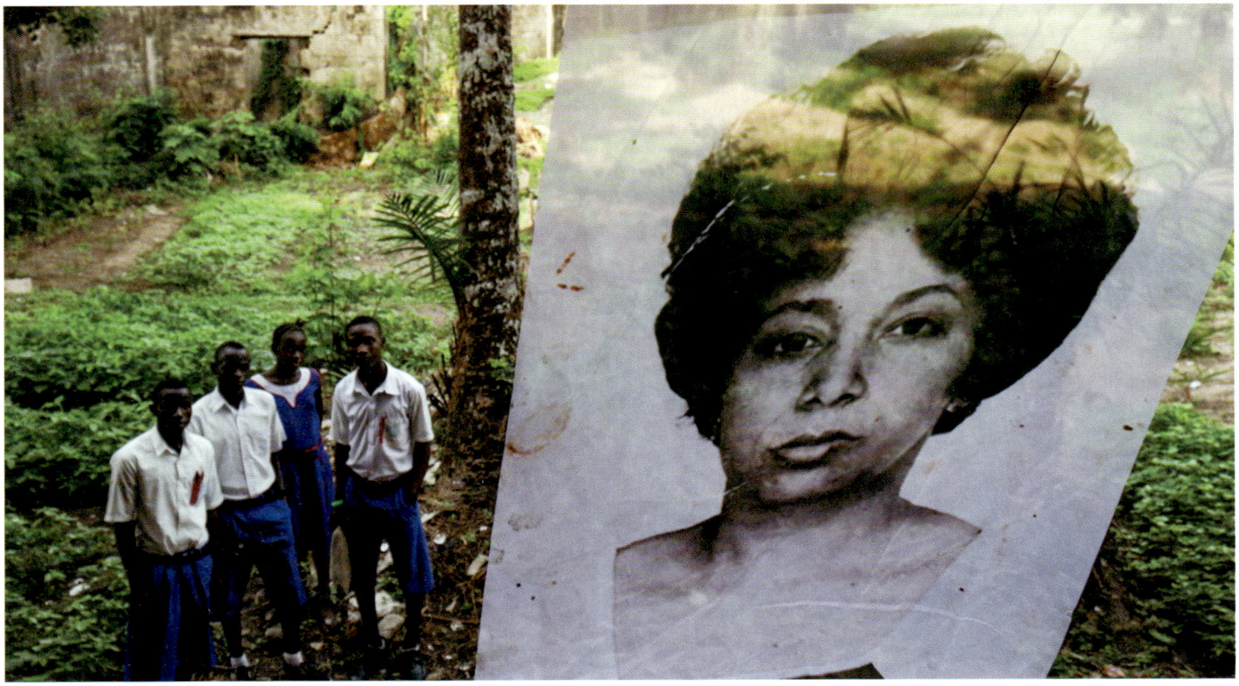

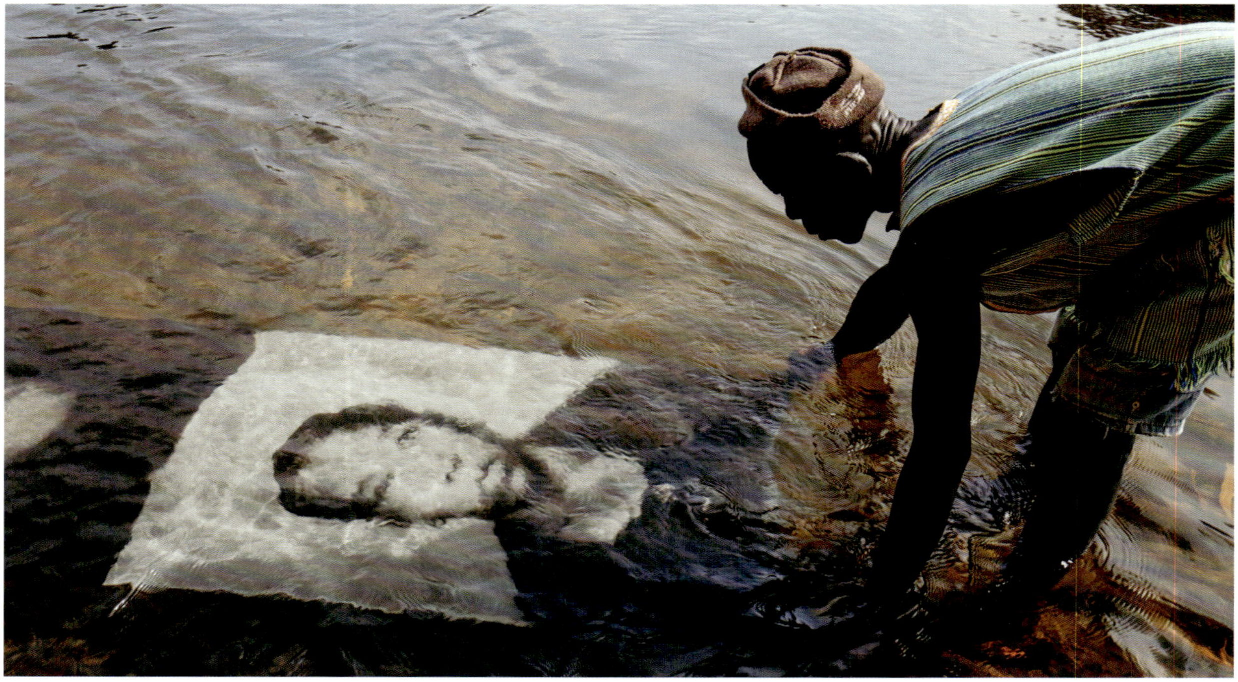

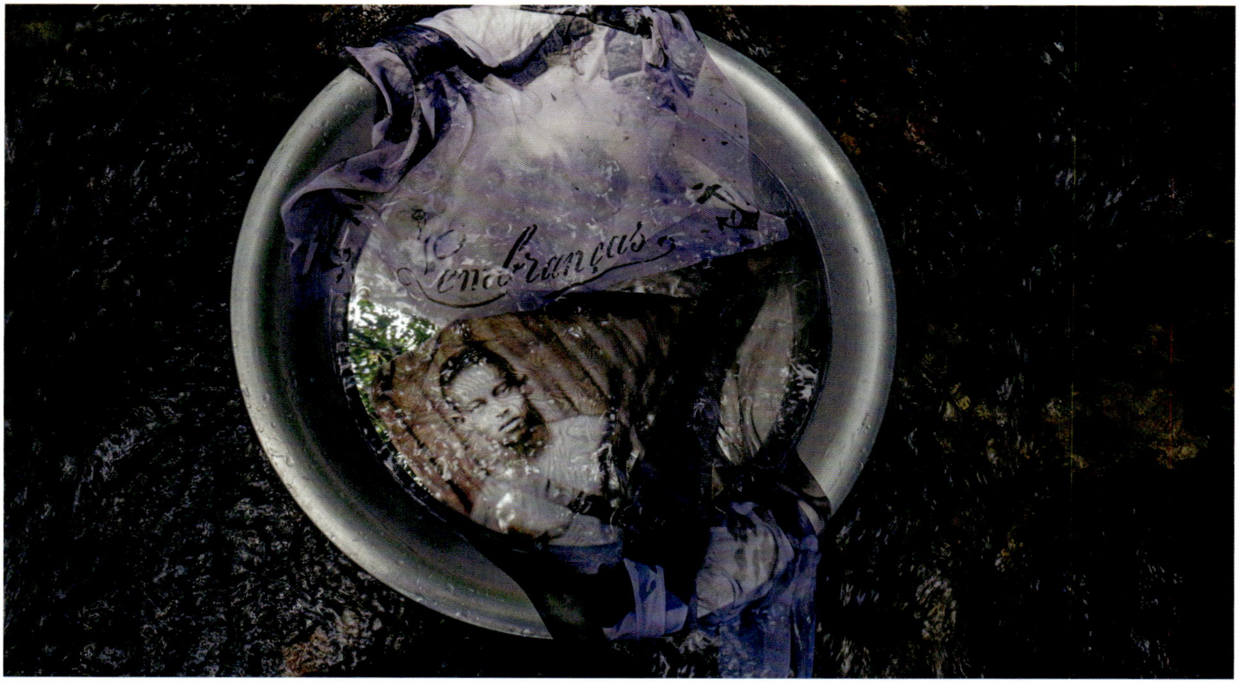

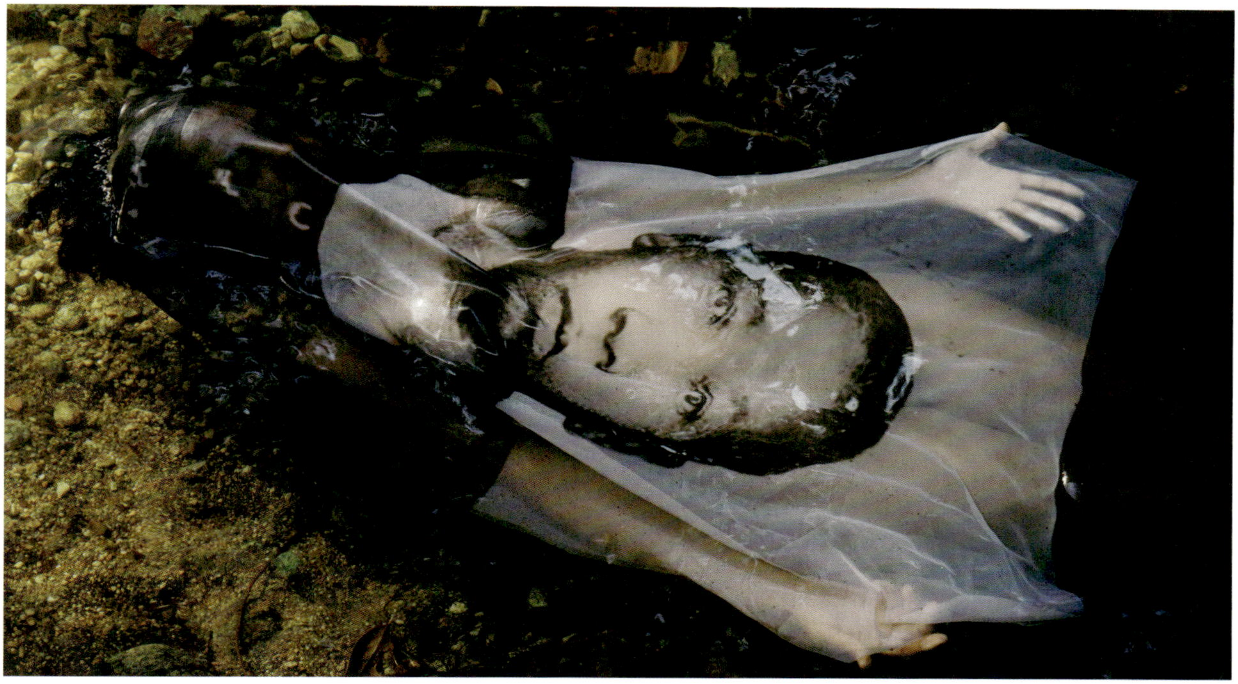

23 Aline Motta
Pontes sobre abismos #6
Bridges over the Abyss #6
2017

24 Aline Motta
Se o mar tivesse varandas #3
If the Sea Had Balconies #3
2017

25 Aline Motta
Se o mar tivesse varandas #4
If the Sea Had Balconies #4
2017

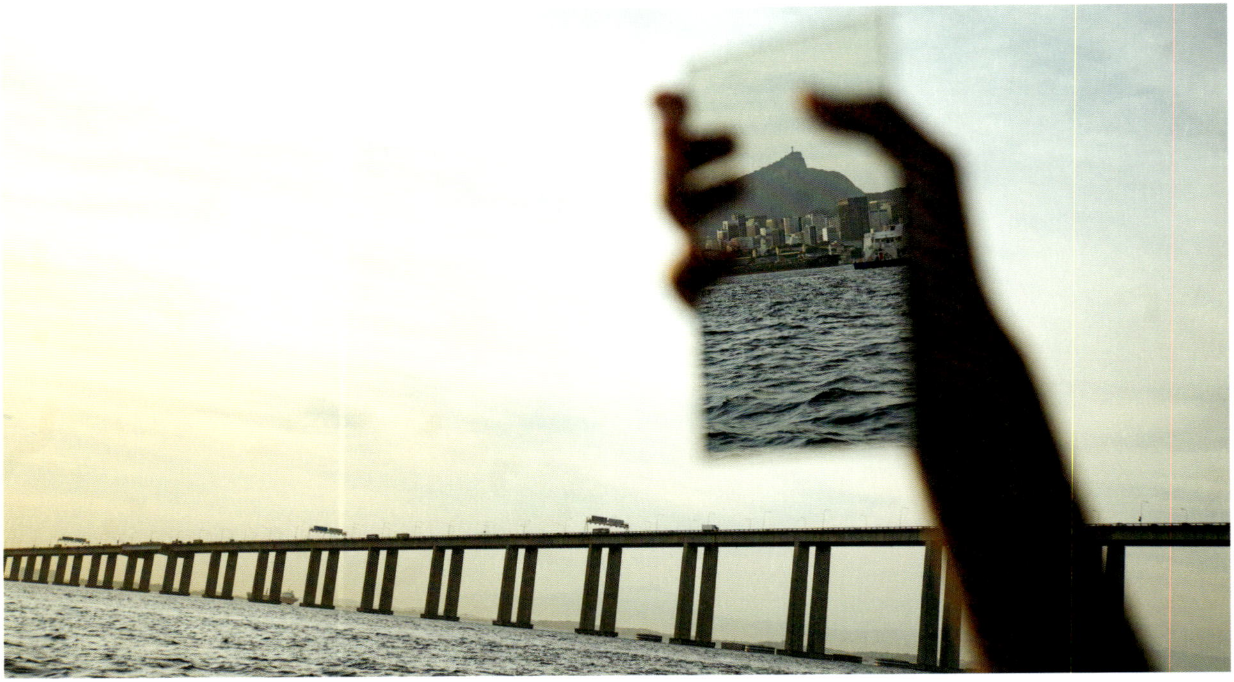

26 Aline Motta
(Outros) Fundamentos #2
(Other) Foundations #2
2017–2019

27 Aline Motta
(Outros) Fundamentos #3
(Other) Foundations #3
2017–2019

28 Aline Motta
(Outros) Fundamentos #4
(Other) Foundations #4
2017–2019

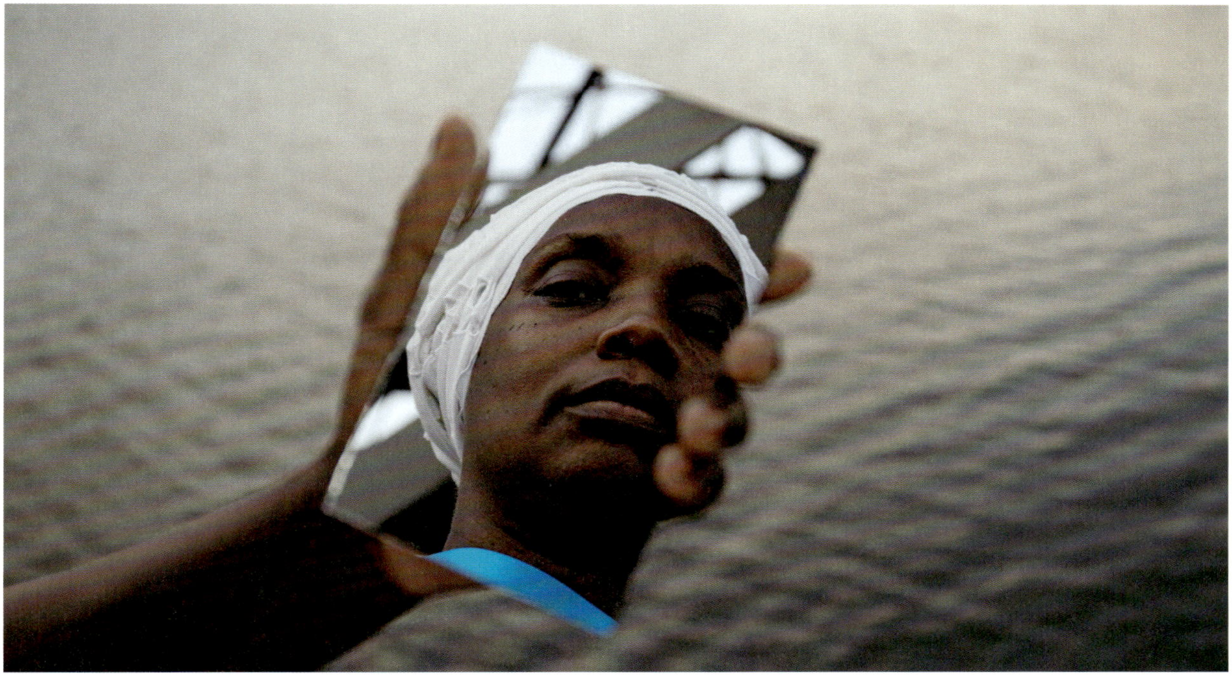

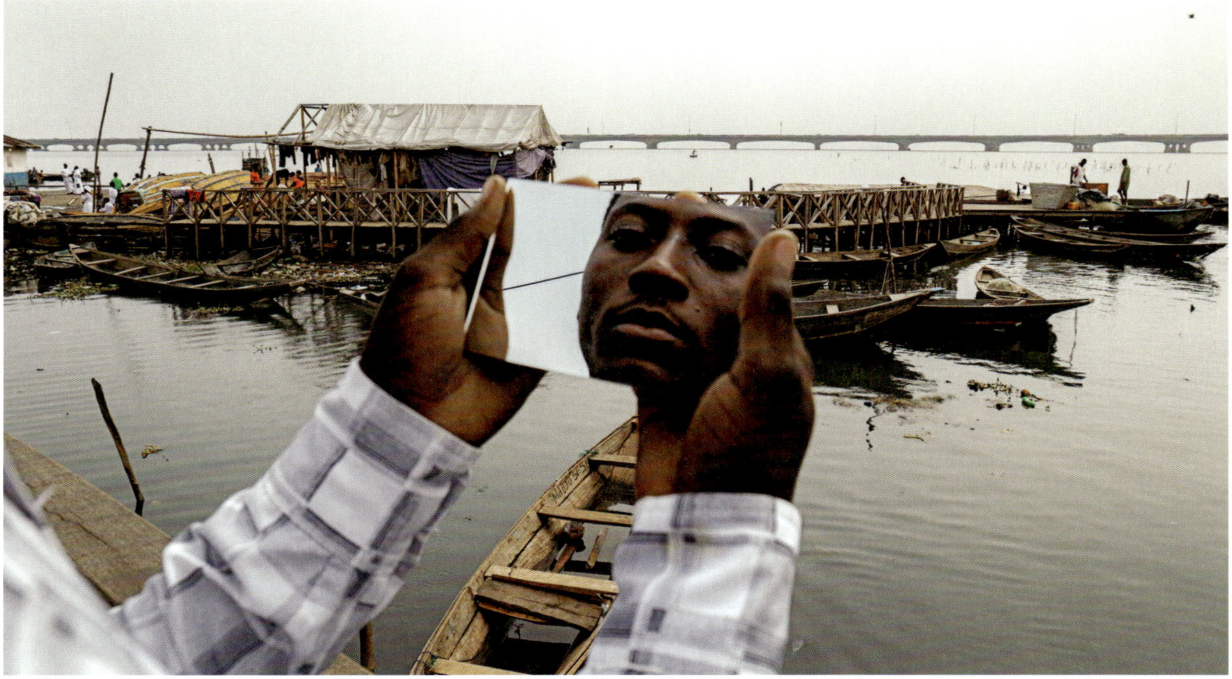

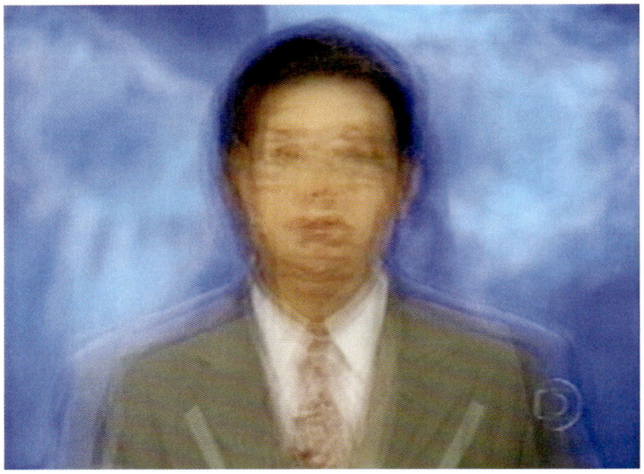

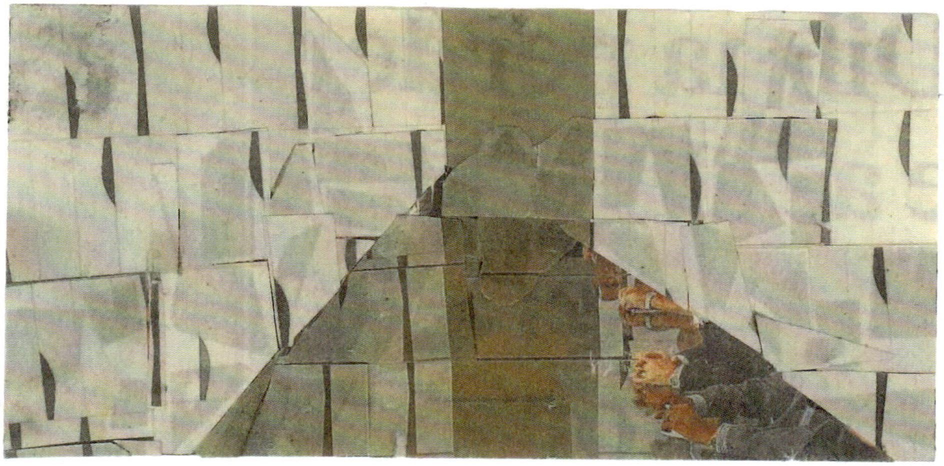

29 Lais Myrrha
Still from *Bestiário*
Still from Bestiary
2005

30 Lais Myrrha
27-04-2016. Articulação (vampiros não aparecem no espelho), da série *Reparação de danos*
27-04-2016. Articulation (Vampires Do Not Appear in the Mirror), from the series Reparation of Damages
2016

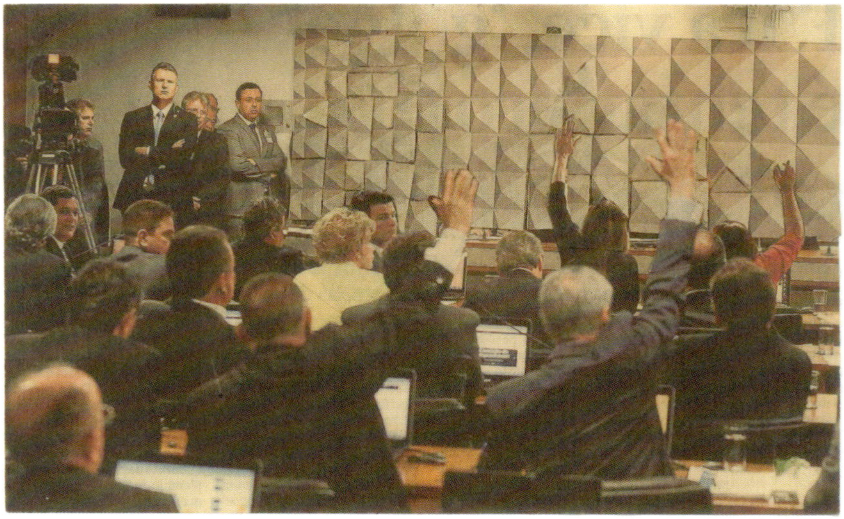

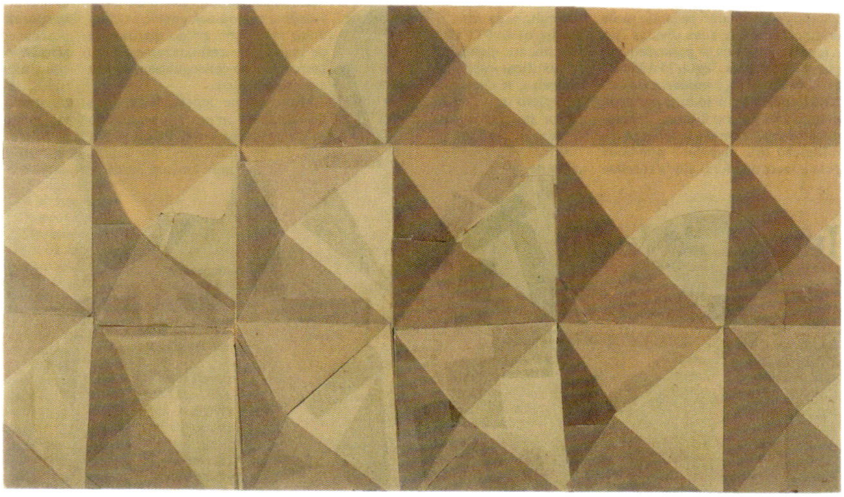

31 Lais Myrrha
27-04-2016. Painel do futuro (Raimundo Lira and others),
da série *Reparação de danos*
27-04-2016. Panel of the Future (Raimundo Lira and Others),
from the series Reparation of Damages
2016

32 Lais Myrrha
27-04-2016. Vultos do Brasil #1 (Aécio Neves and Antonio Anastasia), da série *Reparação de danos*
27-04-2016. Figures from Brazil #1 (Aécio Neves and Antonio Anastasia), from the series Reparation of Damages
2016

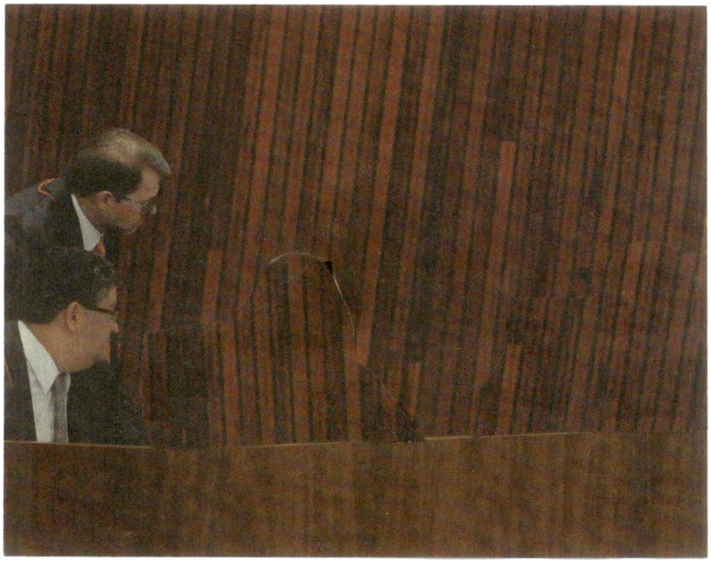

33 Lais Myrrha
04-05-2016. Isola! (Maria Thereza de Assis Moura and Gilmar Mendes), da série *Reparação de danos*
04-05-2016. Isolate! (Maria Thereza de Assis Moura and Gilmar Mendes), from the series Reparation of Damages
2016

34 Lais Myrrha
04-05-2016. Vultos do Brasil #2 (Delcidio do Amaral), da série *Reparação de danos*
04-05-2016. Figures from Brazil #2 (Delcidio do Amaral), from the series Reparation of Damages
2016

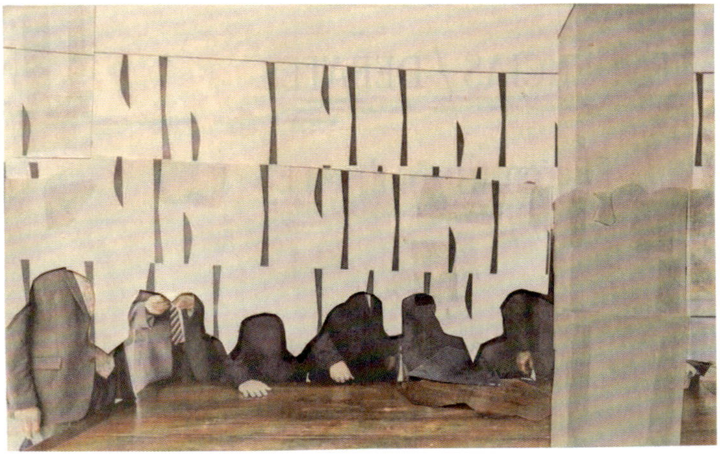

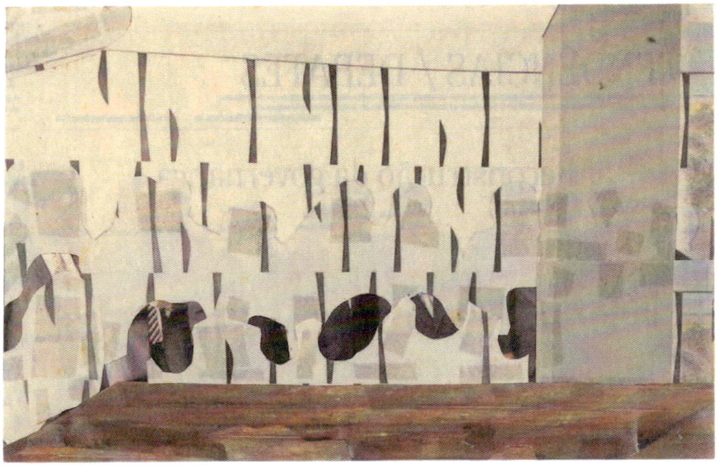

35 Lais Myrrha
13-05-2016. Ratos (andam baixo mas também fazem sombra) (Michel Temer and his ministers), da série *Reparação de danos*
13-05-2016. Rats (Walk Low but Also Cast Shadows) (Michel Temer and His Ministers), from the series Reparation of Damages
2016

36 Lais Myrrha
13-05-2016. Ratos (sempre deixam buracos) (Michel Temer and his ministers), da série *Reparação de danos*
13-05-2016. Rats (Always Leave Holes) (Michel Temer and His Ministers), from the series Reparation of Damages
2016

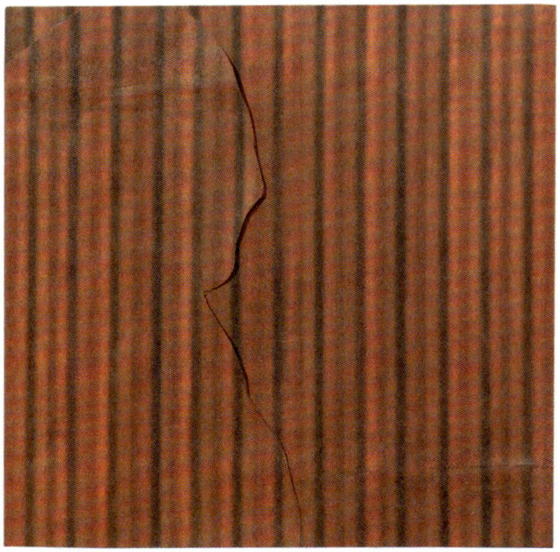

37 Lais Myrrha
16-06-2016. Problema de fundo #1 (Michel Temer), da série *Reparação de danos*
16-06-2016. Background Problem #1 (Michel Temer), from the series Reparation of Damages
2016

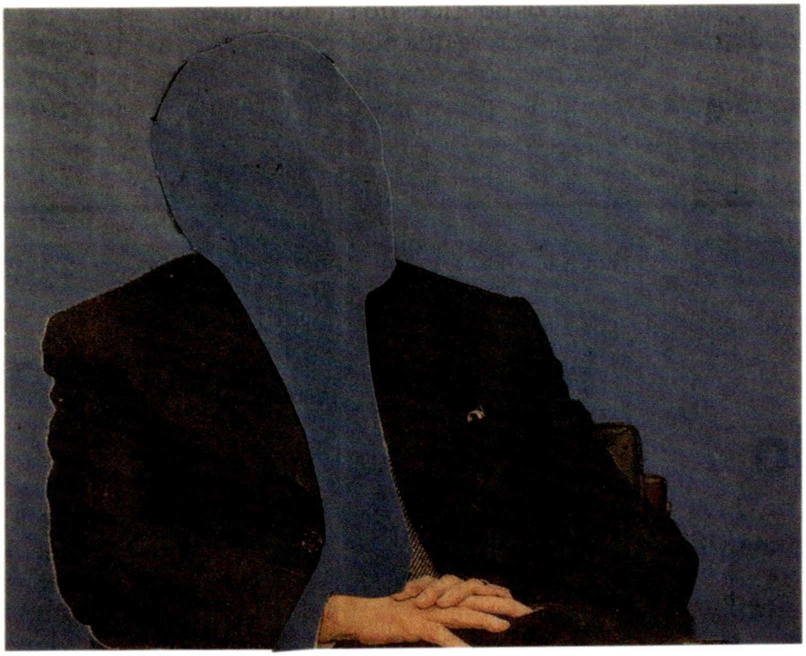

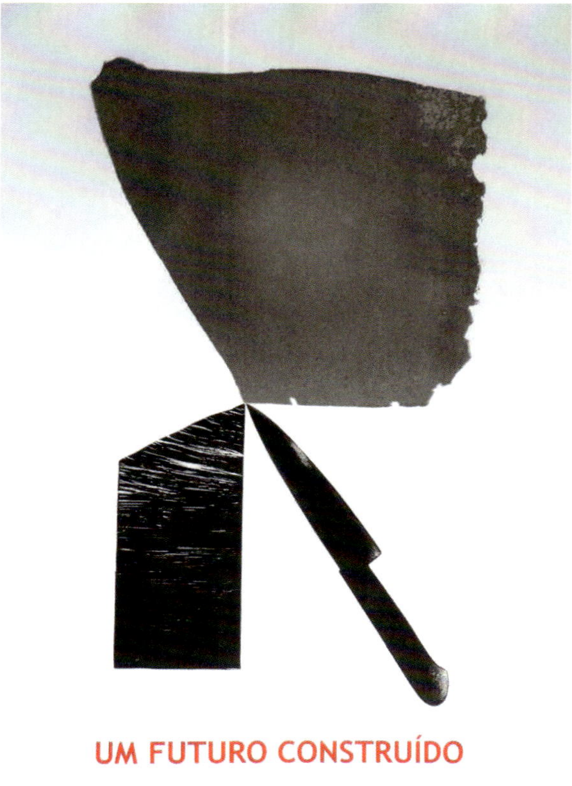

38 Lais Myrrha
16-06-2016. Tudo azul #2 (Michel Temer),
da série *Reparação de danos*
16-06-2016. All Good #2 (Michel Temer),
from the series Reparation of Damages
2016

39 Lais Myrrha
Um futuro construído
A Future Built
2018

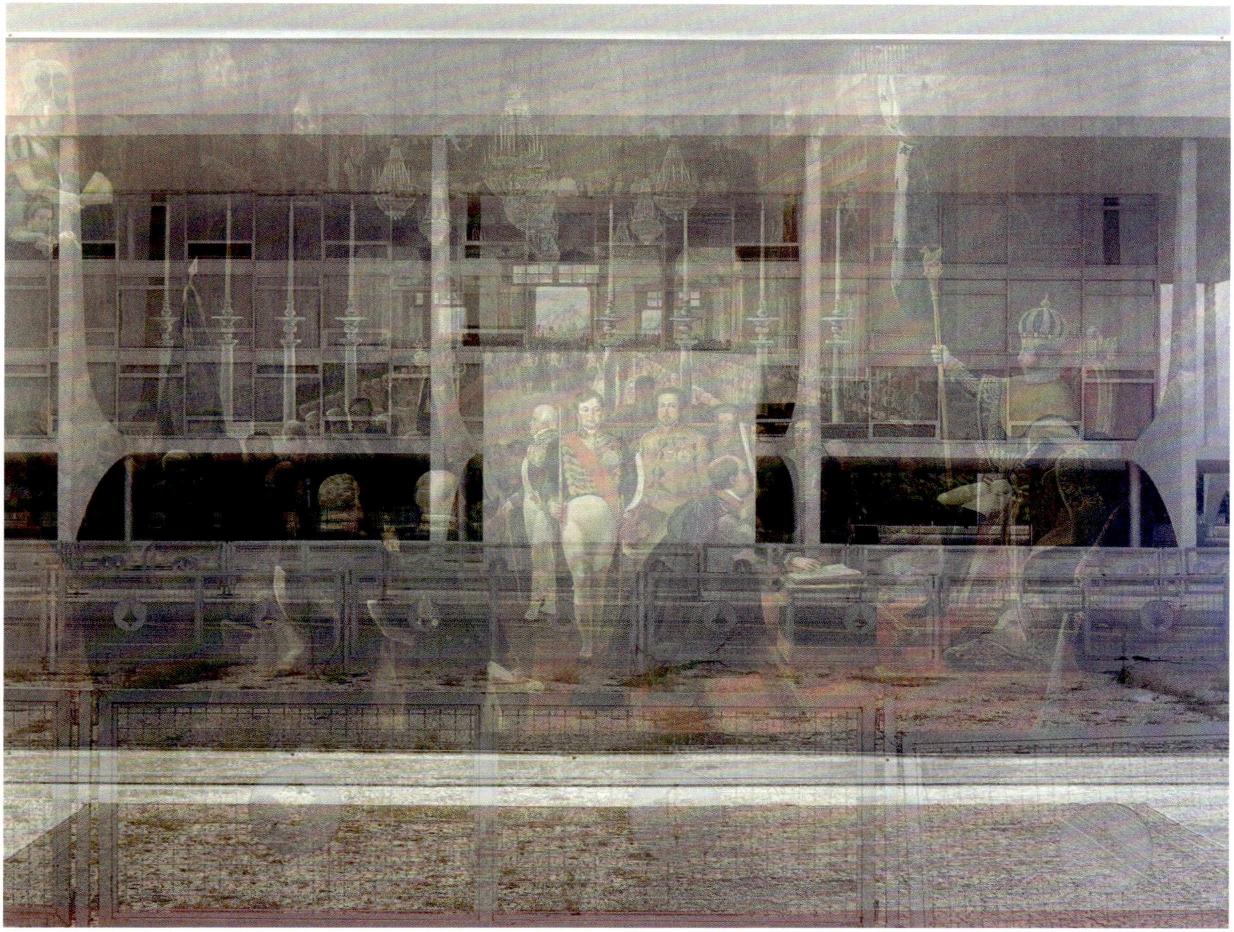

40 Lais Myrrha
Dupla exposição (cena #2). View of Palácio do Planalto and Internal View of Itamaraty with Jean-Baptiste Debret's Painting The Coronation of Dom Pedro I
Double Exposure (scene #2). View of Palácio do Planalto and Internal View of Itamaraty with Jean-Baptiste Debret's Painting *The Coronation of Dom Pedro I*
2022

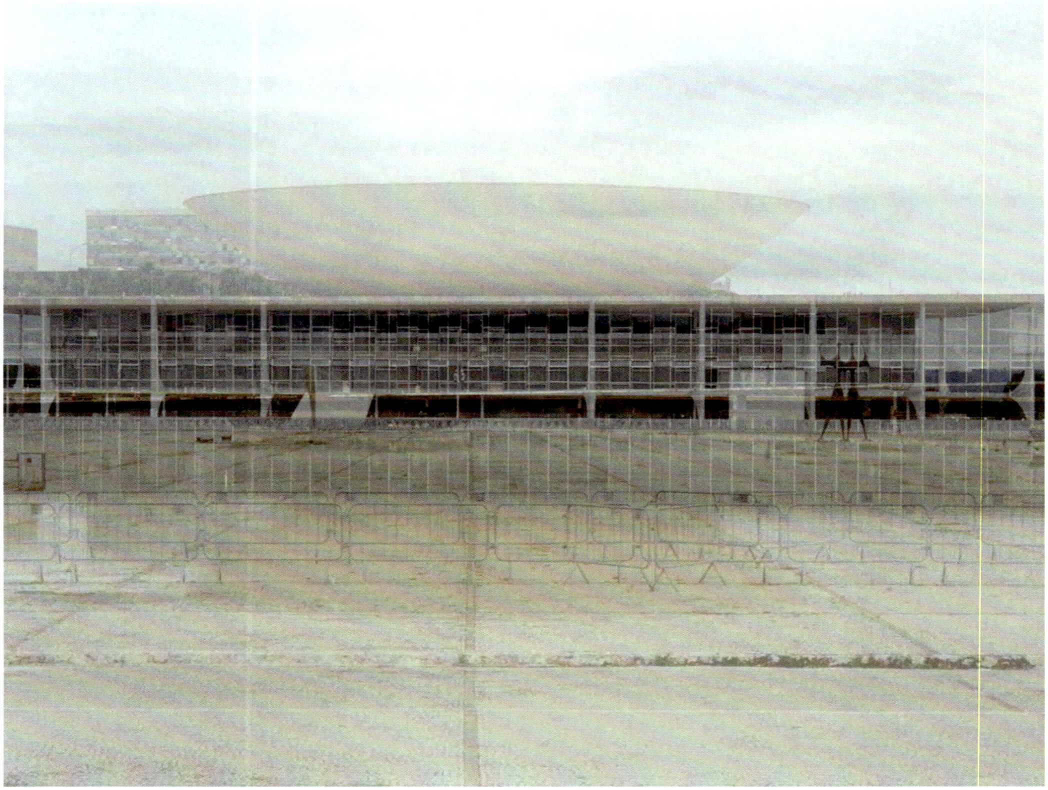

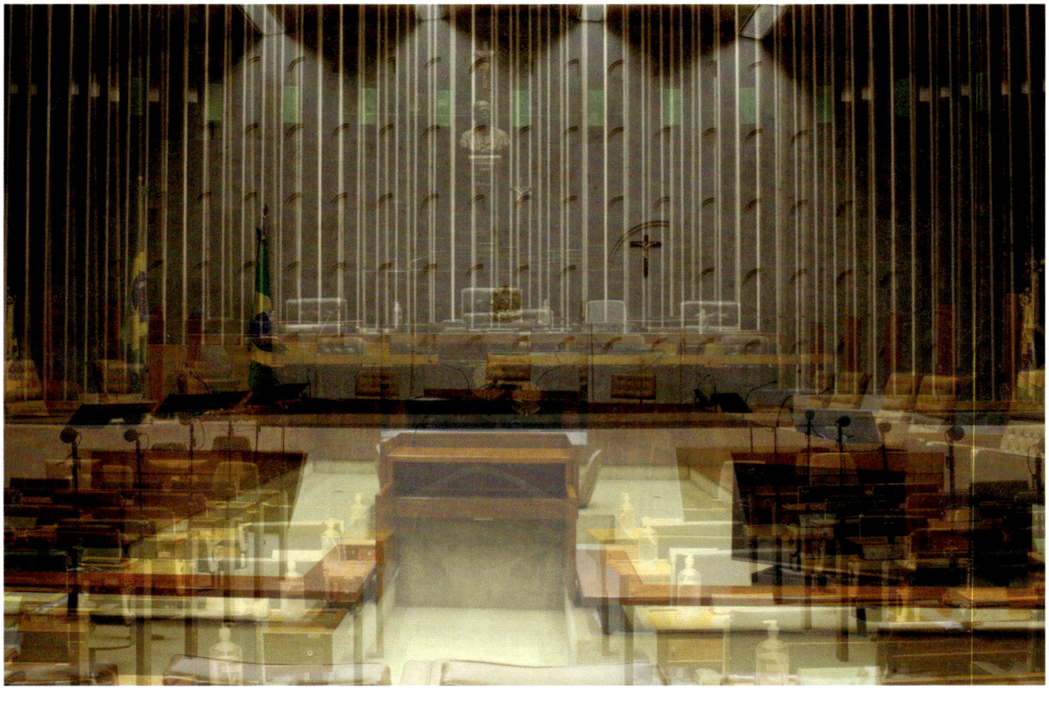

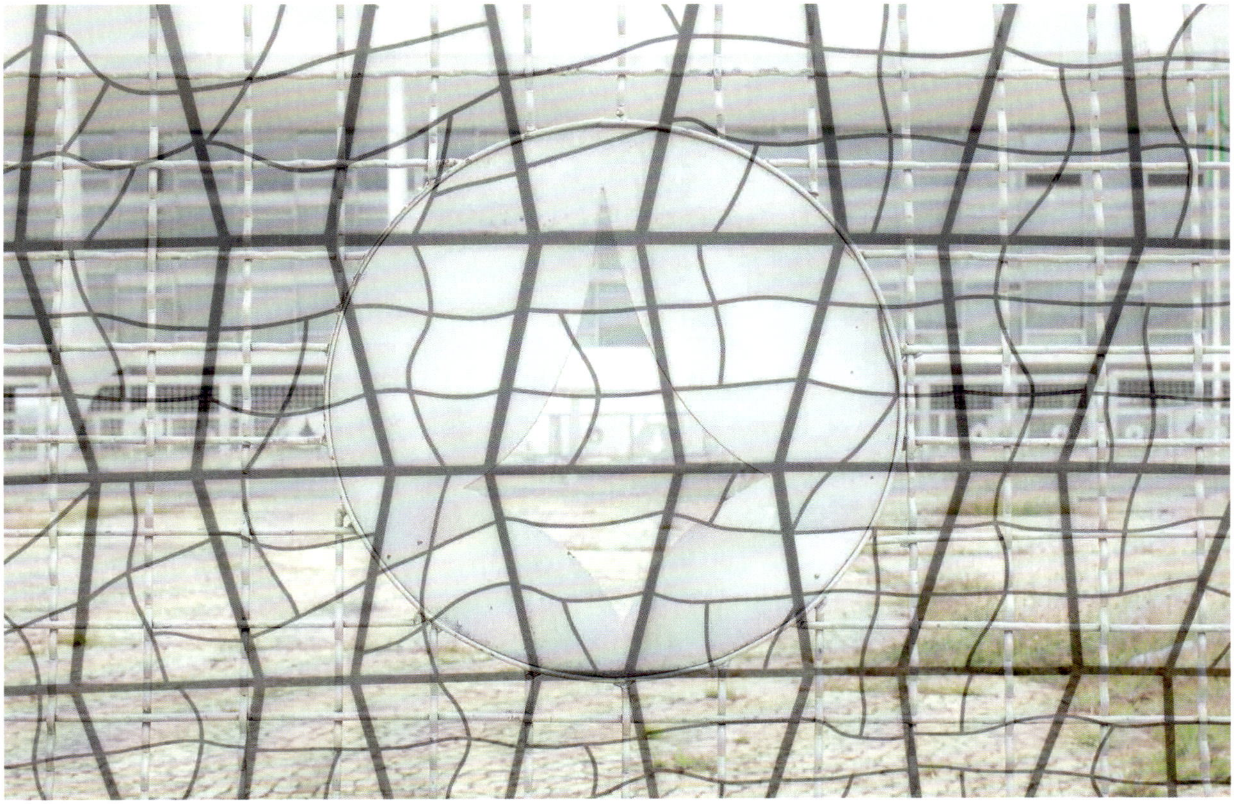

41 Lais Myrrha
Dupla exposição (cena #3). View of Palácio do Planalto and View of the National Congress
Double Exposure (scene #3). View of Palácio do Planalto and View of the National Congress
2022

42 Lais Myrrha
Dupla exposição (cena #5). The Three Plenaries (Senate, Deputy Chamber, and Federal Supreme Court)
Double Exposure (scene #5). The Three Plenaries (Senate, Deputy Chamber, and Federal Supreme Court)
2022

43 Lais Myrrha
Dupla exposição (cena #7). View of Palácio do Planalto and Internal View of the Brasília Cathedral
Double Exposure (scene #7). View of Palácio do Planalto and Internal View of the Brasília Cathedral
2022

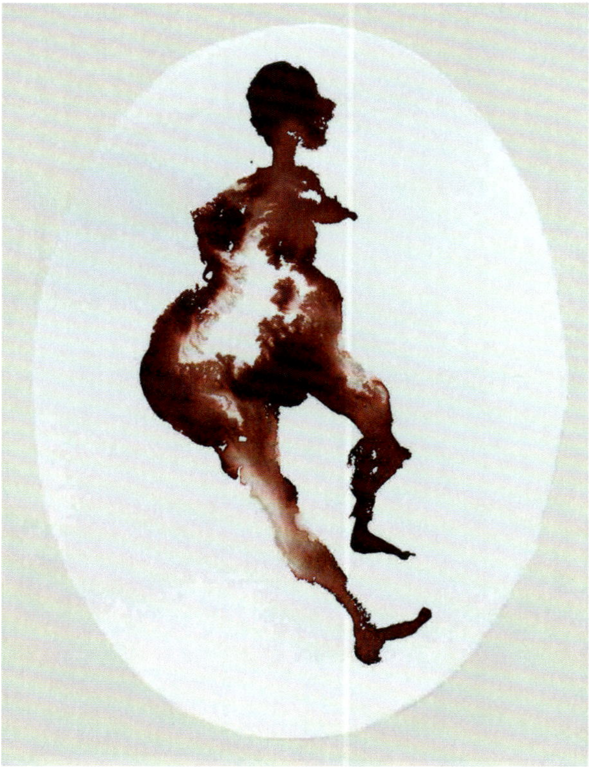

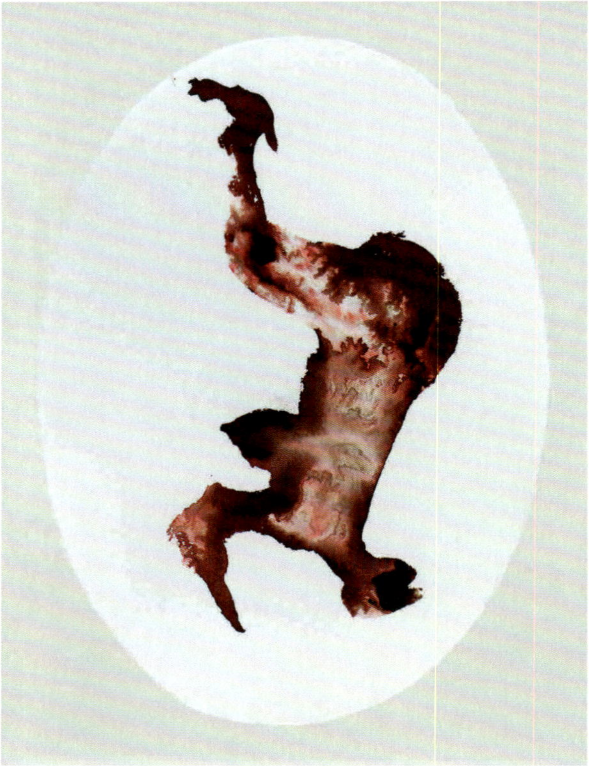

44 Antonio Obá
Mãe
Mother
2017

45 Antonio Obá
Mãe
Mother
2017

46 Antonio Obá
Mãe
Mother
2017

47 Antonio Obá
Mãe
Mother
2017

48 Antonio Obá
Mãe
Mother
2017

49 Antonio Obá
Mãe
Mother
2017

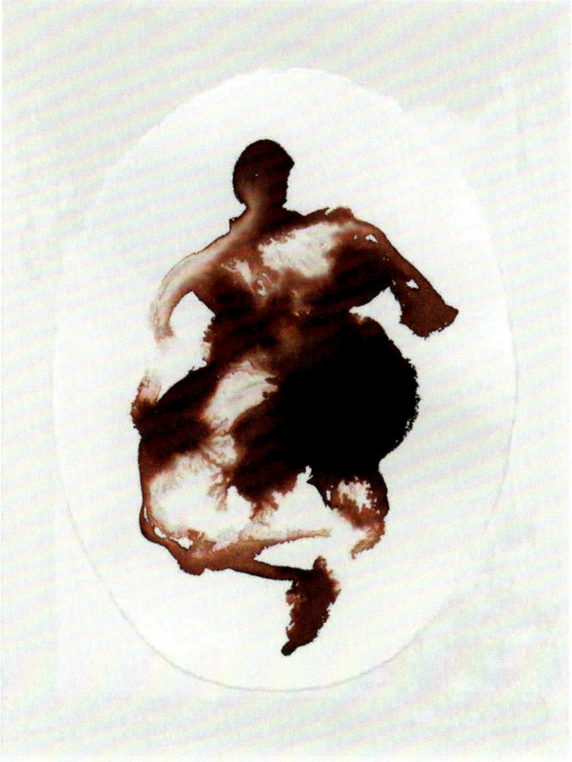
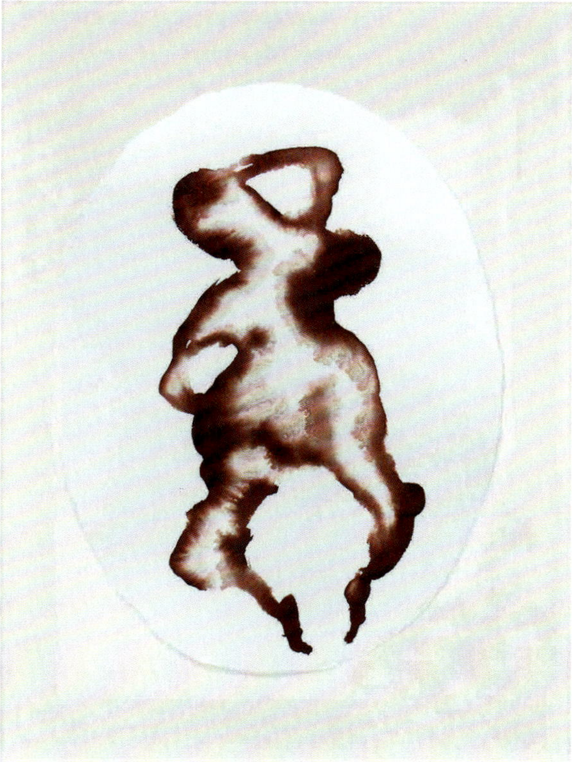
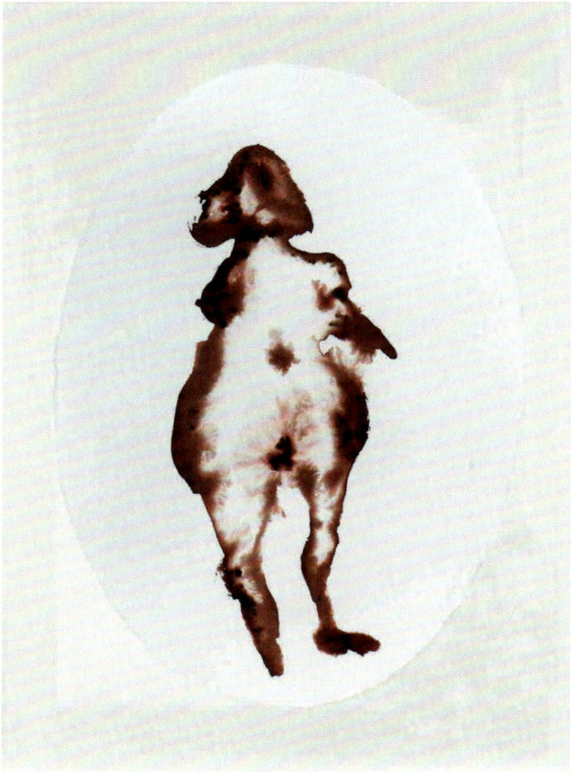
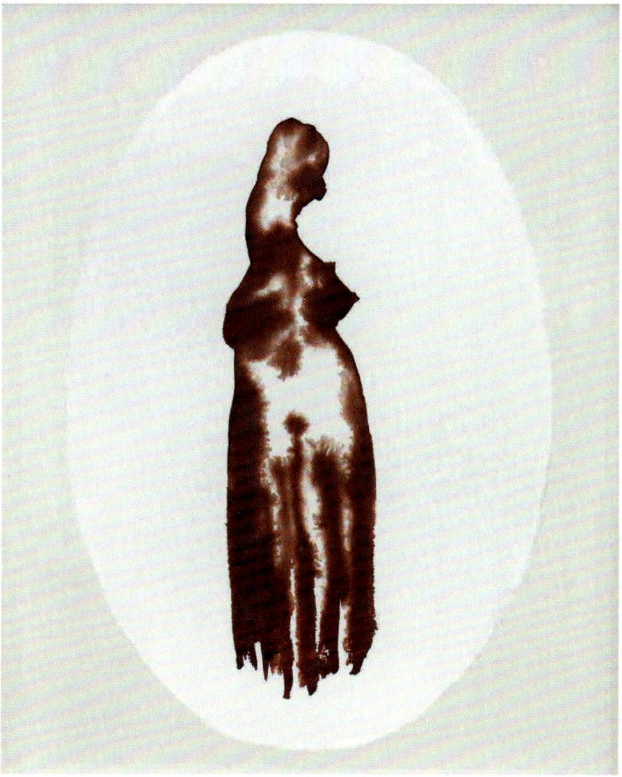

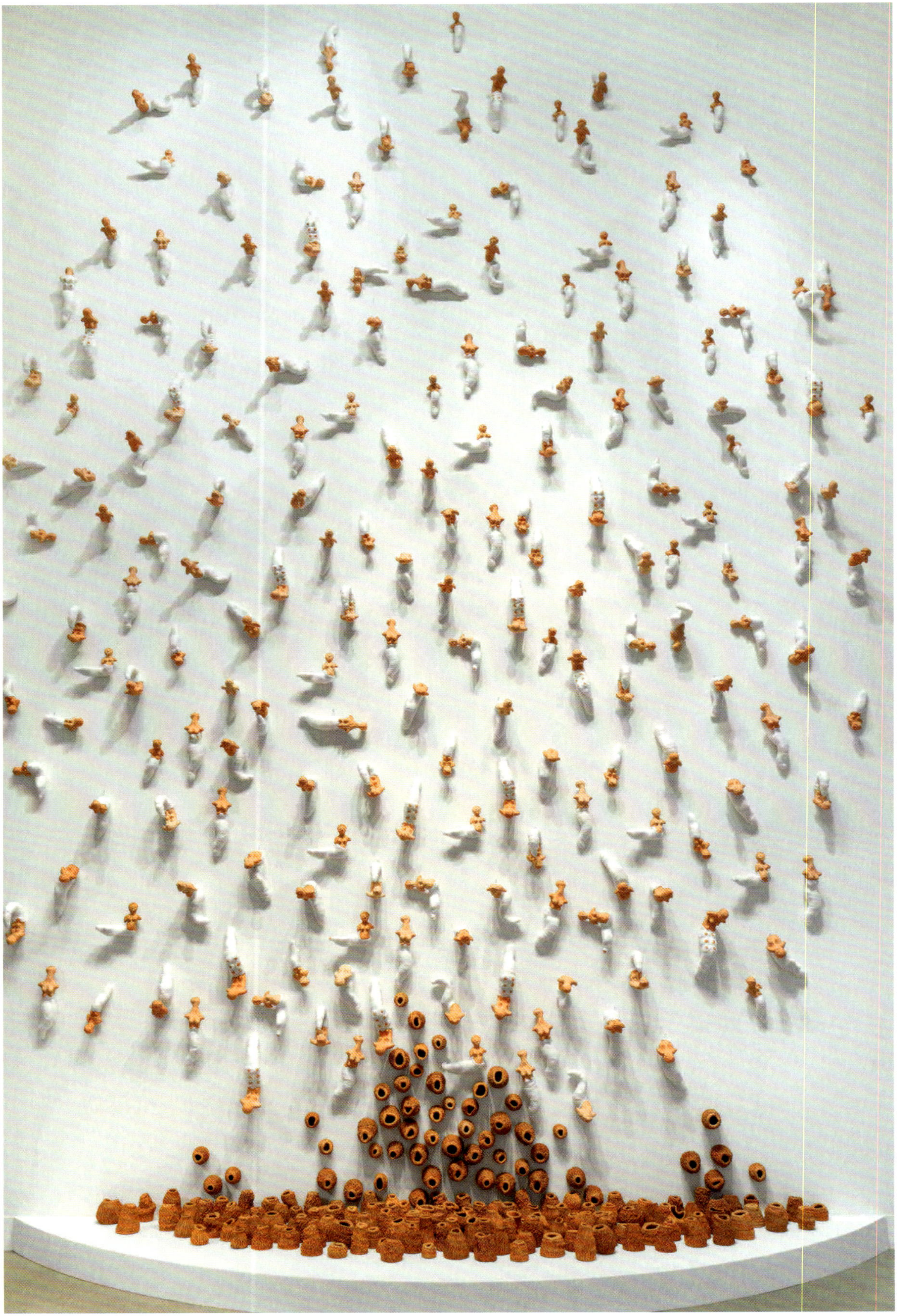

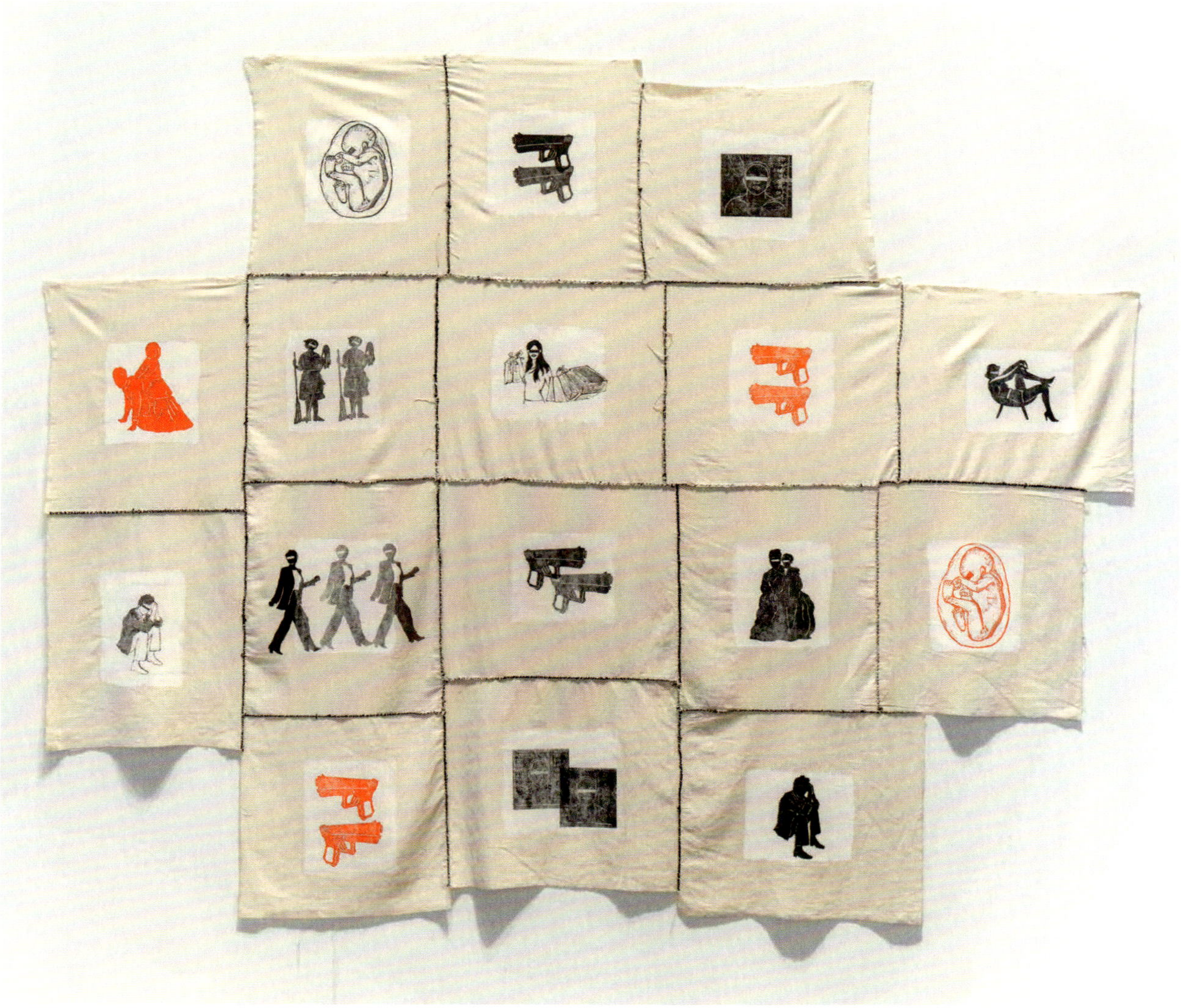

50 Rosana Paulino
Tecelãs
Weavers
2003

51 Rosana Paulino
Tecido social
Social Fabric
2010

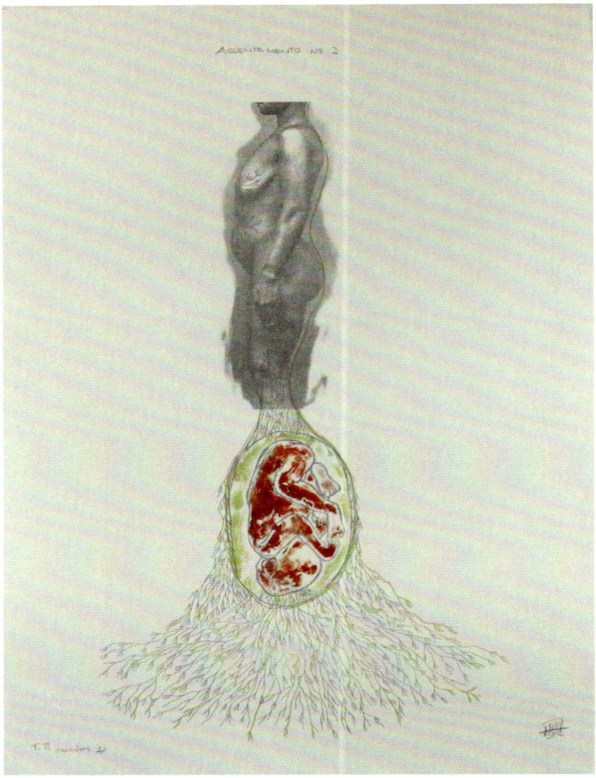

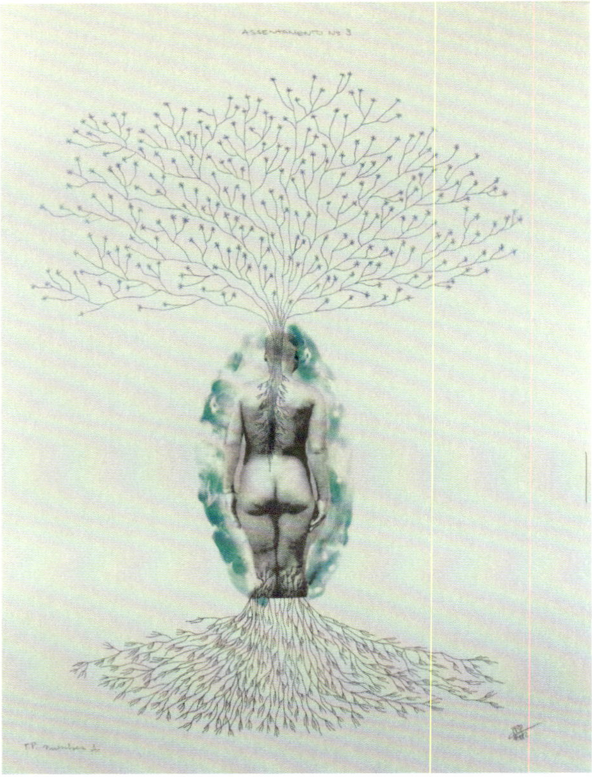

52 Rosana Paulino
Assentamento no. 2
Settlement no. 2
2012–2013

53 Rosana Paulino
Assentamento no. 3
Settlement no. 3
2012–2013

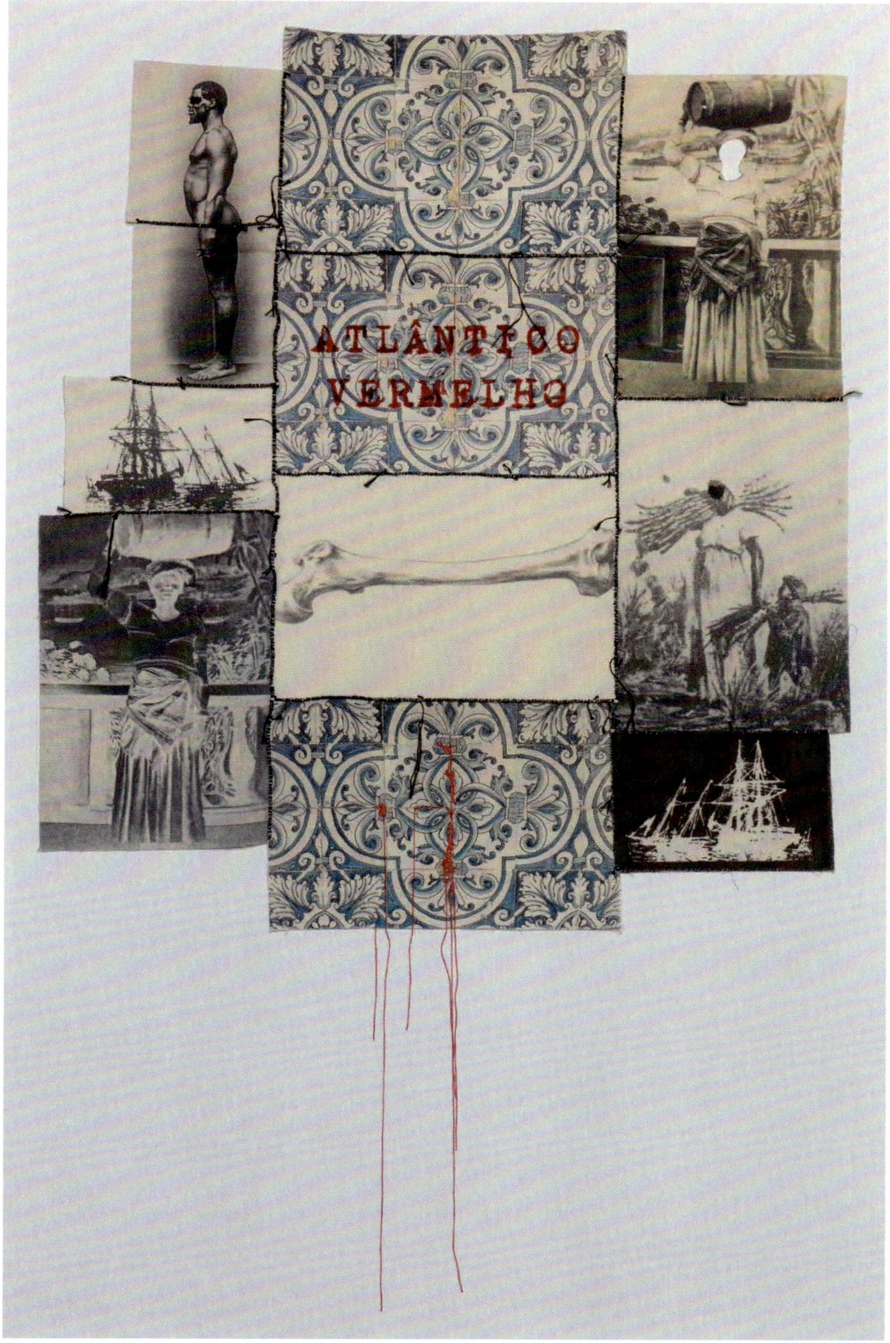

54 Rosana Paulino
Atlântico vermelho
Red Atlantic
2017

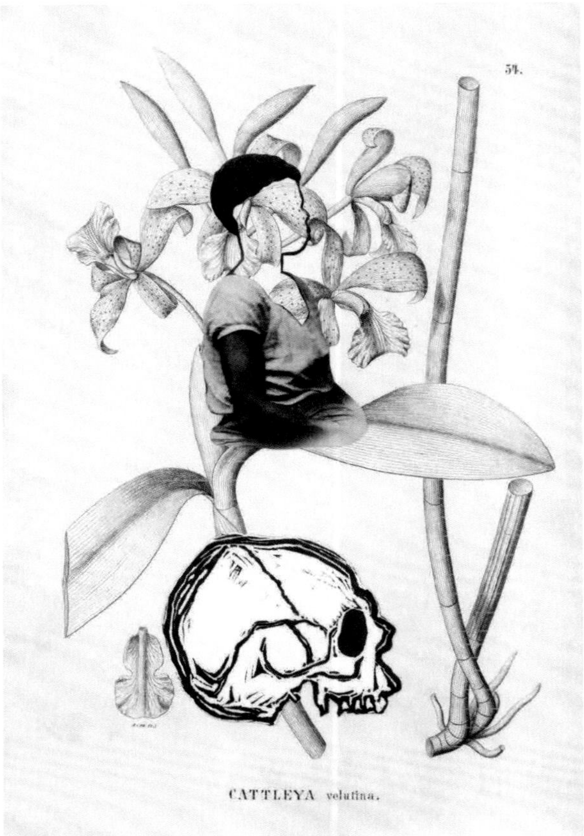

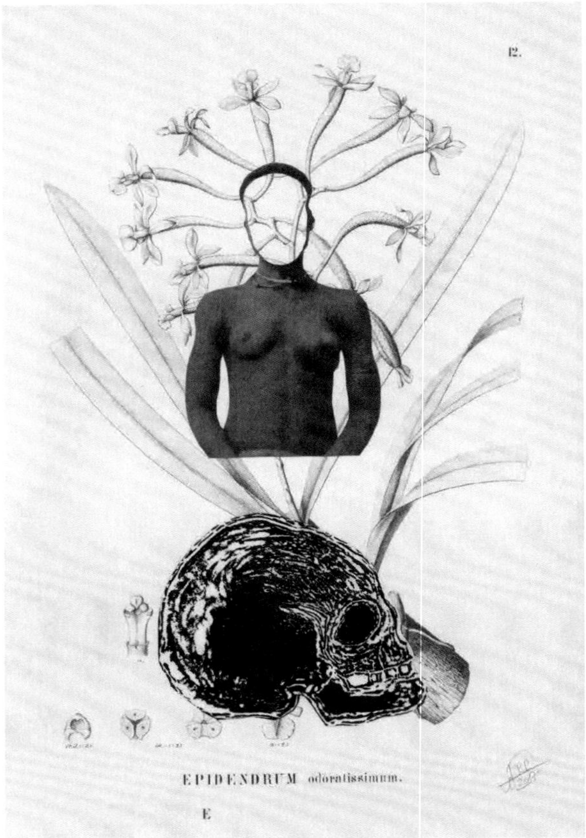

55 Rosana Paulino
Paraíso tropical
Tropical Paradise
2017

56 Rosana Paulino
Paraíso tropical
Tropical Paradise
2017

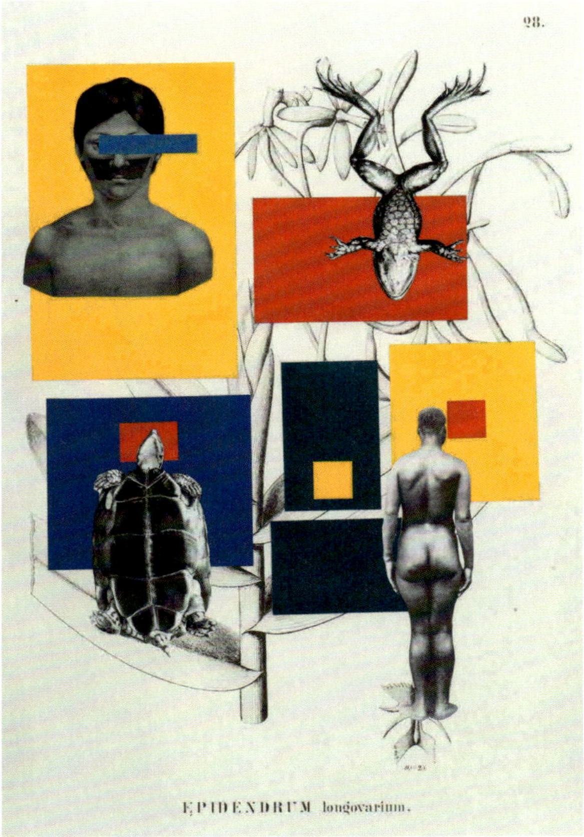

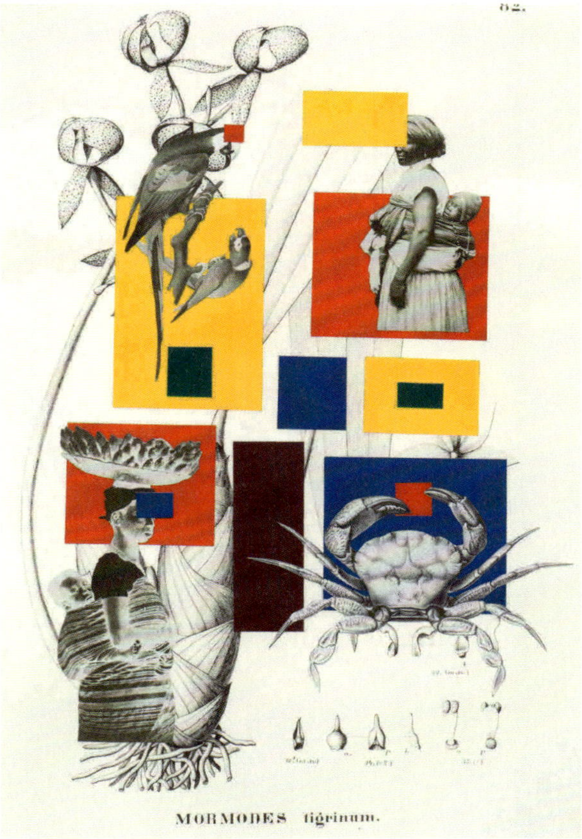

57 Rosana Paulino
A geometria à brasileira chega ao paraíso tropical
Brazilian-Style Geometry Arrives in Tropical Paradise
2018

58 Rosana Paulino
A geometria à brasileira chega ao paraíso tropical
Brazilian-Style Geometry Arrives in Tropical Paradise
2018

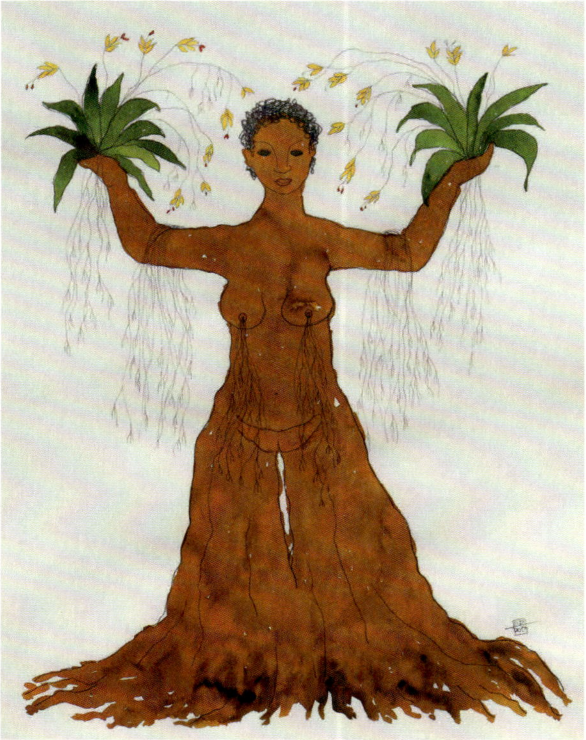

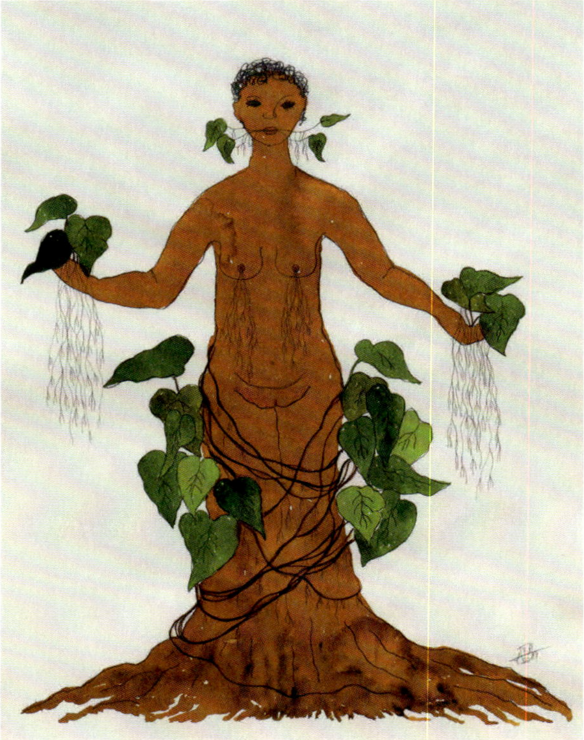

59 Rosana Paulino
Sem título, da série *Jatobá*
Untitled, from the series Jatobá
2019

60 Rosana Paulino
Sem título, da série *Jatobá*
Untitled, from the series Jatobá
2019

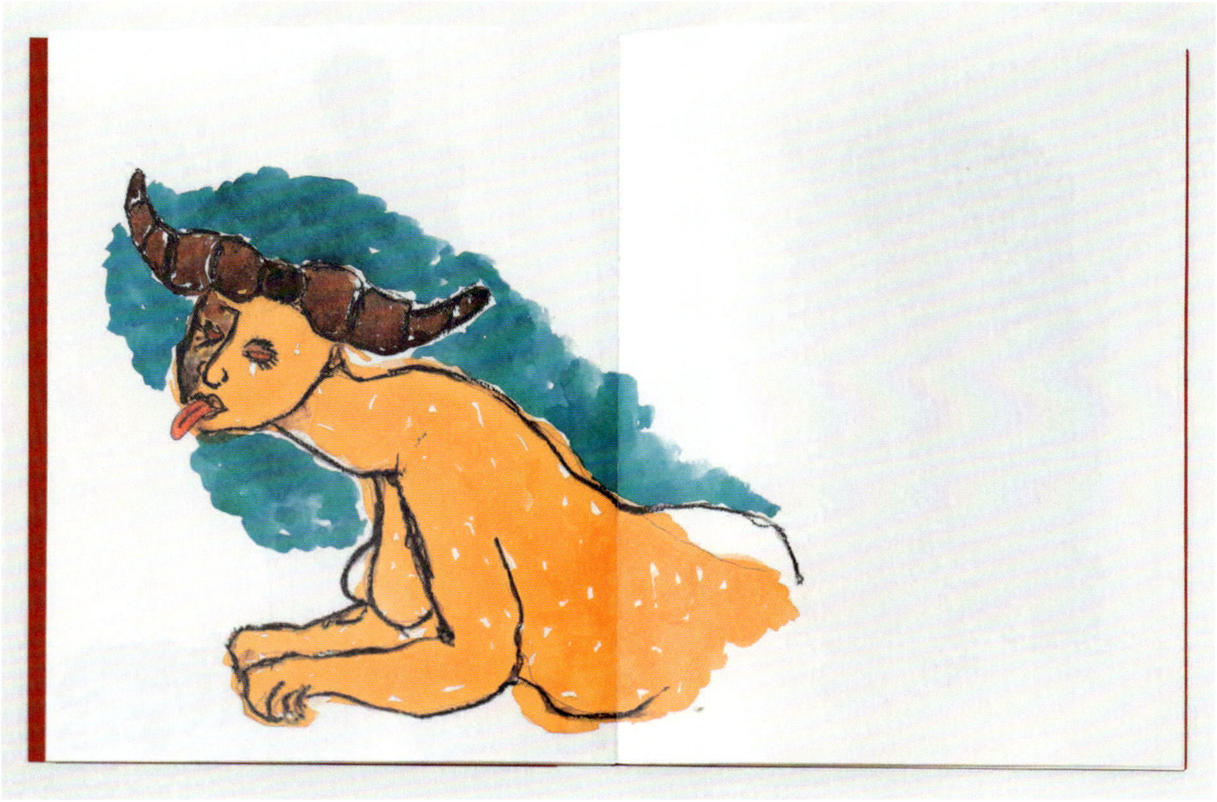

61 Rosana Paulino
Spread from *Búfala e senhora das plantas*
Spread from Buffalo and Lady of Plants
2021

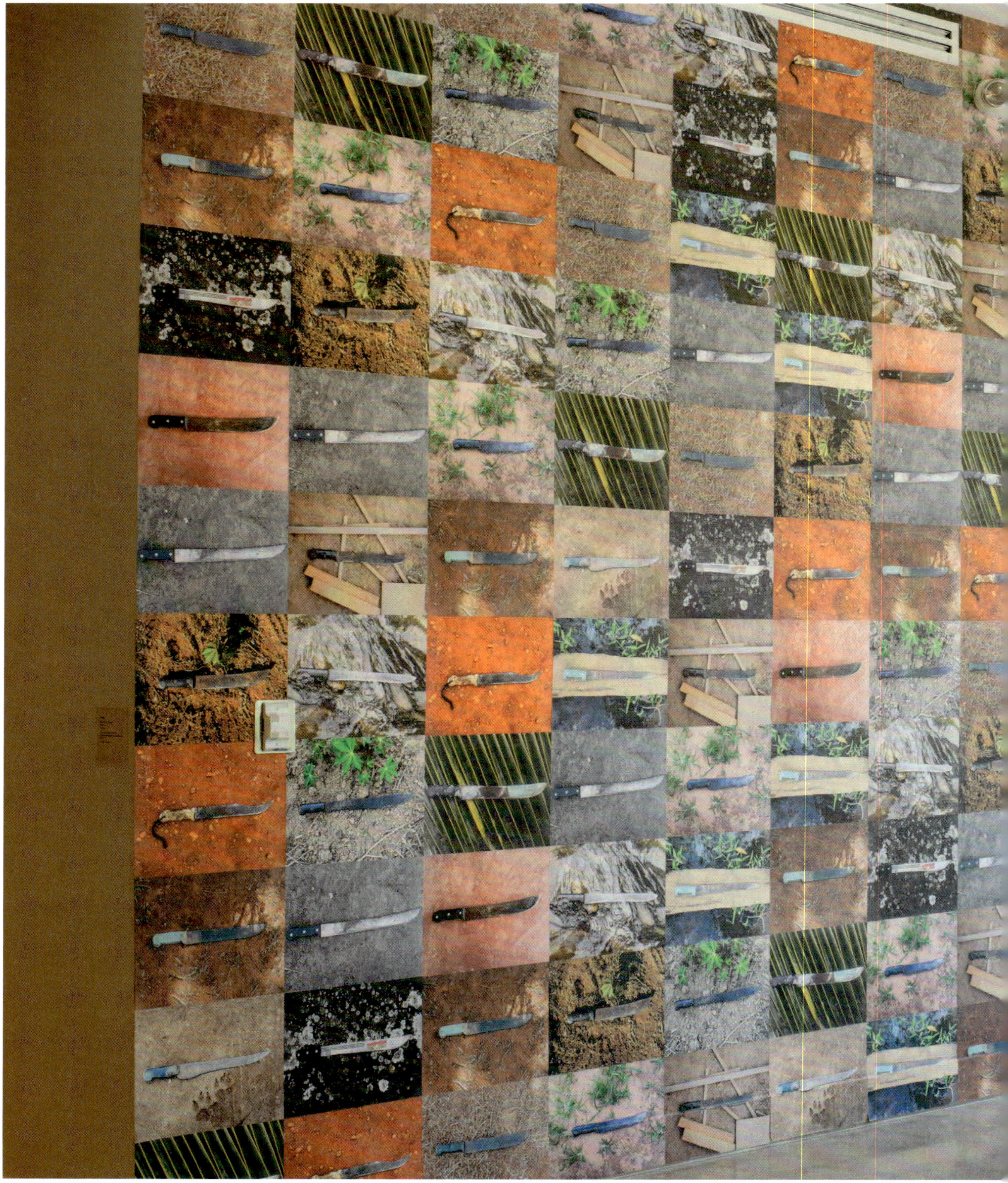

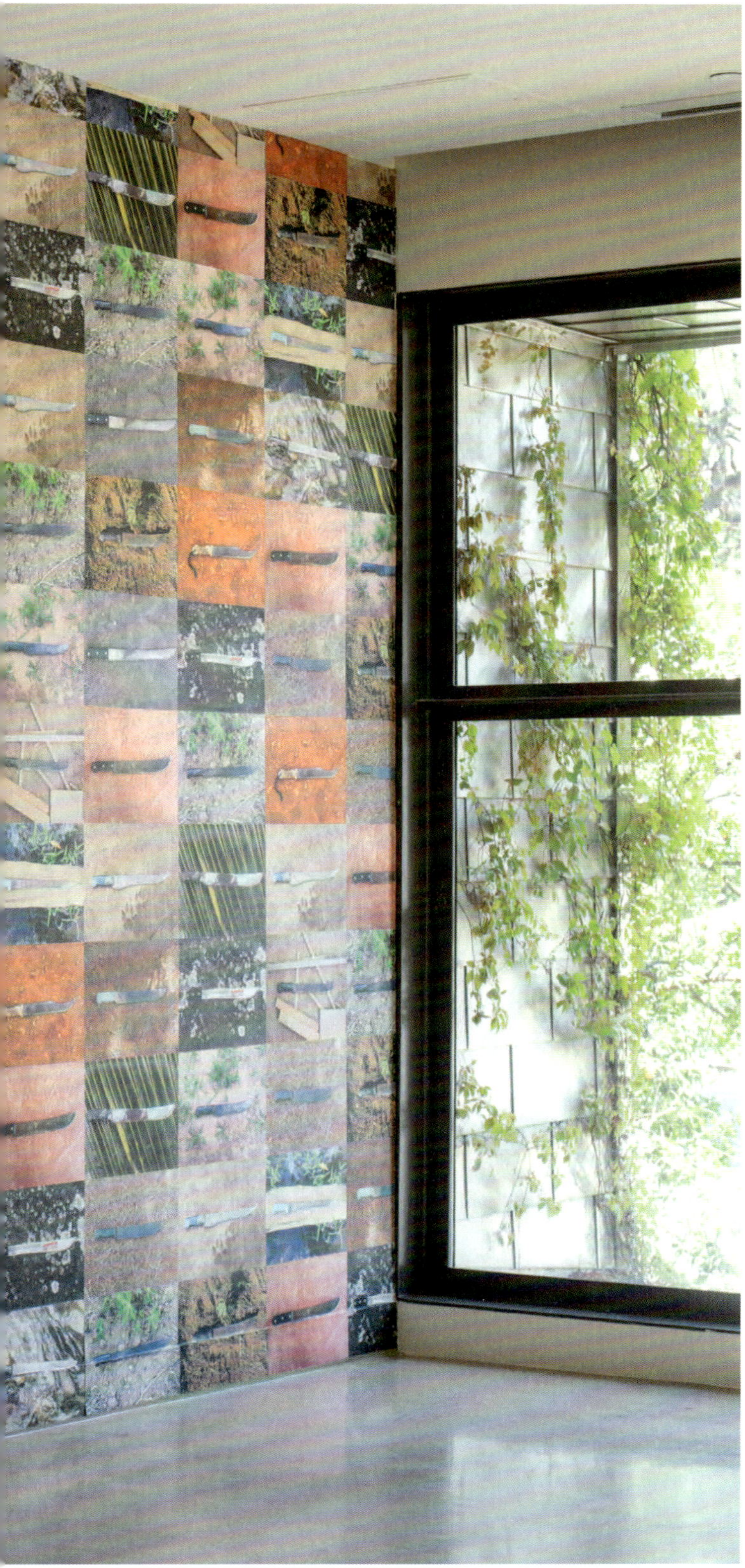

62 Sallisa Rosa
Resistência
Resistance
2017–present

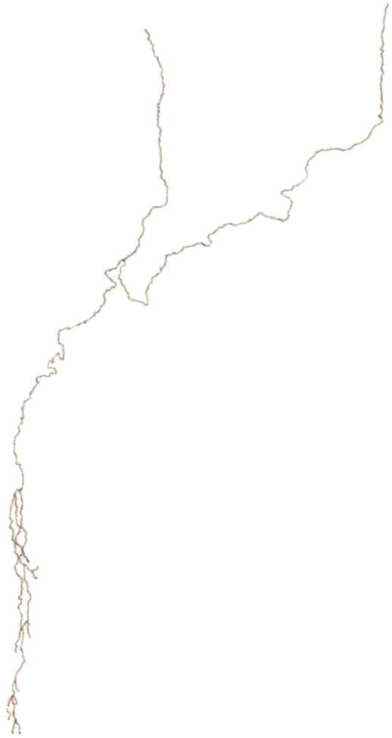

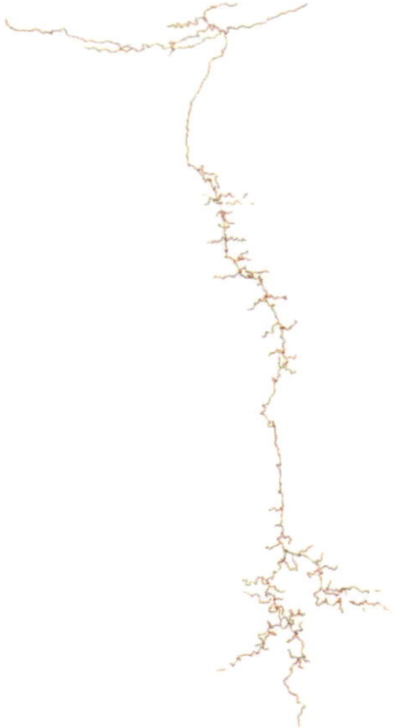

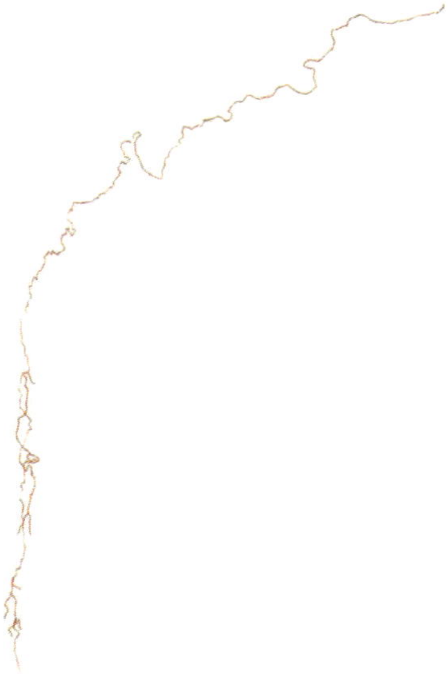

63 Sallisa Rosa
Sem título, da série *Lembranças*
Untitled, from the series Keepsakes
2021

64 Sallisa Rosa
Sem título, da série *Lembranças*
Untitled, from the series Keepsakes
2021

65 Sallisa Rosa
Sem título, da série *Lembranças*
Untitled, from the series Keepsakes
2021

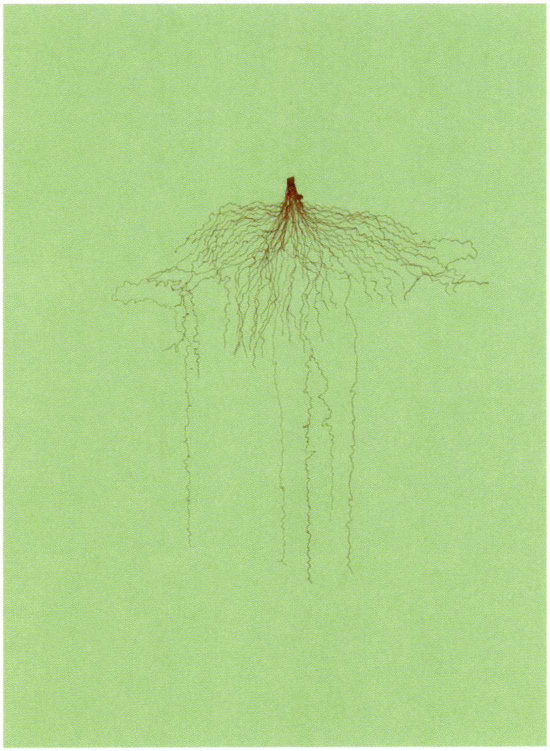

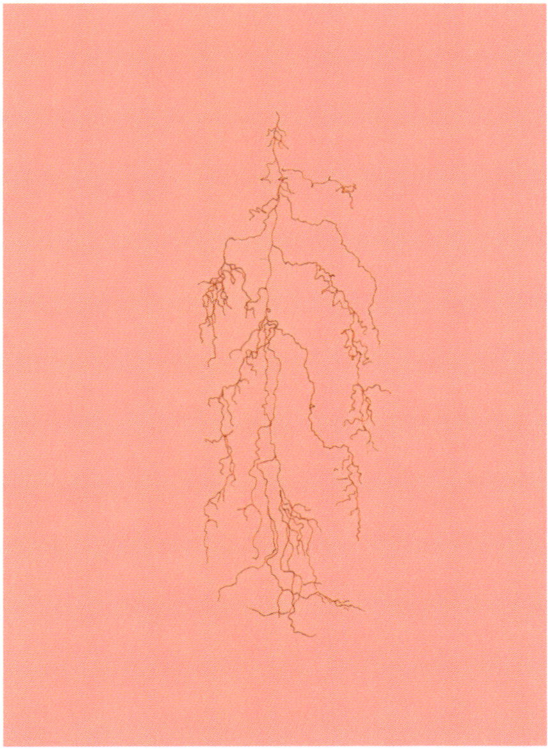

66 Sallisa Rosa
Sem título, da série *Lembranças*
Untitled, from the series Keepsakes
2021

67 Sallisa Rosa
Sem título, da série *Lembranças*
Untitled, from the series Keepsakes
2021

Carta aos indígenas do planeta Marte com códigos de reconhecimento do planeta Terra

Denilson Baniwa

2020

Tradução:
Niterói, Terra Indígena Karioka
Ao parente que vive na Terra Indígena Marte.
Do amigo e parente, Denilson Baniwa

Oi, bom tempo! Seja manhã, tarde, noite ou madrugada. Espero que hoje tenha chovido aí, nenhuma chuva ácida nenhum temporal. Só uma chuva mesmo, sabe? Daquelas que molham o chão e refresca a quentura. Sim, essa. Aquela que faz um barulho quando cai na terra, que molha as plantas e tira o calor do solo. Daquela que dá esperança e não desespero. Pode ser um sol também, se você está num dia gelado ou numa tempestade que não passa. Seja um dia que revigore suas energias e fé.

Queria te contar uma coisa engraçada, na TV está passando um programa chamado Largados e Pelados, o nome é engraçado, e a sinopse diz que: "a cada semana um homem e uma mulher são levados a um dos ambientes de clima mais extremo do mundo. Os dois ficarão literalmente expostos, já que serão deixados sem comida, sem água e sem roupas". Neste episódio duas pessoas são levadas para a savana da Guiana, e lá com um facão, uma pederneira e uma panela têm a chance de provar que conseguem sobreviver sem a ajuda de equipamentos da vida na cidade. Não é o primeiro episódio que vejo, então consegui circular um padrão, te conto aqui porque é engraçado, e pode ser útil para mim e de que forma pretendo terminar esta carta.

Letter to the Indigenous Peoples of Planet Mars with Recognition Codes from Planet Earth

Denilson Baniwa

2020

Translation:
Niterói, Indigenous Land of the Kariokas
To our relatives living on Indigenous Martian Land.
From your friend and relative, Denilson Baniwa

Greetings and fair weather! Whether it be morning, afternoon, or evening where you are. I hope it rained there today. Not a storm or acid rain. Just normal rain, you know? The kind of rain that wets the ground and cools everything off. Yes, that kind. The kind that makes noise when it hits the earth, that wets the plants and removes heat from the soil. The kind that brings hope, not desperation. Or I wish you sunny weather, if it's a cold day or one with a storm that just won't pass. May it be a day that reinvigorates your energy and faith.

I wanted to tell you something funny. On TV there's a show called *Naked and Afraid*—the name is funny—and the synopsis says that "every week a man and a woman are taken to one of the most extreme environments in the world. They are left there completely exposed, without food, water or clothes." On this episode, two people are taken to the Guianan savanna, and there with just a machete, some flint, and a pot they are given a chance to prove that they can survive without the help of the modern appliances of the city. It's not the first episode I've seen, and I've begun to notice some patterns, which I'll tell you about here because they're funny and since they could be useful to me and the way I intend to end this letter.

Bom, o padrão que percebi foi: as pessoas que desistem na primeira semana, são as que chegam contando vantagem e falando sobre suas experiências nas forças armadas ou no domínio das adversidades; os homens desistem mais rápido; a água e fogo são essenciais para manter a sanidade mental; apesar da carne ser muito importante como fonte de proteína, a falta dela não é certeza de continuar firme no programa. As mulheres que vi nos episódios, conseguem ser mais práticas e inteligentes; elas não desistem fácil e encontram soluções engenhosas. No que estou assistindo agora, não foi diferente, o homem desistiu no segundo dia e a mulher está se mantendo firme, apesar das adversidades. Ela pegou um Bauari agora, um peixinho de água doce. Estou torcendo por ela.

Assistindo este episódio, tenho pensado no que é realmente essencial na vida moderna. O que precisamos pra viver bem? Talvez essa TV que está ligada não seja essencial, talvez ela me afaste ainda mais do que é a natureza. Natureza da qual nós, eu e você, fazemos parte. Já faz um tempo que não pesco um Bauari. É, já faz um tempo.

Outra coisa que pensei foi, imagina se não tivesse mais floresta, nem rios, nem savanas, nem nada ... como seria o programa? Talvez ao invés de largados e pelados na natureza, seria um "largados e pelados" no apocalipse, né? Vai saber.

Outro dia vi que os planos de morar em outros planetas estão avançando, quer dizer, essa gente lá da NASA, já sabe que pelo ritmo que destruímos tudo, não vai sobrar nada aqui neste planeta. Quer dizer, quando acabarmos tudo por aqui, vamos acabar o que tem em outros planetas. Descobriram ouro e diamante em Marte, é uma nova corrida do garimpo. A Serra Pelada Marciana. É o que temos planejado. Então, fiquem alertas, os terráqueos não são confiáveis. Te conto mais . . .

Aqui onde estou, chama-se Brasil. Viviam aqui cerca de três milhões de parentes meus, era uns mil povos diferentes. Hoje sobraram trezentos e cinco povos e aproximadamente oitocentos e noventa e sete mil pessoas. Somos aqui 0,47% da população desta fronteira chamada Brasil. É o que sobrou do contato com o outro mundo. Fico pensando como será o contato aí com vocês, mas pelo que leio as notícias aqui o objetivo é apenas um: explorar e dominar. O que não foi diferente do contato aqui.

Aqui, nós os indígenas estamos cada vez mais lutando por uma volta ancestral, sabe? Como uma volta a um tempo antes da colonização, mas sabemos que é impossível. Então vivemos numa certa redução de danos. Redução de danos da colonização. Ou como eu, conversando com amizades, cheguei a conclusão de que é um retorno à terra. Terra essa que chamamos de comunidade, território e memória. É isso, aqui estamos no retorno da memória. Espero que você e teu povo não tenham que passar por tudo o que passamos aqui. Para isso eu desenhei alguns códigos que servem como modelo e modo

Here are some of the patterns I've noticed: the people who give up in the first week are the ones who arrive bragging about their experiences in the military or with adversity; the men give up faster; water and fire are essential to maintain mental health; and in spite of meat's importance as a source of protein, a lack of it doesn't mean you won't continue doing well in the competition. The women I've seen throughout the series manage to be more practical and intelligent; they don't give up so easily and instead find clever solutions to their problems. The episode I'm watching now hasn't been any different: the man gave up on the second day and the woman is staying strong in the face of adversity. Just now she grabbed a *bauari*, a little freshwater fish. I'm rooting for her.

Watching this episode, I've been thinking about what's really essential in modern life. What do we need to live well? Maybe this turned-on TV isn't essential; maybe it distances me further from nature. Nature that we, you and I, are both a part of. It's been a while since I've fished for *bauari*. Yes, it's been quite a while.

Another thing I thought was: imagine if all the forests, rivers, and savannas all disappeared. What would the show be like then? Instead of being naked and afraid in nature, it would be naked and afraid in the apocalypse, wouldn't it? Who knows.

The other day I saw that the plans to live on other planets are advancing, that is, that the people working for NASA, aware of the speed with which we destroy everything, know there will be nothing left on this planet. That is to say that, once we've used up everything here, we're going to use up what they have on other planets too. They've discovered gold and diamonds on Mars; it's a new gold rush. The Martian Serra Pelada. That's what we're planning. So be on the lookout—earthlings aren't trustworthy. Let me tell you more . . .

Here where I am they call it Brazil. Around 3,000,000 of my relatives lived here. There were around 1,000 different cultural groups/peoples. Today, 305 of these groups and approximately 897,000 people remain. We are only 0.47 percent of the population of this frontier called Brazil. This is all that's left after we came into contact with the other world. I keep thinking about what the first contact with you will be like, but from what I read in the news there's just one objective: exploit and dominate. Which is no different than the first contact here.

Here, we Indigenous are fighting harder each day for a return to the ways of our ancestors. Like a return to the time before colonization, but we know it's impossible. So we live in an era of harm reduction. Mitigating damages wrought by colonization. Or like me, talking with friends, I arrived at the conclusion that it's a return to the earth. That earth that we call community, territory, and memory. That's what it is; here we're in the midst of a return of memory. I hope that you and your people don't have to go through de pensar a vida e a caminhada do meu povo. Também alguns desenhos que apresentam este planeta pra você. Caso quando você venha nos visitar, não tenha mais o que temos hoje: florestas, rios, oxigênio, animais; vida.

Grande abraço! Nos vemos no Universo.

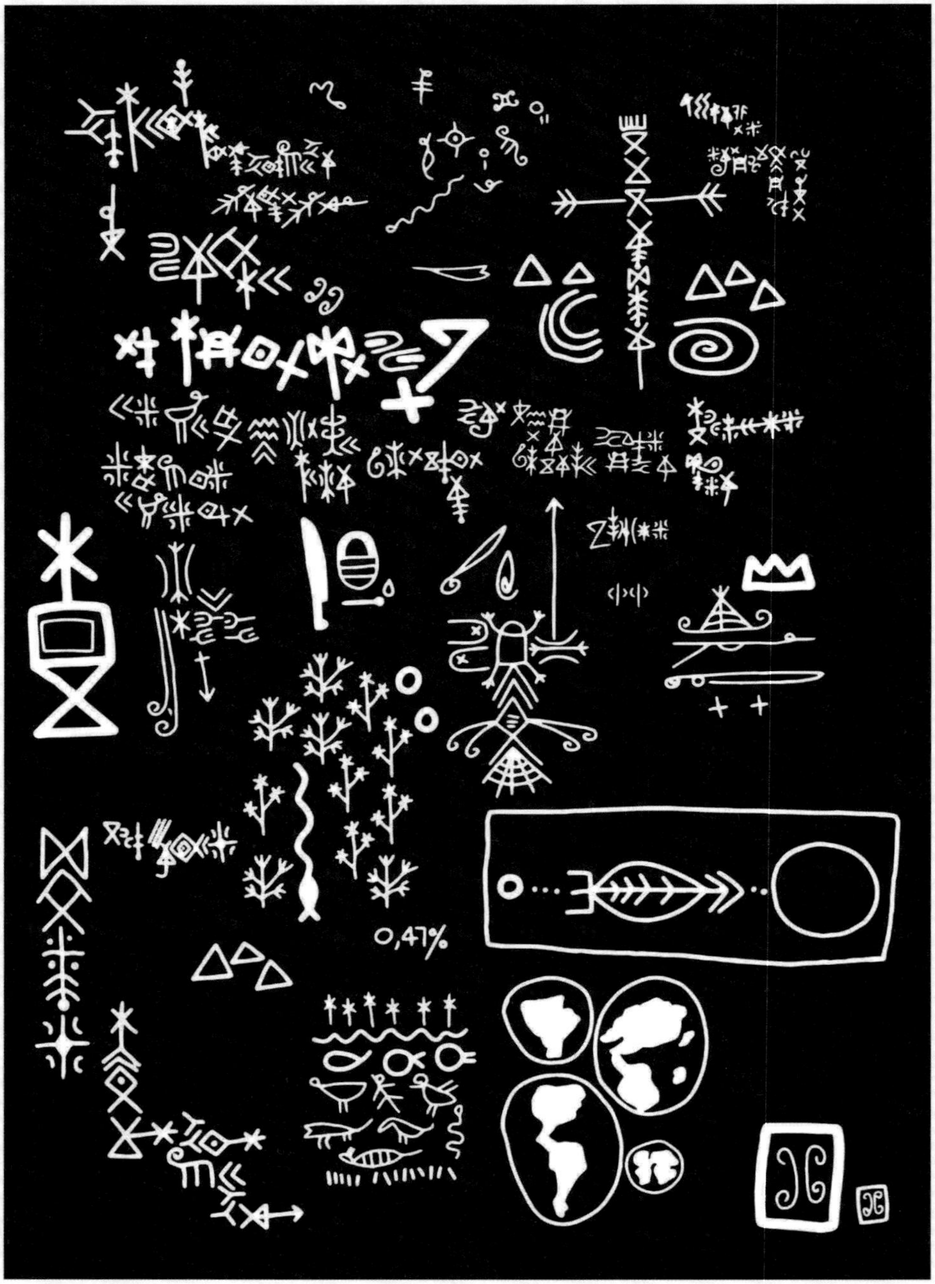

everything we've been through here. In order to prevent that, I drew some codes that serve as a model and way to think about life and the path of my people. Also some drawings that represent this planet for you. So that, in case you visit, we don't have what we have now: forests, rivers, oxygen, animals, life.

A big hug! We'll see each other in the Universe.

NOTE

Translation from Portuguese to English by Maria Emilia Fernandez and Sean McPherson.

Denilson Baniwa. *Carta aos indígenas do planeta Marte com códigos de reconhecimento do planeta Terra* (Letter to the Indigenous Peoples of the Planet Mars with Recognition Codes of the Planet Earth), 2020/2022. Acrylic. 7 × 10 ft. (219 × 310 cm).

Jupiter is Here. Celestial is Everything.

Castiel Vitorino Brasileiro

2022

A liberdade me trouxe até aqui. E essa sensação de ser alienígena dentro do próprio planeta também me fez criar essa obra.

O que acontece nessas outras zonas que a colonialidade nomeia de "outro mundo"? Não se trata de uma questão antropológica, mas uma questão de fé.

Acredito que sim, existem outras formas de se viver. E essa obra é um pedaço do meu mundo, do meu planeta, de onde eu vim.

Um espaço perecível de liberdade. Para construí-lo, utilizei os chamados "pontos riscados de Umbanda" como linhas arquitetônicas.[1]

Também estudei história aquática do Texas, que em algum momento já foi um mar.

Eu acredito em Kalunga como esse poder líquido de transmutação, por isso fico muito emocionada em ter um fóssil de animal marinho ancestral dentro de minha obra.

Acredito na água como um elemento espiritual, um condutor de energia, capaz de limpar e alimentar, então criei esse grande caminho em direção à sua contemplação.

Essa obra é um espaço para permanecer, sentar, deitar e olhar, com respeito, cuidado, intuição e amor.

Júpiter é uma condição relativa. Quando assistimos a vida fora deste planeta, Júpiter é apenas uma palavra, assim como o termo "o outro" também é.

Júpiter pode ser aqui, este planeta. Porque tudo é celestial, cósmico. Tudo está em tudo.

NOTA

1 "Pontos riscados de Umbanda" são complexos sistemas comunicacionais de origem bantu localizados no limite entre palavra e desenho. São signos que contam a história da alma.

Jupiter is Here. Celestial is Everything.

Castiel Vitorino Brasileiro

2022

Freedom brought me here. And the feeling of being alien on my own planet also made me create this project.

What is happening in these other zones that coloniality calls the "other world"? This is not an anthropological question, but one of faith.

I believe there are other ways of living. And this installation is a piece of my world, of the planet from which I came.

A perishable space of freedom. To create it, I used the so-called *pontos riscados de Umbanda* as architectural lines.[1]

I also studied the aquatic history of Texas, which at one time was a sea.

I believe in *Kalunga* as the liquid power of transmutation, and therefore am thrilled to have the fossil of an ancestral marine animal in this project.

I believe in water as a spiritual element, as an energy conductor, capable of cleaning and nourishing, so I created this great path unfolding toward its contemplation.

This work is a space to linger, sit, lie down, and look with respect, care, intuition, and love.

Jupiter is a relative condition. When we observe life beyond this planet, Jupiter is only a word, just as the term "other" also is.

Jupiter can be here, on this planet. Because everything is celestial, cosmic. Everything is in everything.

NOTES

Translation from Portuguese to English by Sean McPherson.

1 The *pontos riscados de Umbanda* are complex communication systems of Bantu origin, located on the border between words and drawings. They are signs that tell the story of the soul.

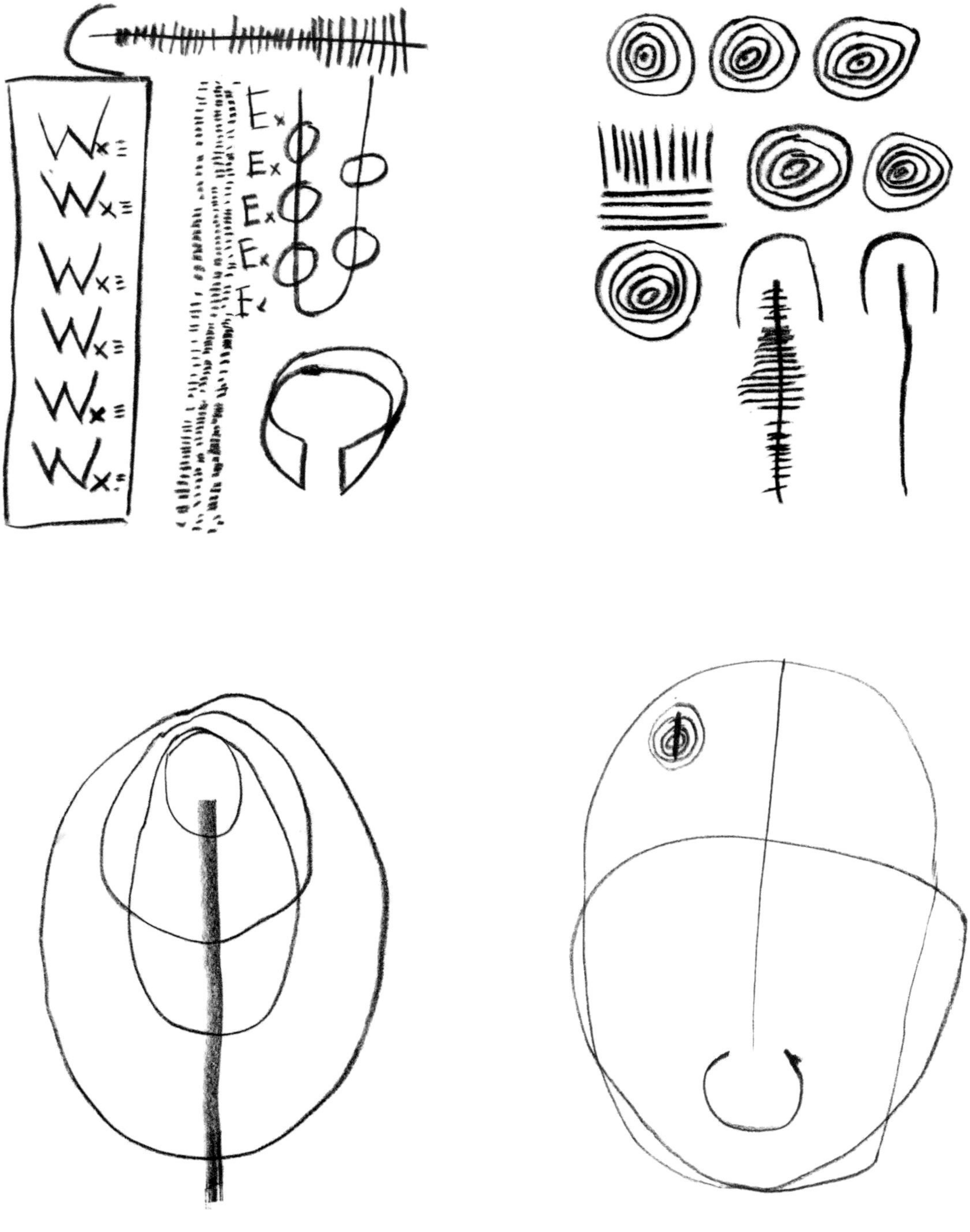

Castiel Vitorino Brasileiro. Preliminary drawings for the installation *Jupiter is Here. Celestial is Everything.*, 2022. Charcoal on paper. $3\frac{15}{16} \times 5\frac{15}{16}$ in. (10 × 15 cm). Courtesy of the artist.

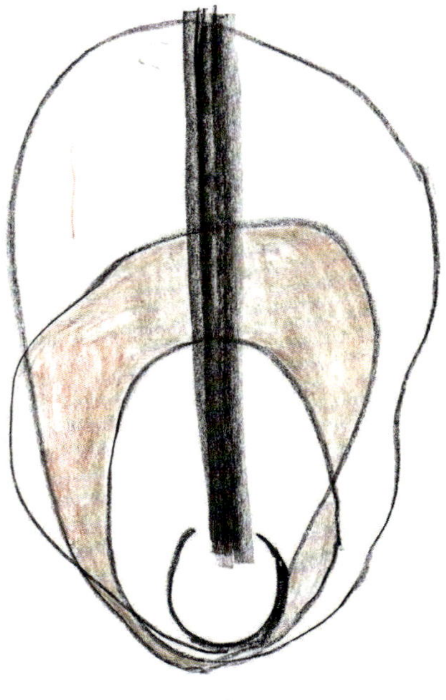

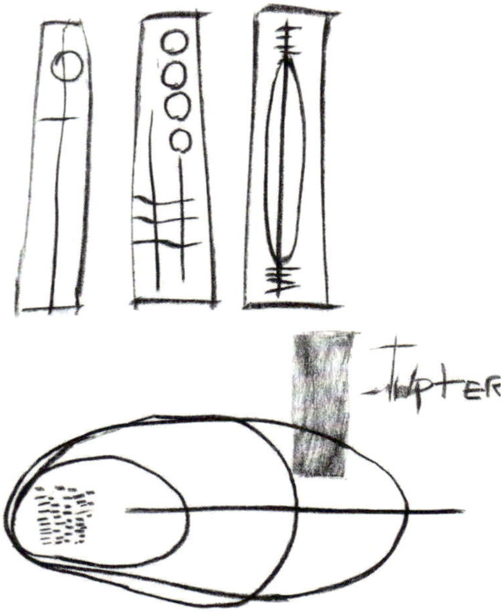

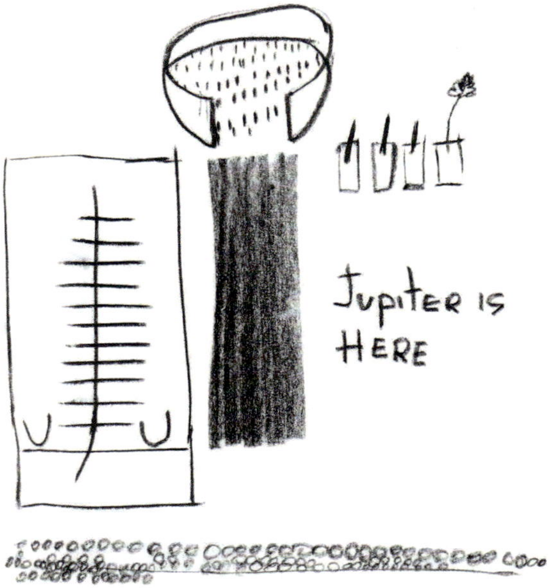
Jupiter is
HERE

Fundamento

Maré de Matos

2019

Antes de cruzarem as fronteiras da nossa humanidade
antes do desejo de nos esmagarem com o peso monolítico
dos seus costumes e sistemas de pensamento;
antes da súbita invenção das normas e modelos
antes da produção e aprimoramento
das técnicas de gerenciamento de medo;
nascemos

Embora contraiam pátria e língua
assim como impunham facas e táticas;
embora construam obstáculos em
caminhos estreitos que nos querem arquipélagos;
embora mantenham corações apegados
a órgãos que produzem pirâmides das diferenças;
por audácia mesmo embora deteriorem as pontes que nos ligam o
nosso direito à existência,
nascemos

Mesmo que supostamente frágeis afirmem-se
no delírio colonial da universalidade,
mesmo que estrategicamente violentos se
apoiem na escrita e outros projetos de esquecimento

Nos resta sensibilidade, vozes e gestos
ainda que não saibam, mas nos digam "sinto muito"
Existimos antes de não terem tempo
para outras configurações de mundo

Foundation

Maré de Matos

2019

Before crossing the borders of our humanity
before the desire to crush us with the monolithic weight
of their customs and systems of thought;
before the sudden invention of norms and models
before the production and refinement
of the management techniques of fear;
we are born

Even though they conflate motherland and language
just as they impose knives and tactics;
even though they construct obstacles on
narrow paths to turn us into archipelagos;
even though they maintain hearts attached
to organs that produce pyramids of differences;
by sheer audacity, even though
they deteriorate the bridges that connect us to
our right to existence,
we are born.

Even if, supposedly fragile, they affirm themselves
in the colonial delirium of universality,
even if, strategically violent, they
rely on writing and other projects of forgetfulness

We still have sensibility, voices, and gestures
even if they don't know but tell us "I'm sorry"
We exist before not having time
for other world configurations

NOTE

Translation from Portuguese to English by Maria Emilia Fernandez and Sean McPherson. Translation editing from Portuguese to English by Stephanie Alvarado. See detail on p. 80: Maré de Matos, *Fundamento* (Foundation), 2019.

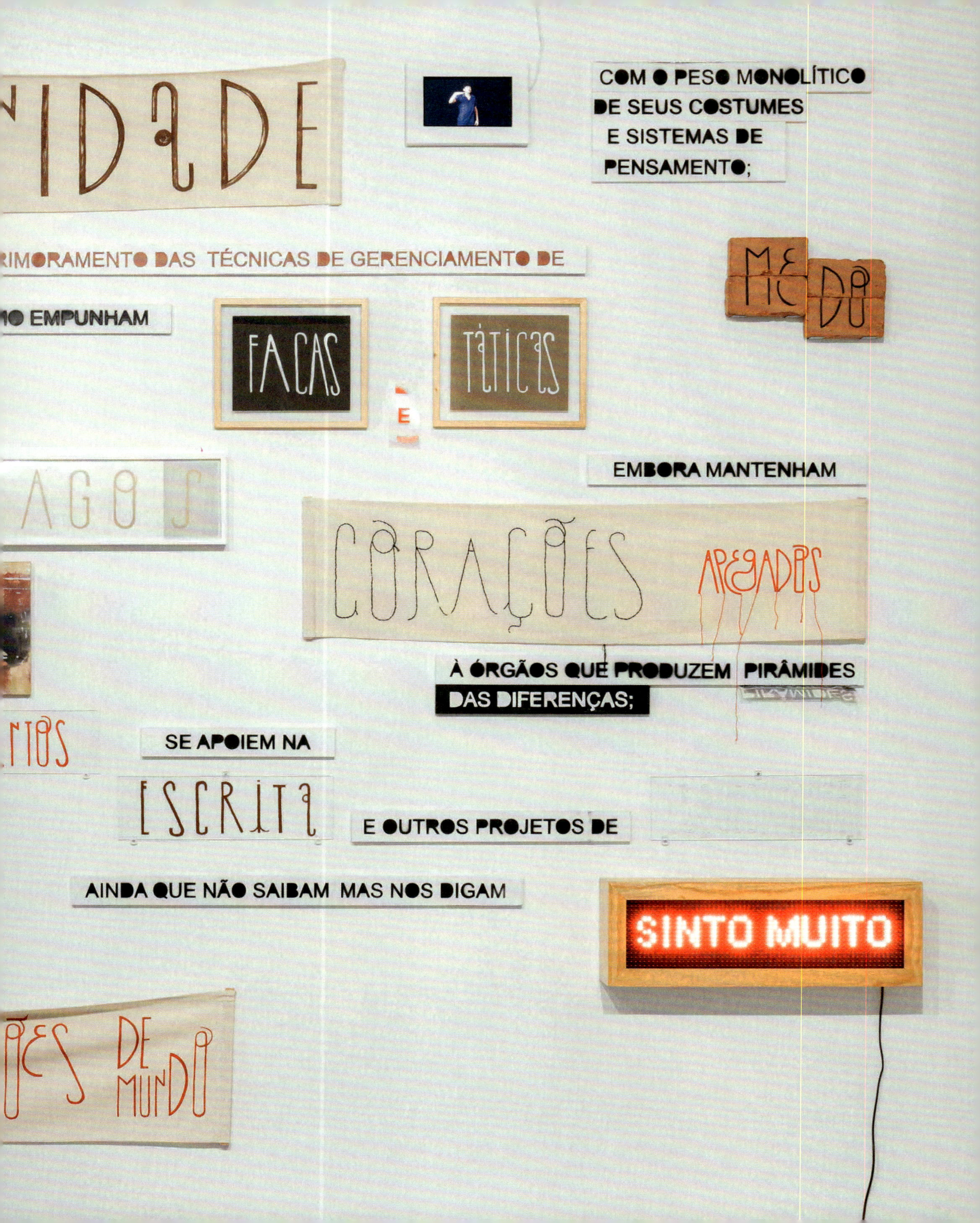
COM O PESO MONOLÍTICO
DE SEUS COSTUMES
E SISTEMAS DE
PENSAMENTO;
RIMORAMENTO DAS TÉCNICAS DE GERENCIAMENTO DE
MEDO
O EMPUNHAM
FACAS
E
TÁTICAS
EMBORA MANTENHAM
CORAÇÕES
APEGADOS
À ÓRGÃOS QUE PRODUZEM PIRÂMIDES
DAS DIFERENÇAS;
SE APOIEM NA
ESCRITA
E OUTROS PROJETOS DE
AINDA QUE NÃO SAIBAM MAS NOS DIGAM
SINTO MUITO
DE MUNDO

Installation Views

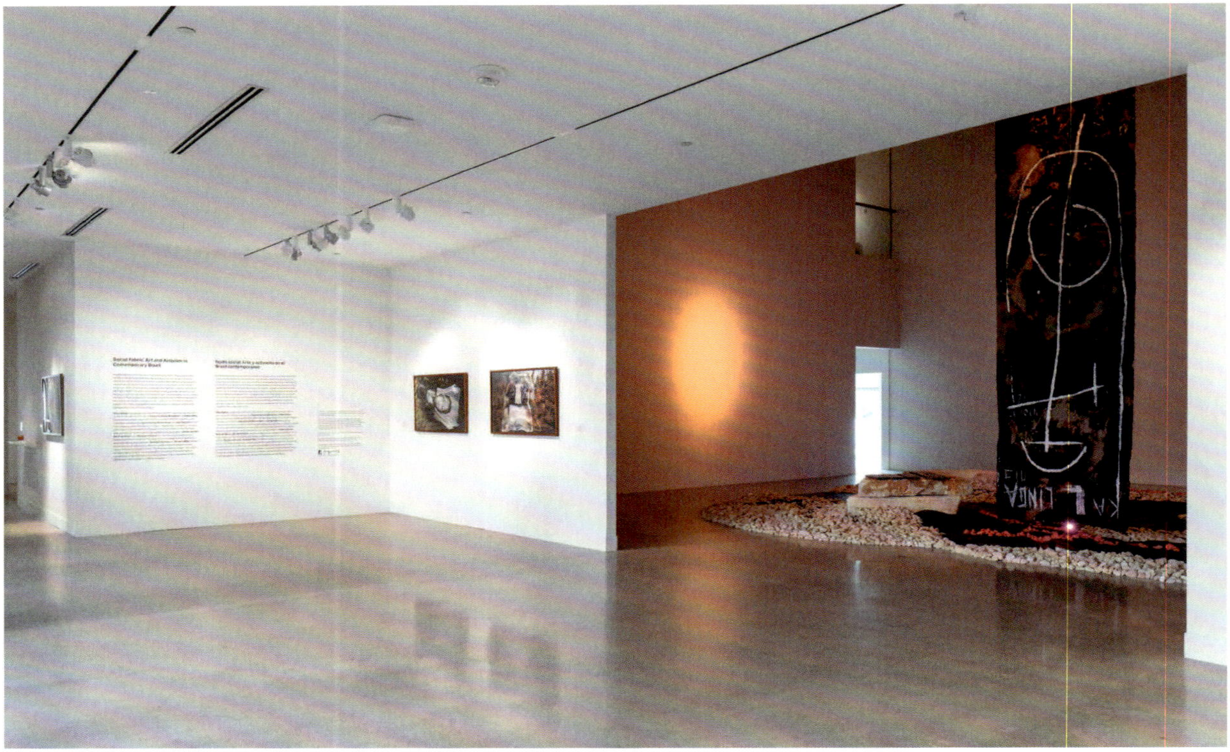

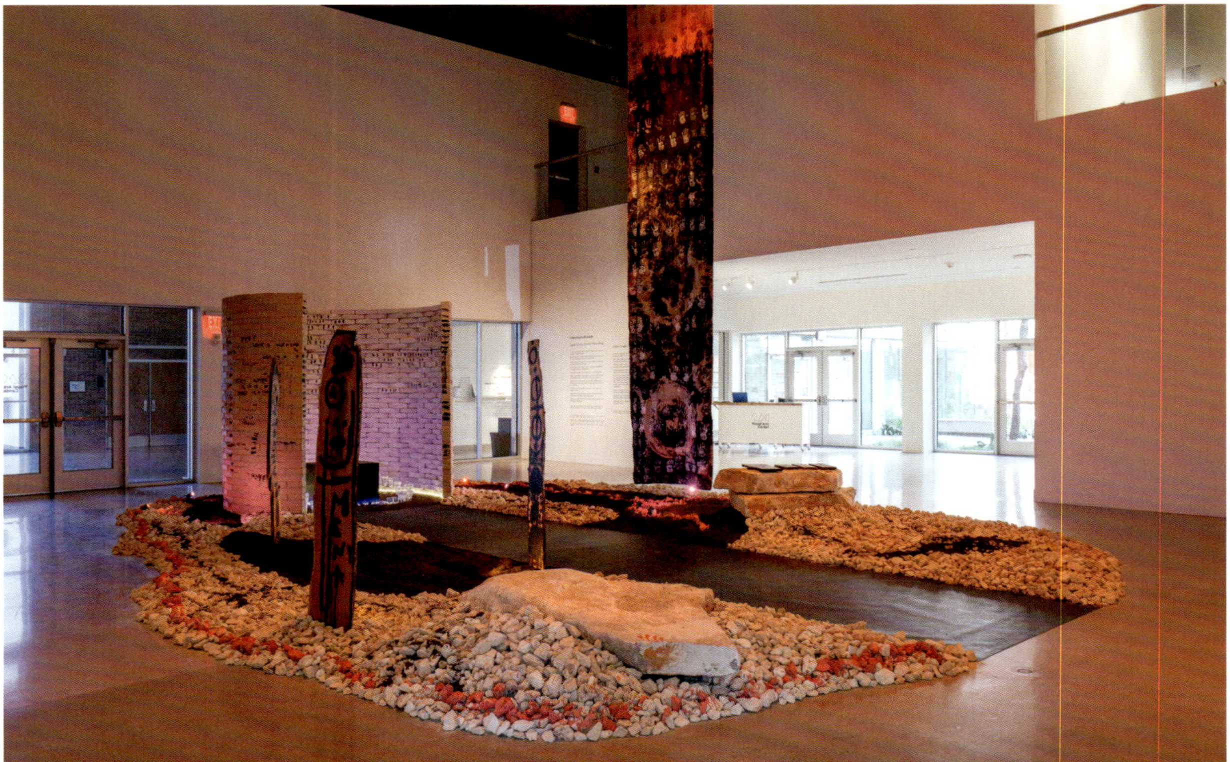

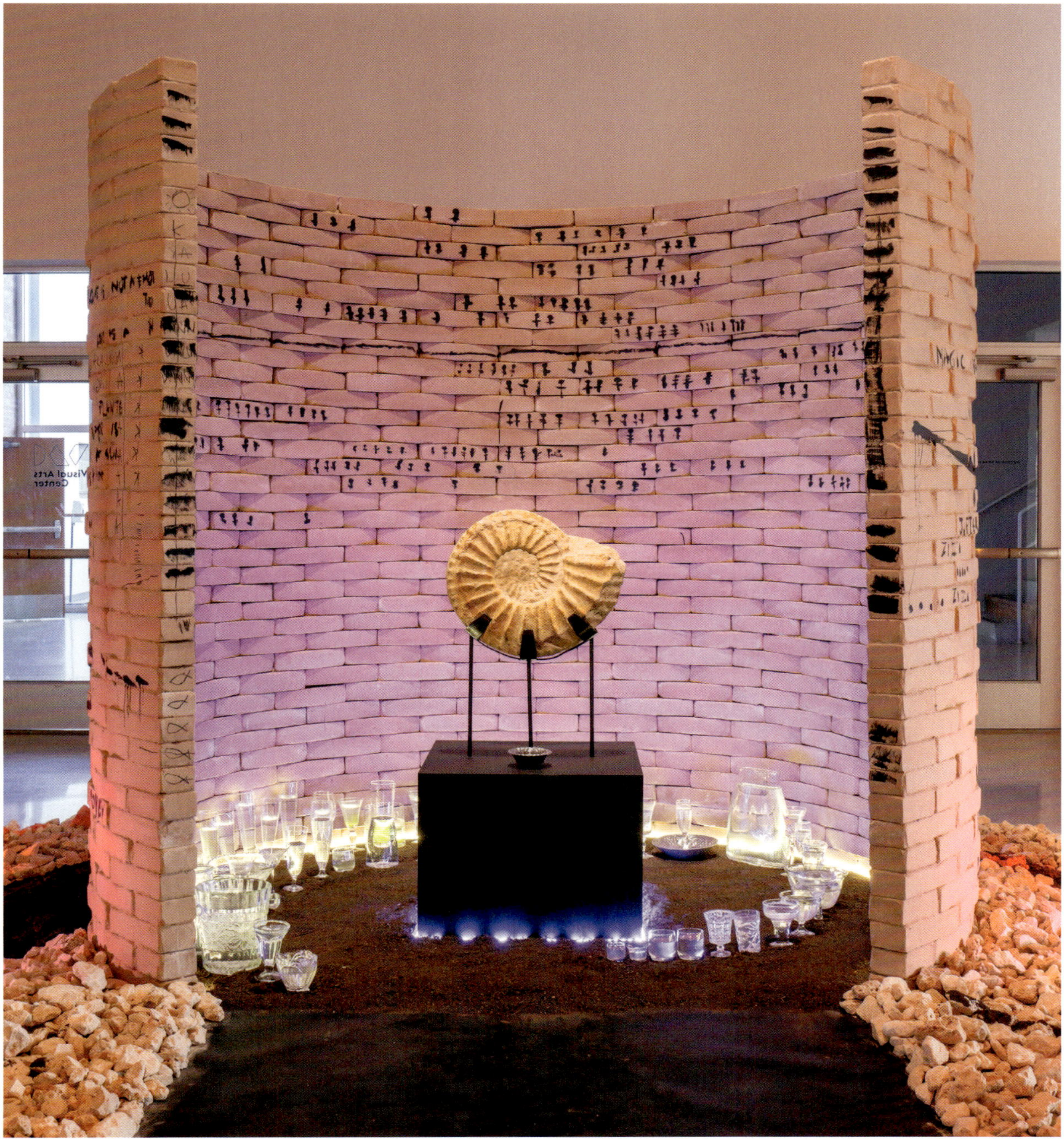

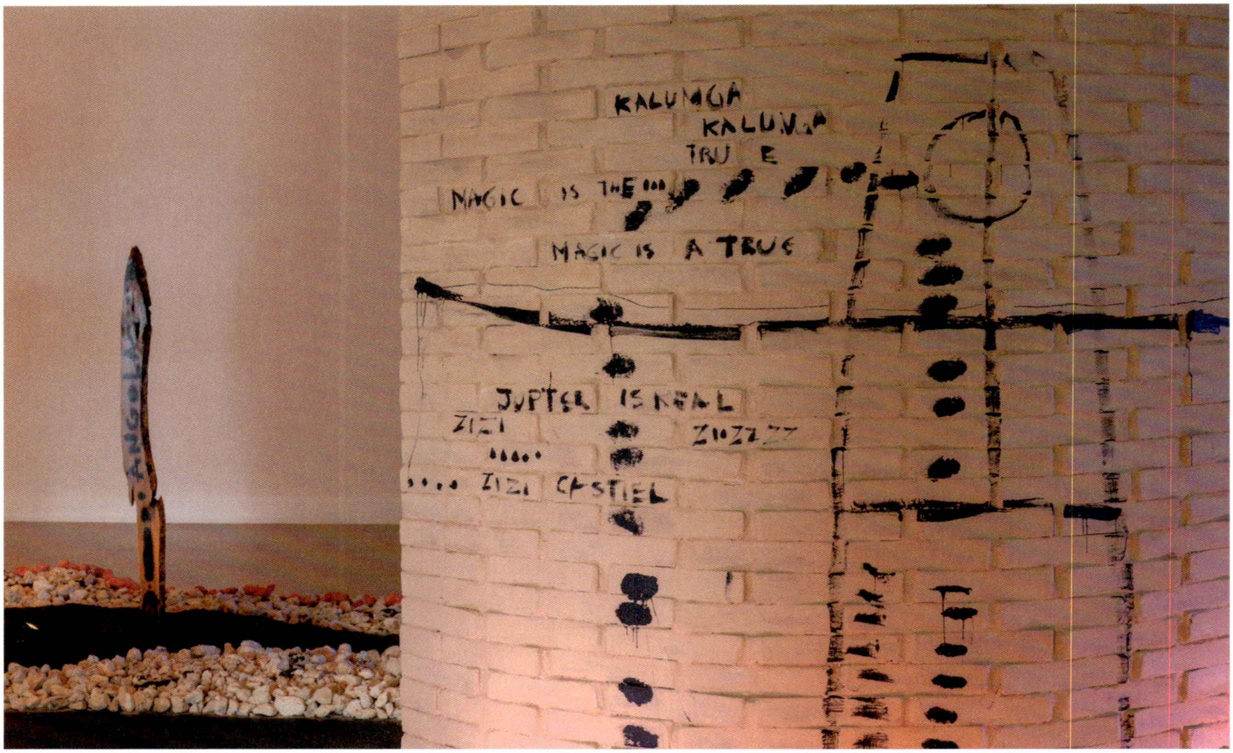
KALUNGA
KALUNGA
TRU E
MAGIC IS THE
MAGIC IS A TRUE
ZIZI
ZIZI CASTIEL
ANGOLA

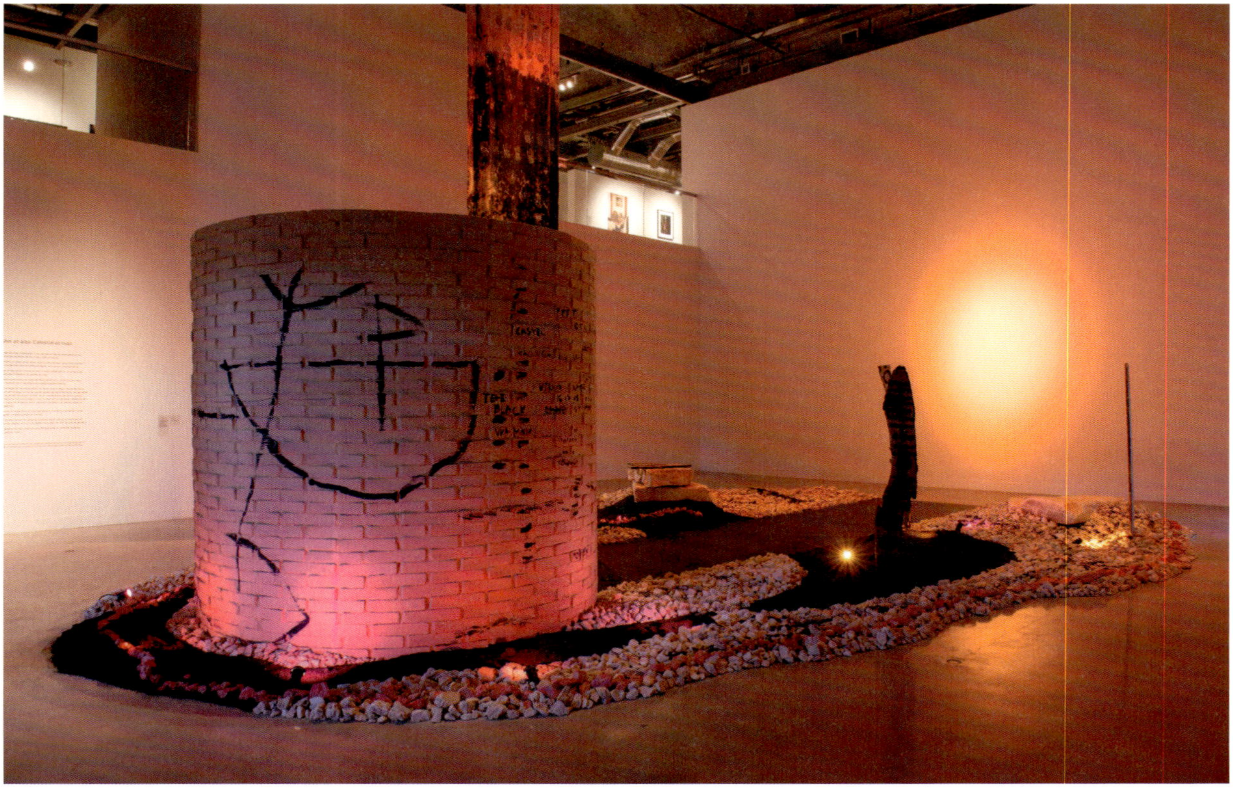

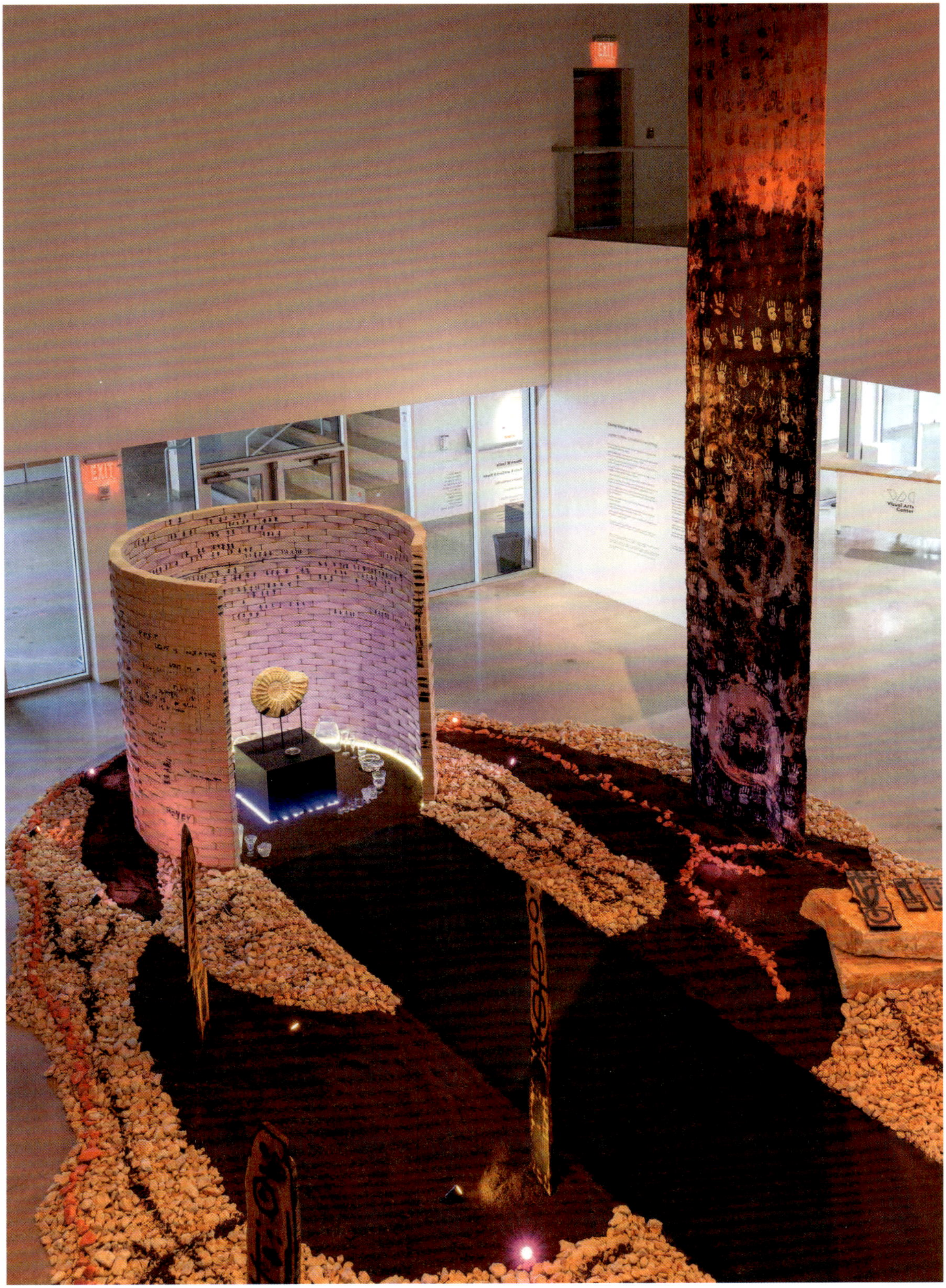
EXIT

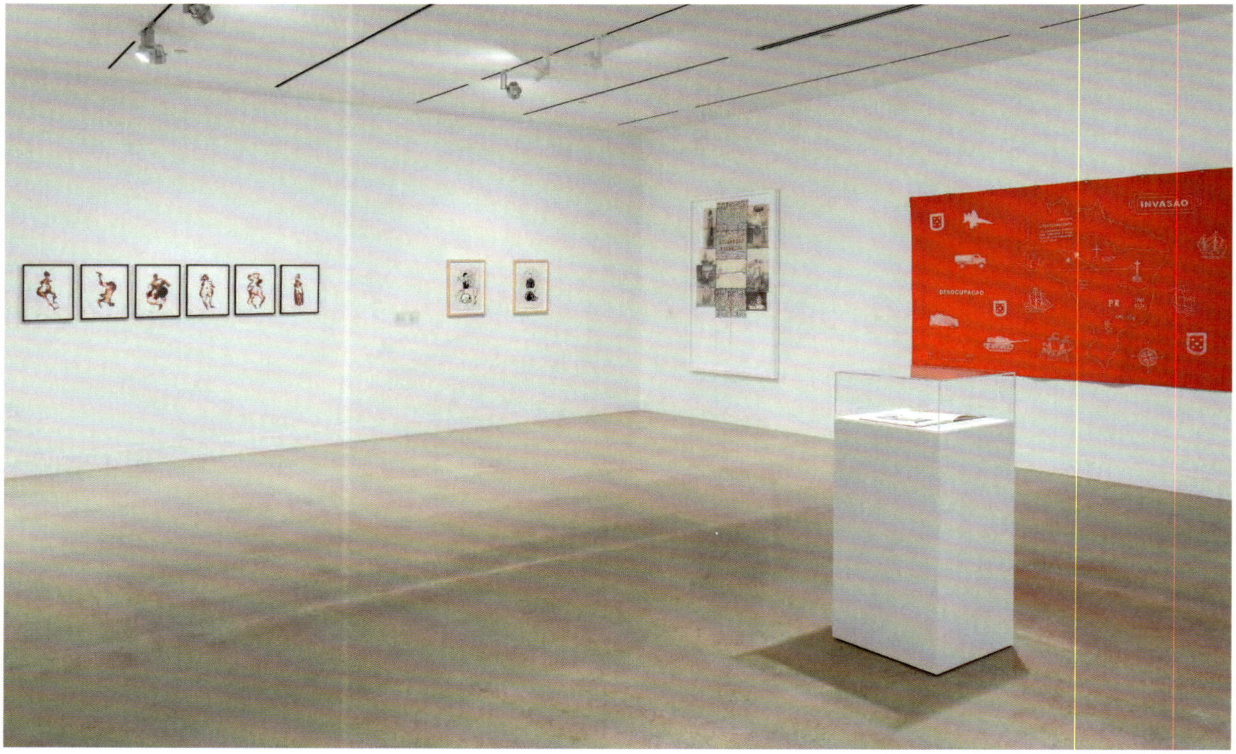

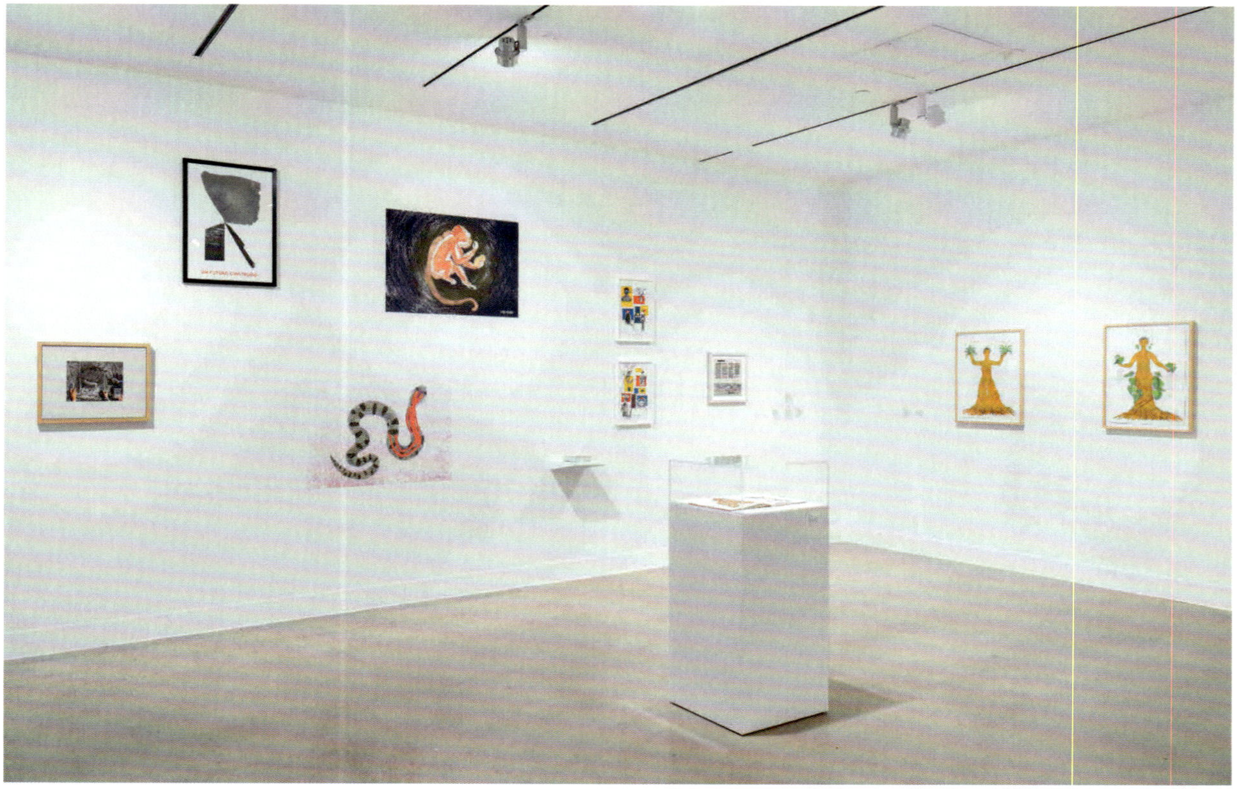

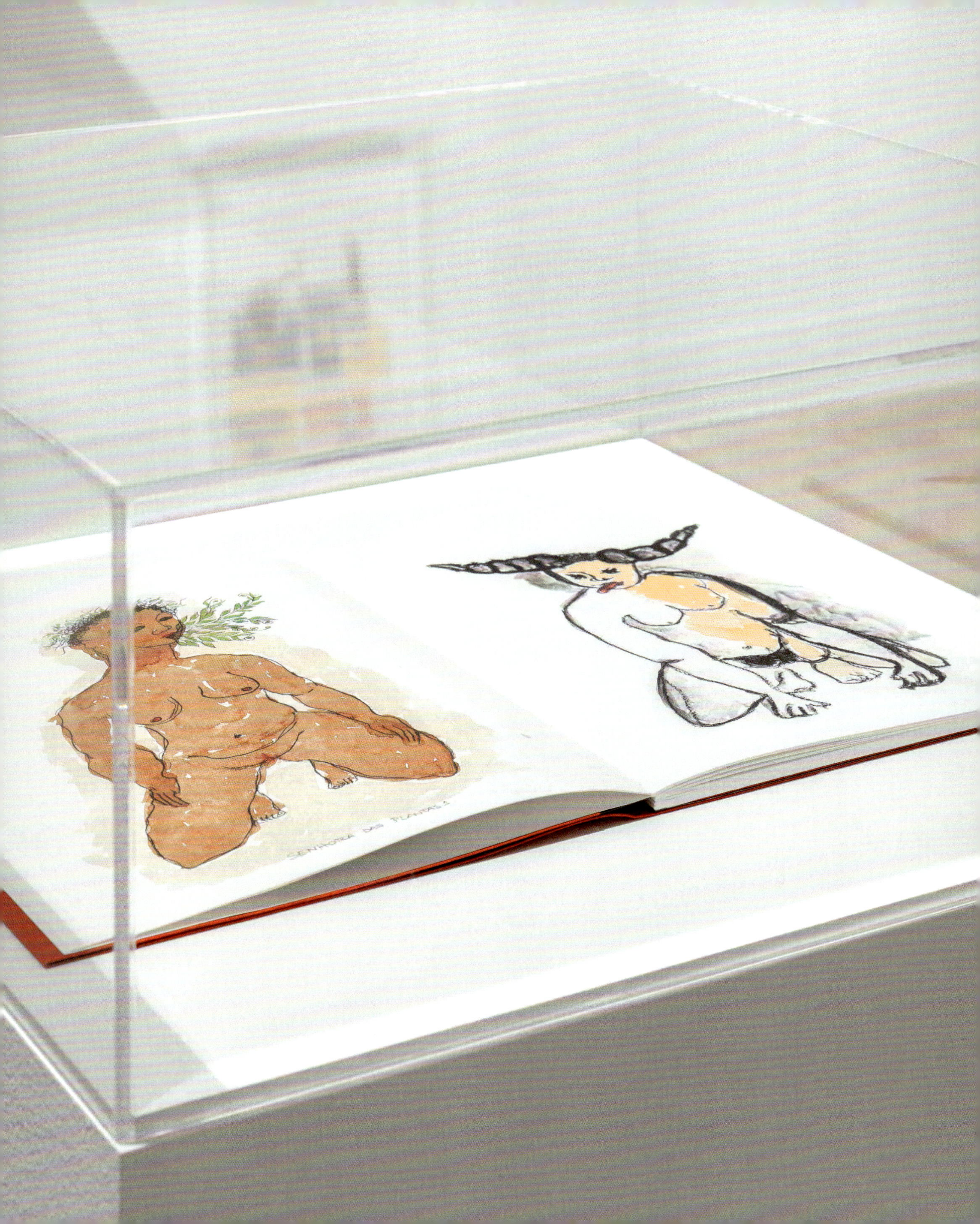
SENHORA DAS PLANTAS

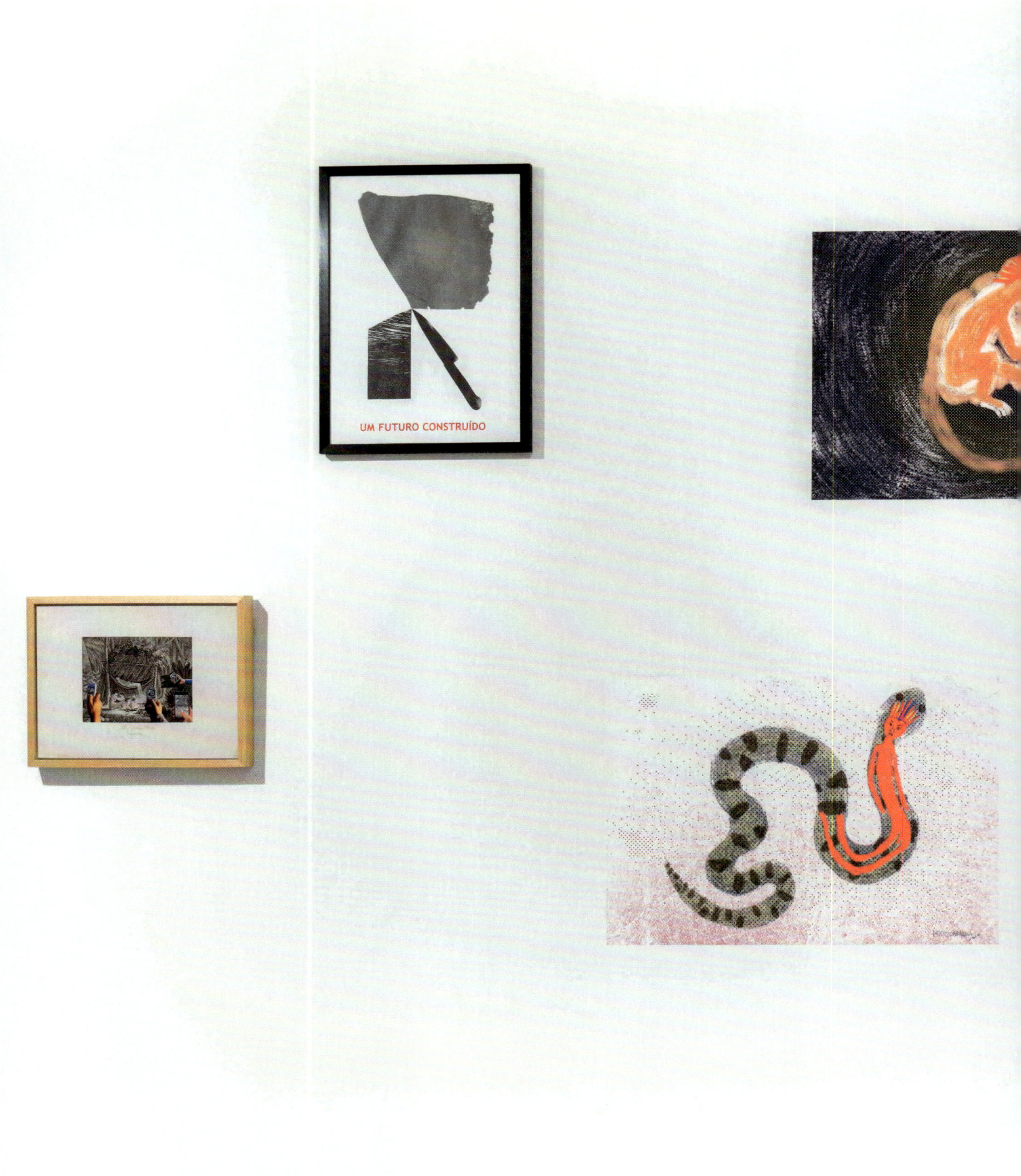
UM FUTURO CONSTRUÍDO

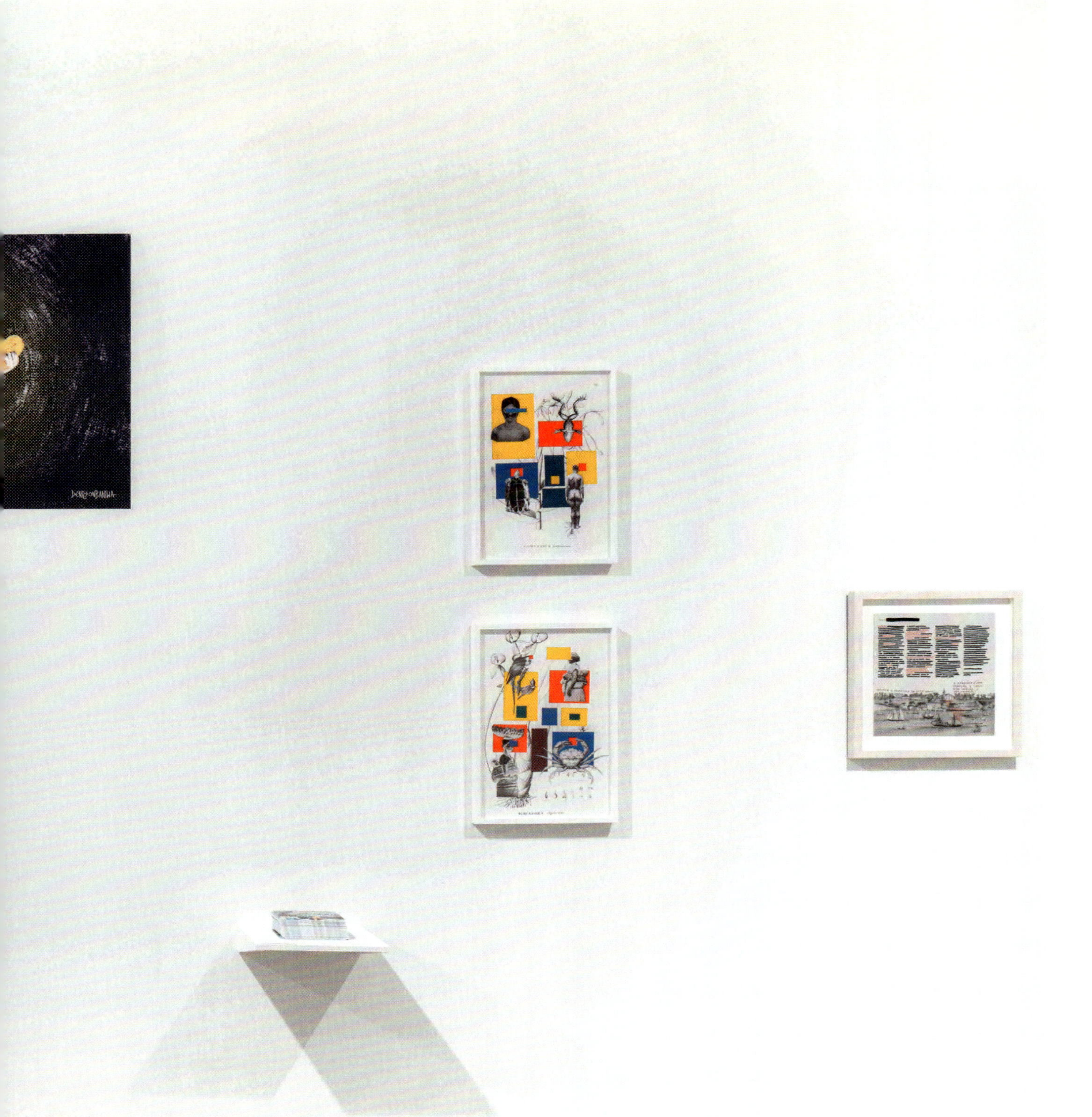

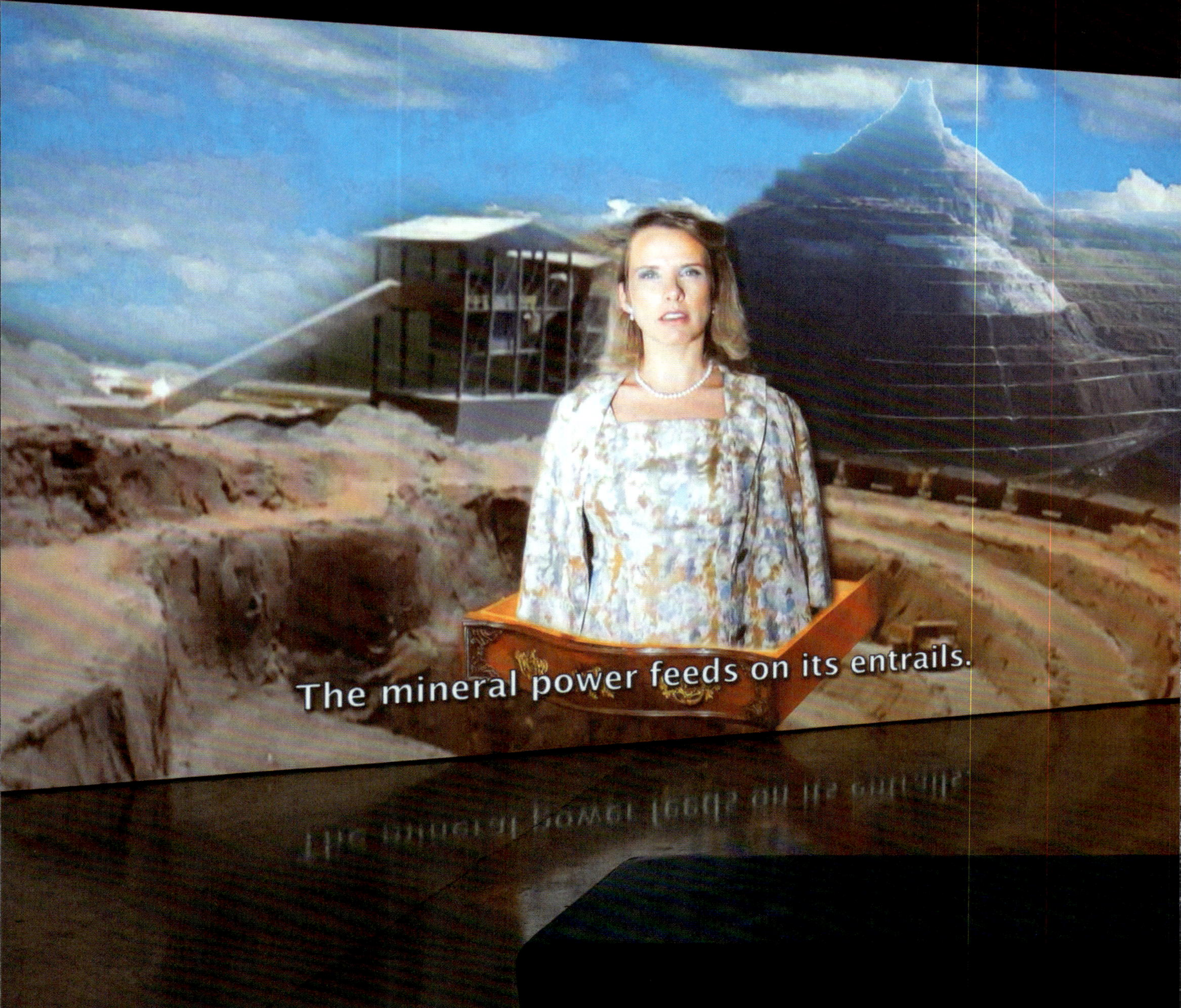
The mineral power feeds on its entrails.

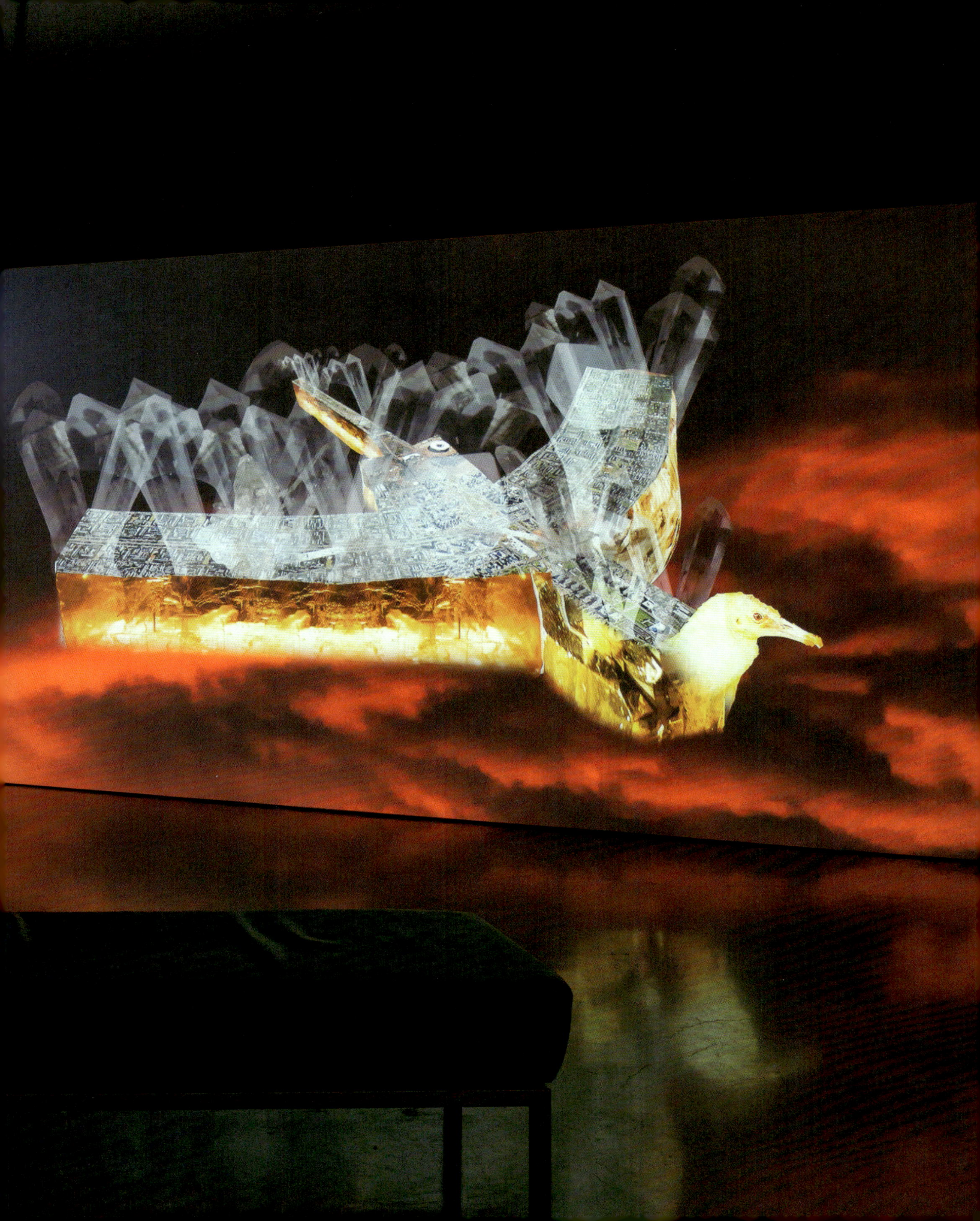

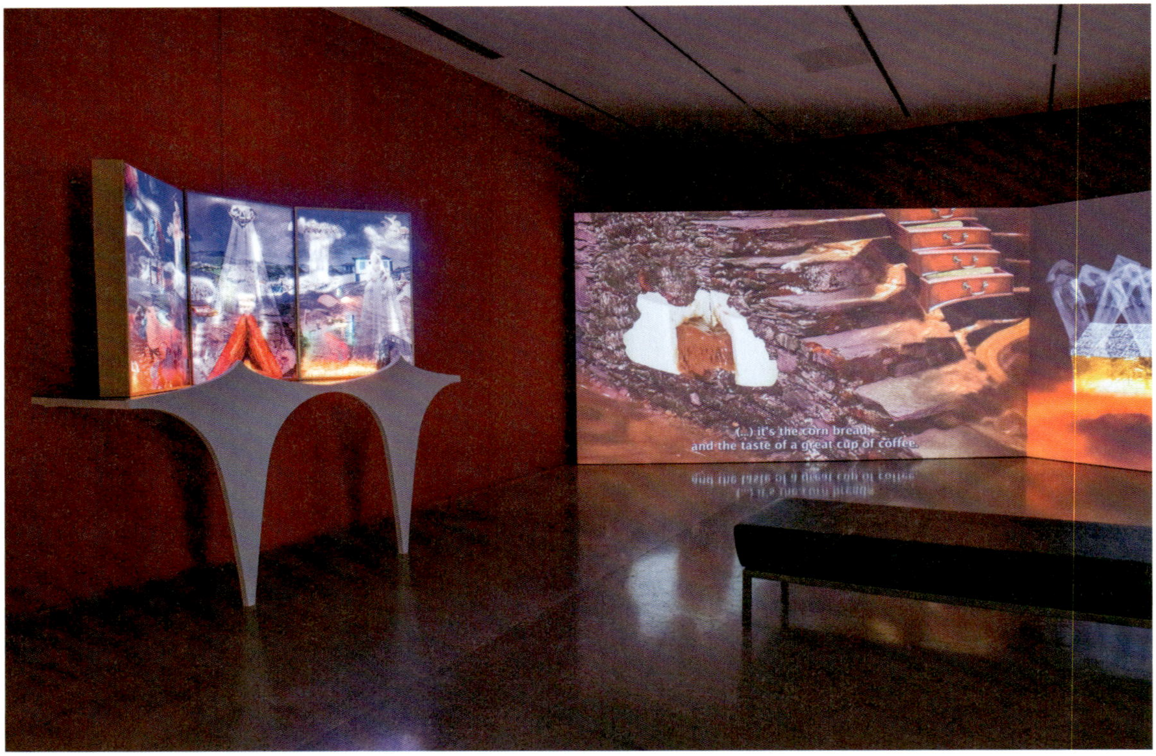
(...) it's the corn bread
and the taste of a great cup of coffee.

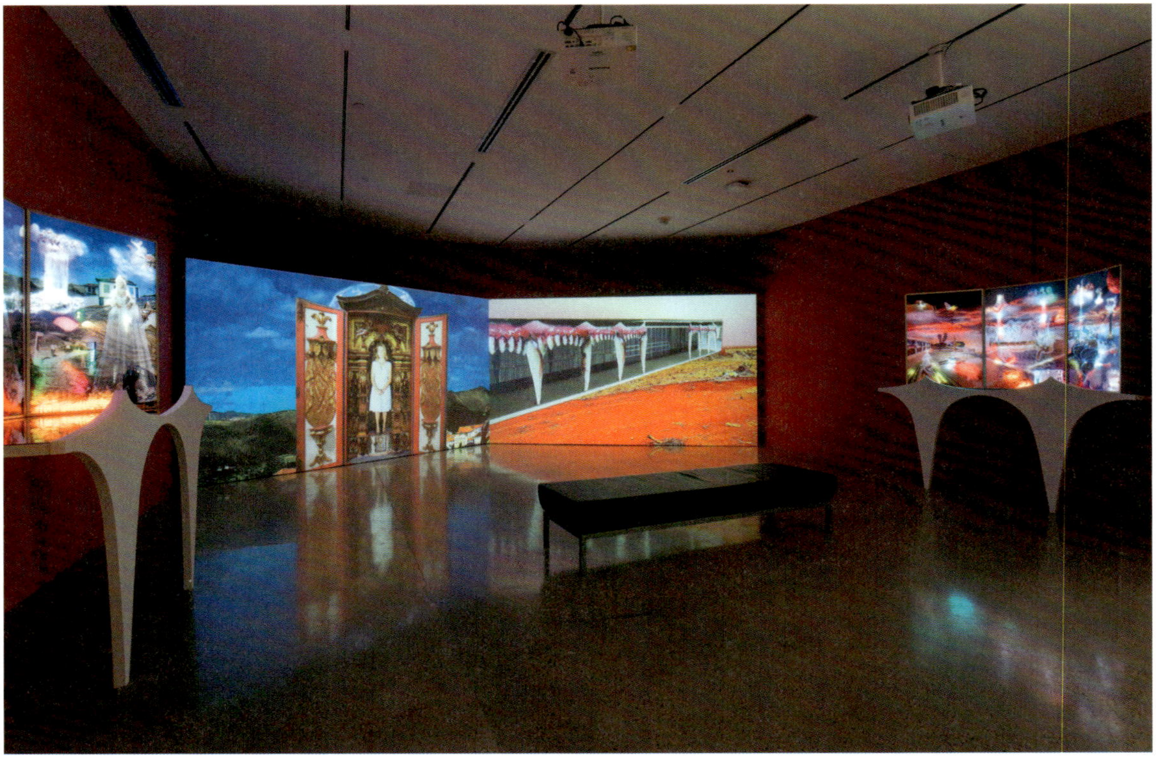

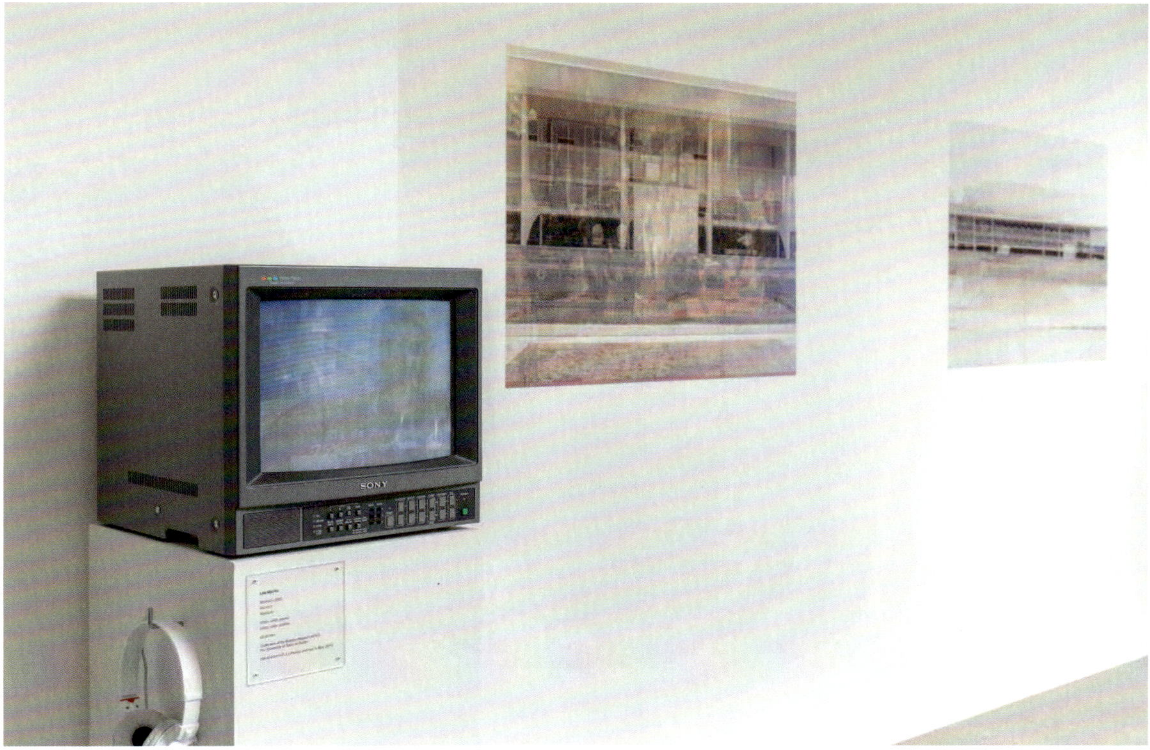
SONY

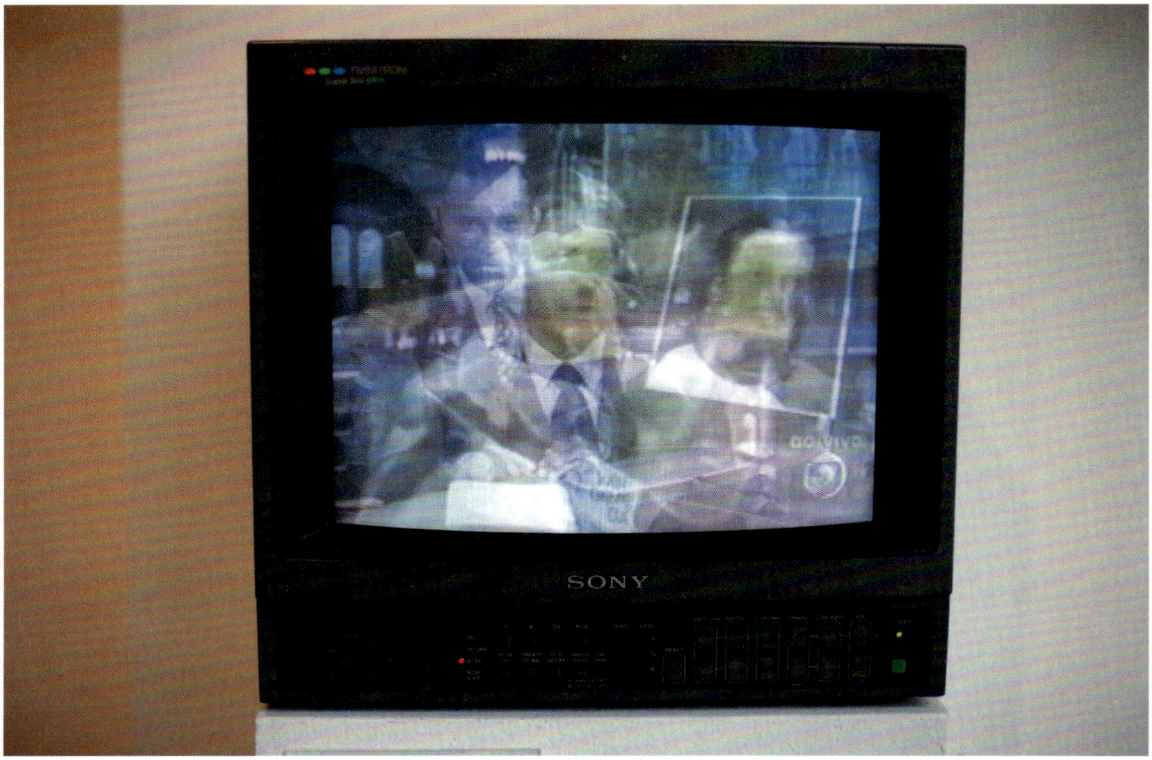
SONY

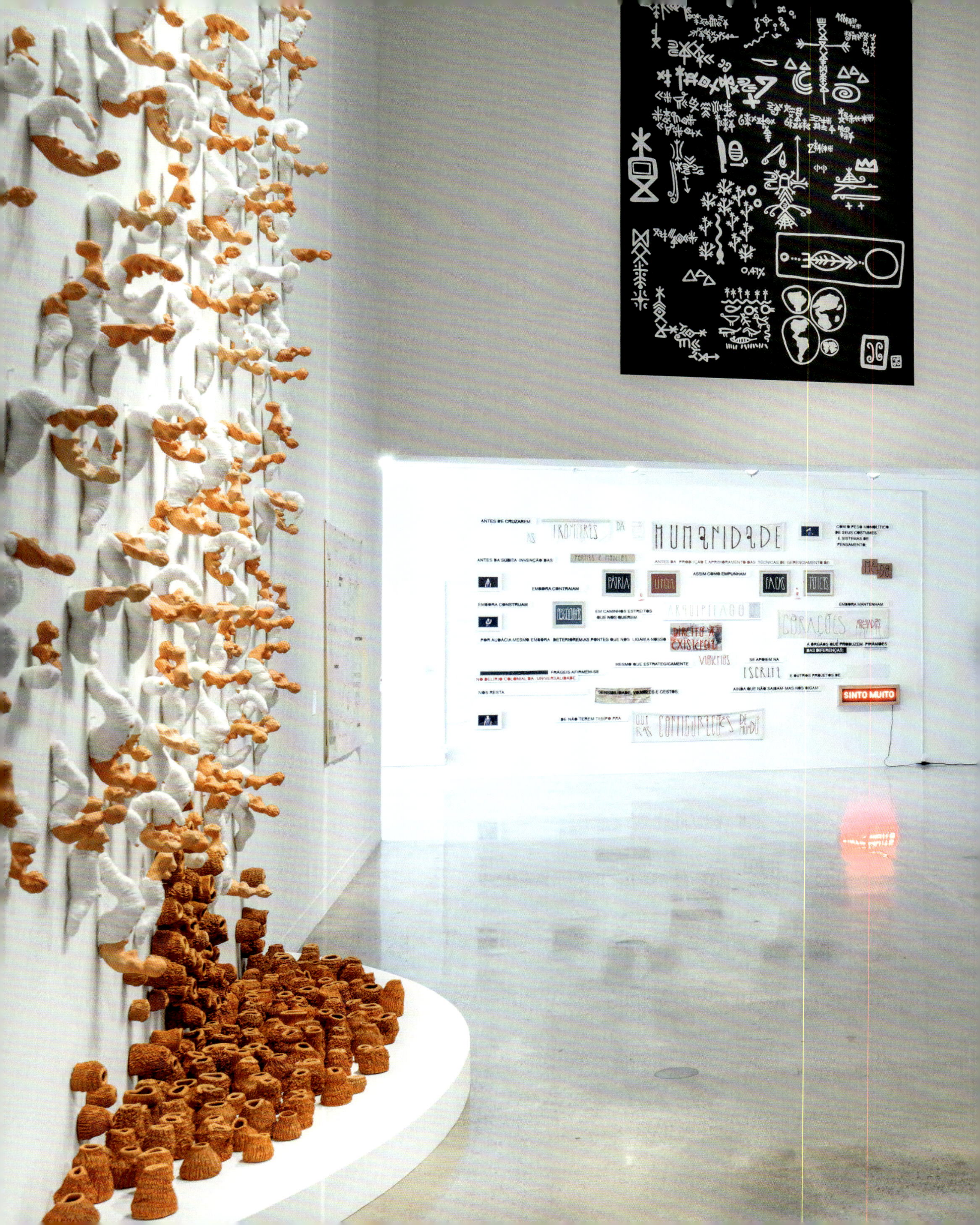

ANTES DE CRUZAREM
AS
DA
HUMANIDADE
COM O PESO MONOLÍTICO DE SEUS COSTUMES E SISTEMAS DE PENSAMENTO;
ANTES DA SÚBITA INVENÇÃO DAS
ME DO
ASSIM COMO EMPUNHAM
EMBORA CONTRAIAM
PÁTRIA
FACAS
EMBORA CONSTRUAM
EM CAMINHOS ESTREITOS QUE NOS QUEREM
EMBORA MANTENHAM
CORAÇÕES
POR AUDÁCIA MESMO EMBORA DETERIOREM AS PONTES QUE NOS LIGAM A NOSSO
DIREITO À EXISTÊNCIA
A ÓRGÃOS QUE PRODUZEM PIRÂMIDES DAS DIFERENÇAS;
MESMO QUE ESTRATEGICAMENTE
SE APOIEM NA
ESCRITA
FRÁGEIS AFIRMEM-SE
NO DELÍRIO COLONIAL DA UNIVERSALIDADE
E OUTROS PROJETOS DE
NOS RESTA
E GESTOS.
AINDA QUE NÃO SAIBAM MAS NOS DIGAM
SINTO MUITO
DE NÃO TEREM TEMPO PRA
OUT RAS CONFIGURAÇÕES DE MUNDO

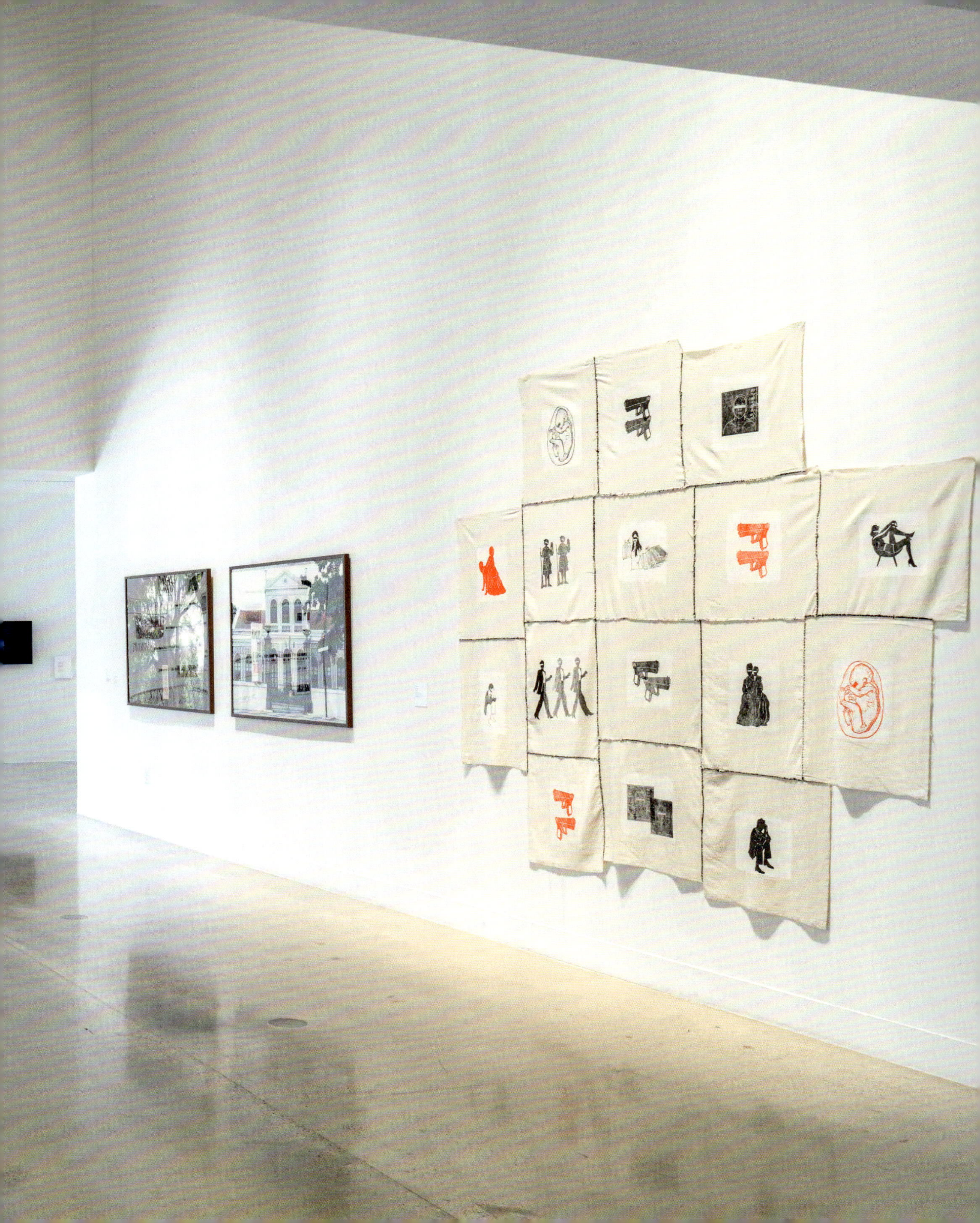

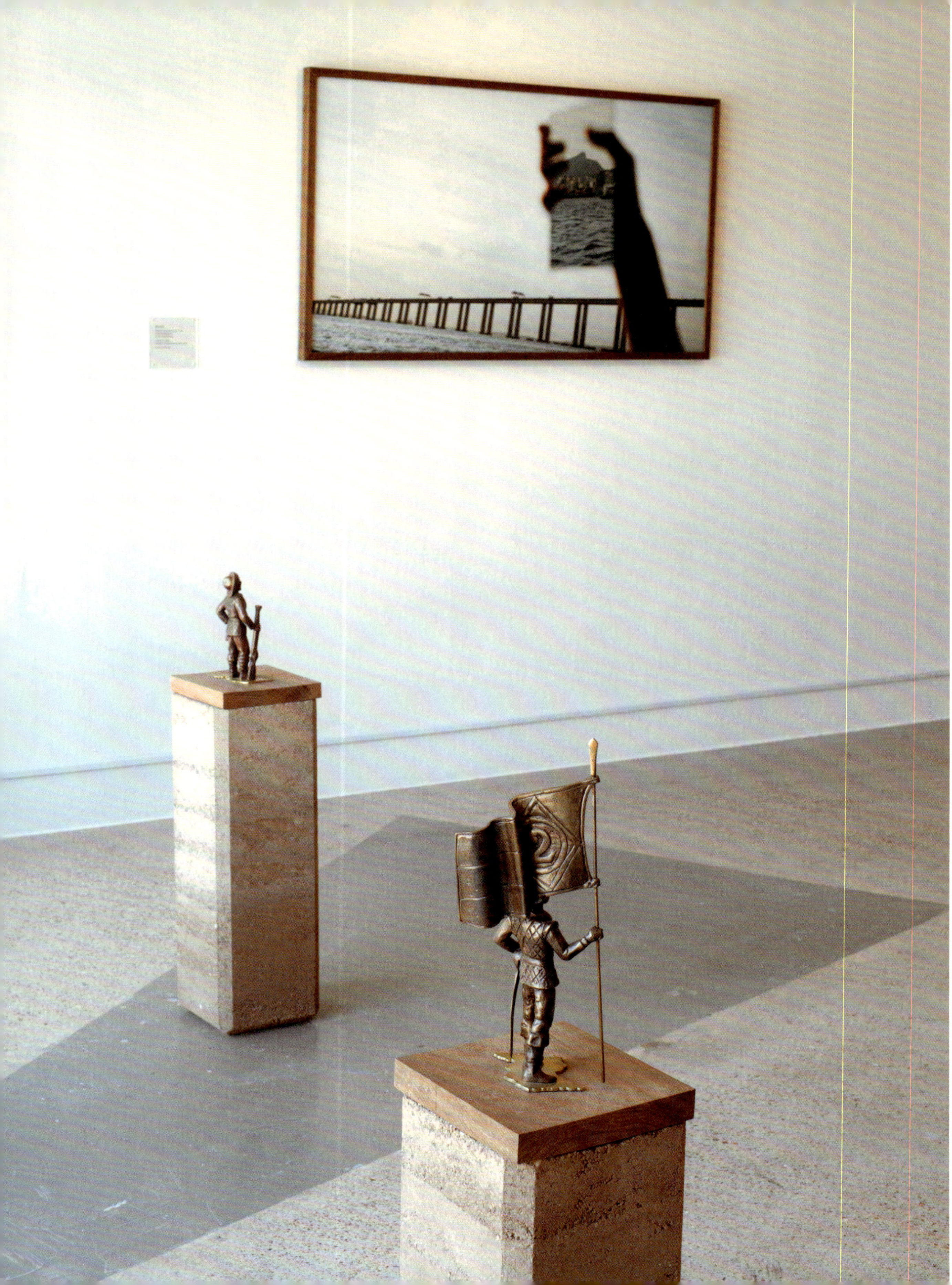

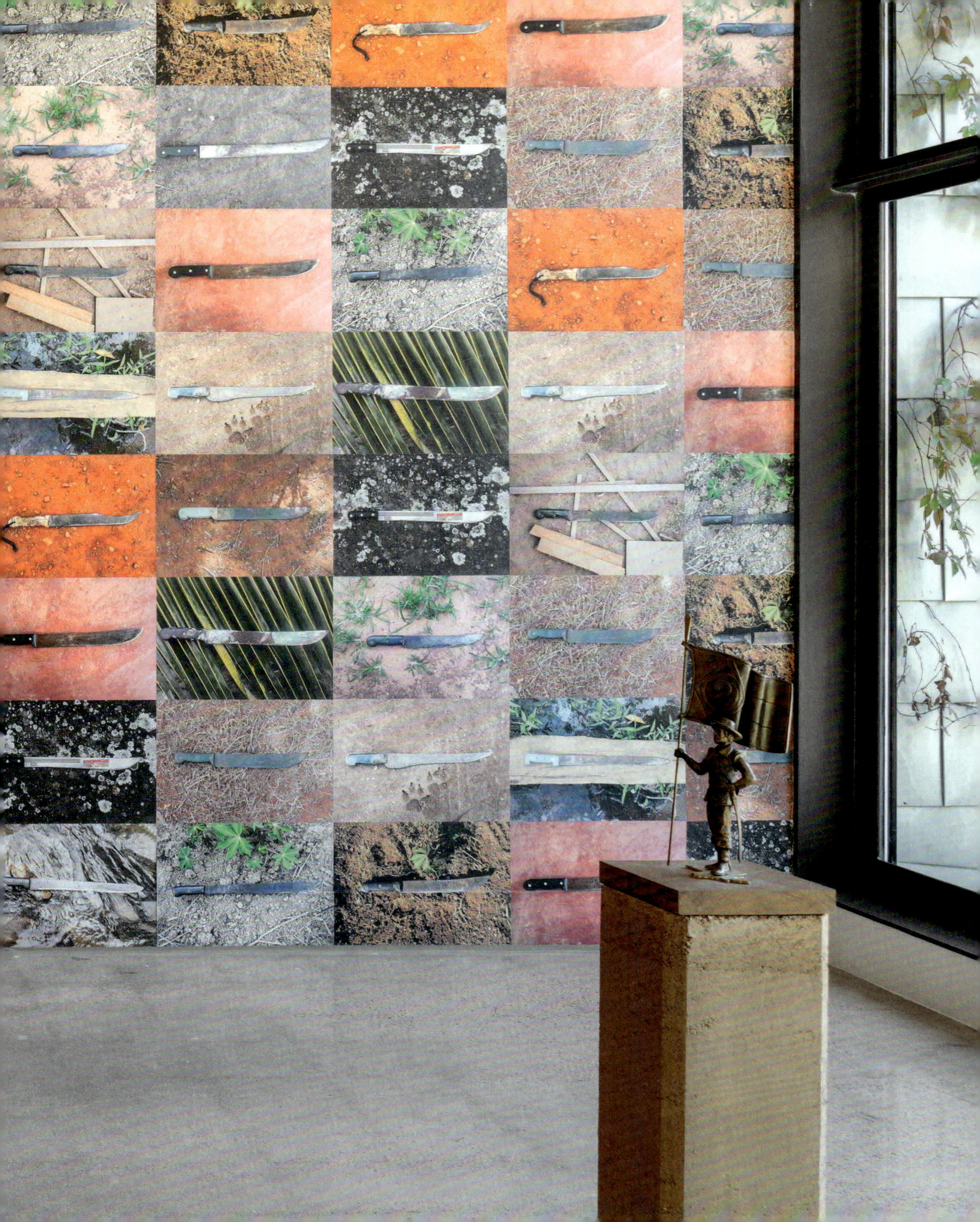

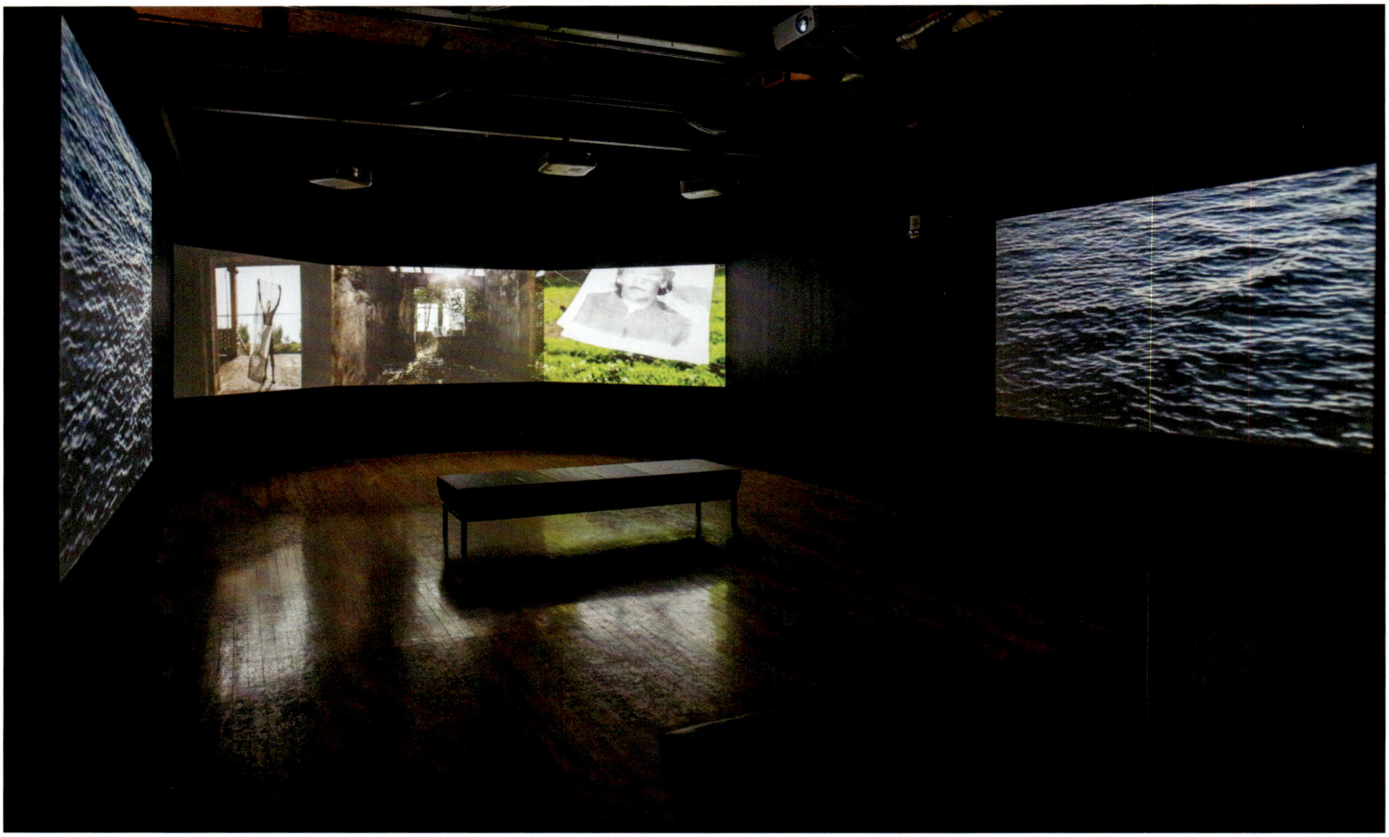

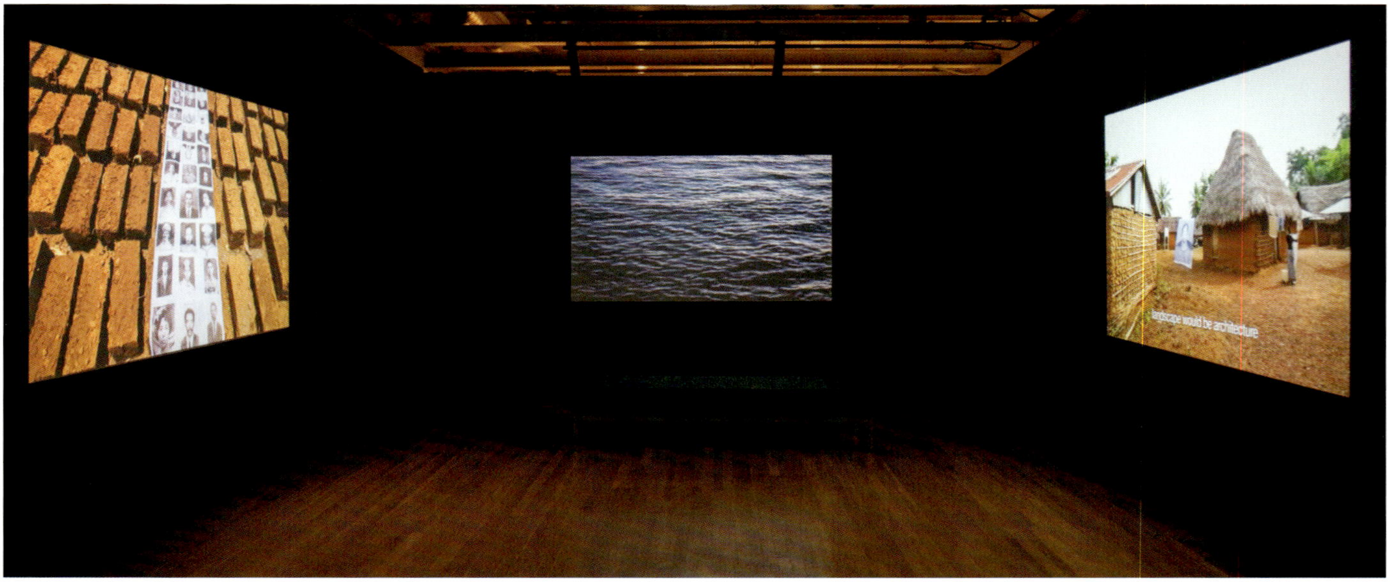
landscape would be architecture

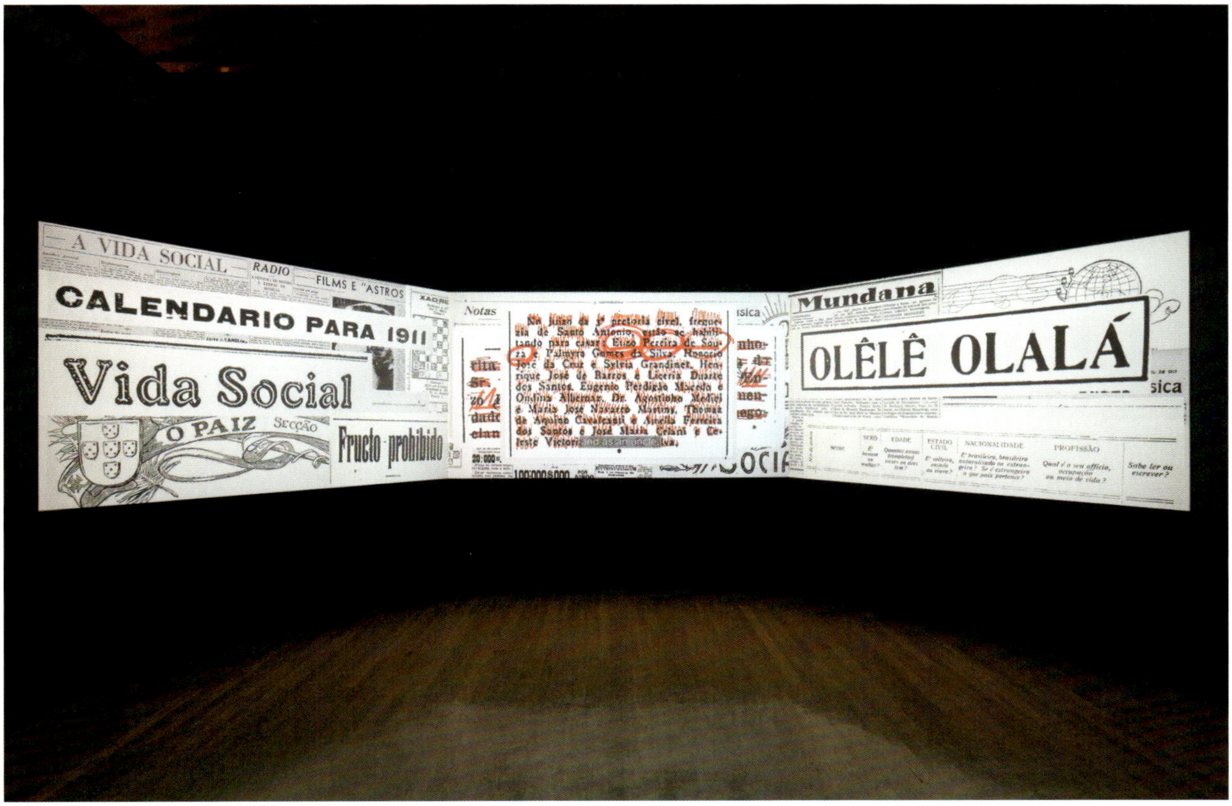
A VIDA SOCIAL
RADIO
FILMS E "ASTROS
CALENDARIO PARA 1911
Vida Social
O PAIZ
SECÇÃO
Fructo prohibido
Notas
Mundana
OLÊLÊ OLALÁ

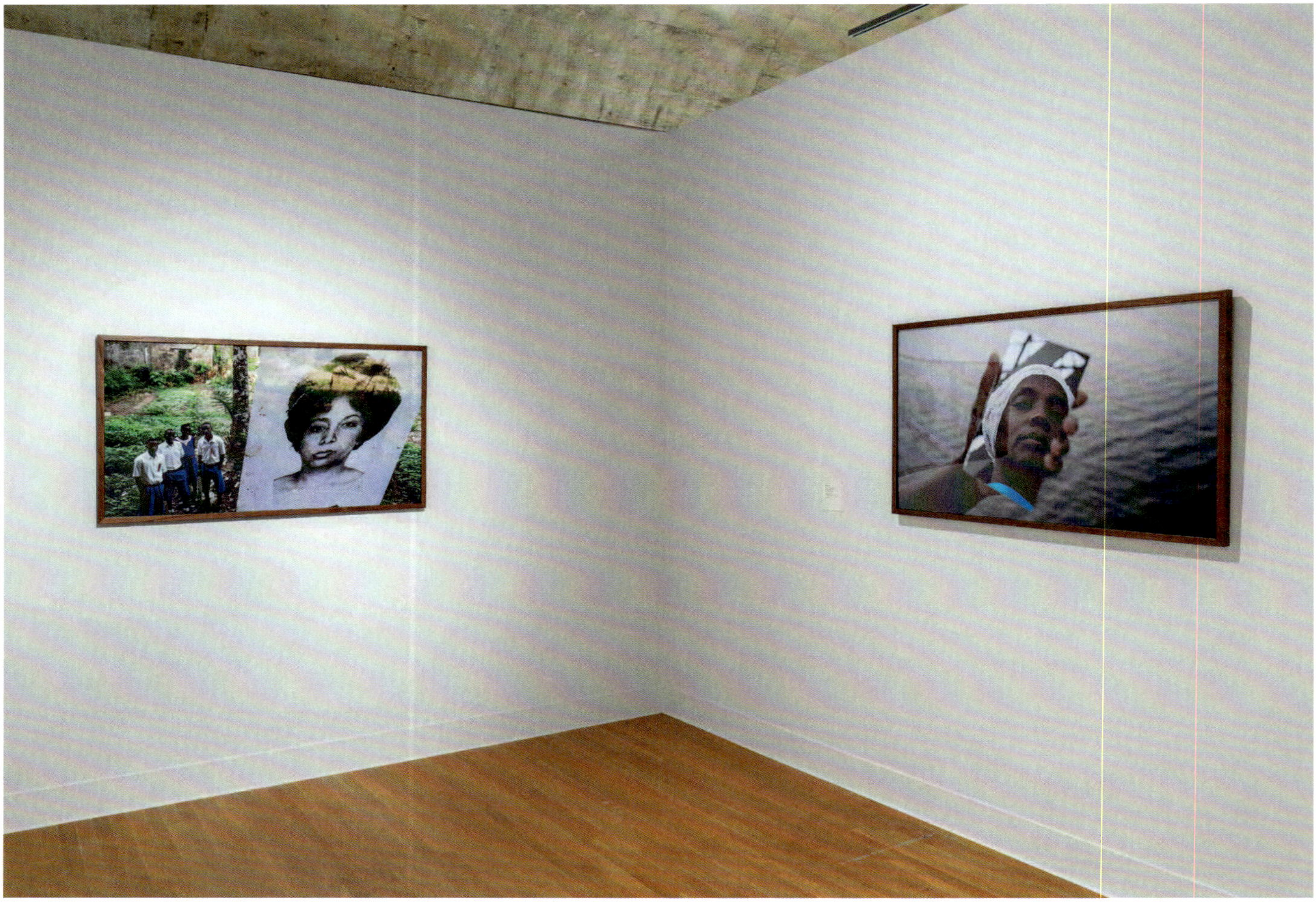

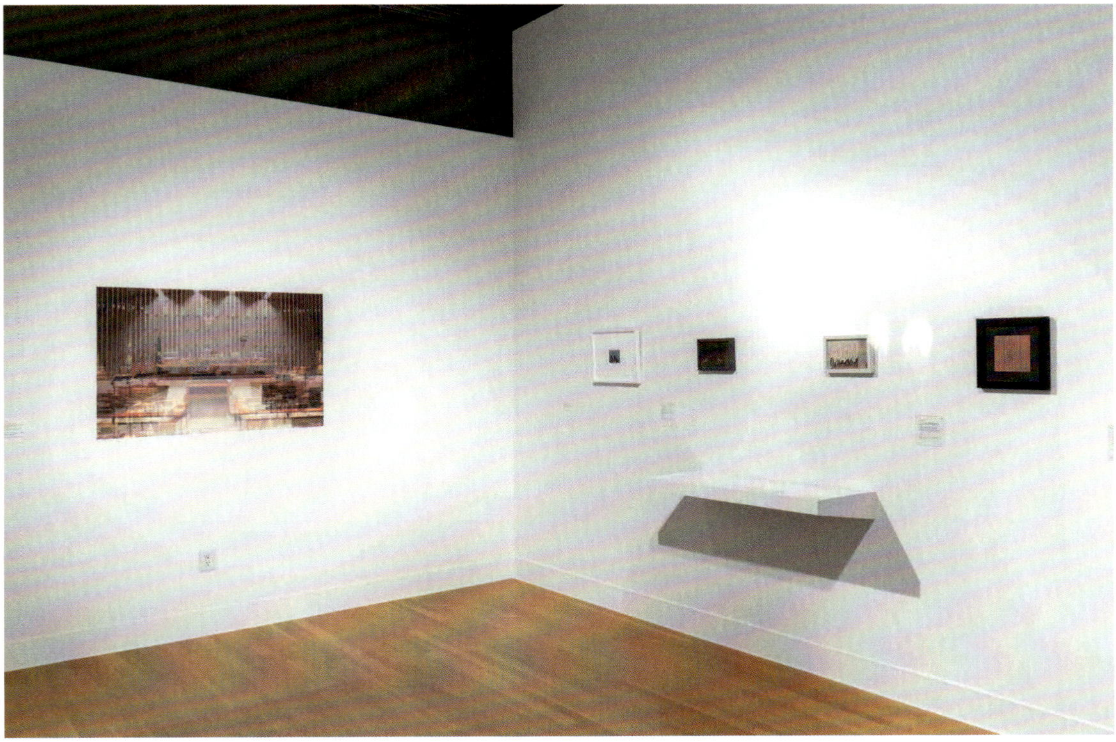

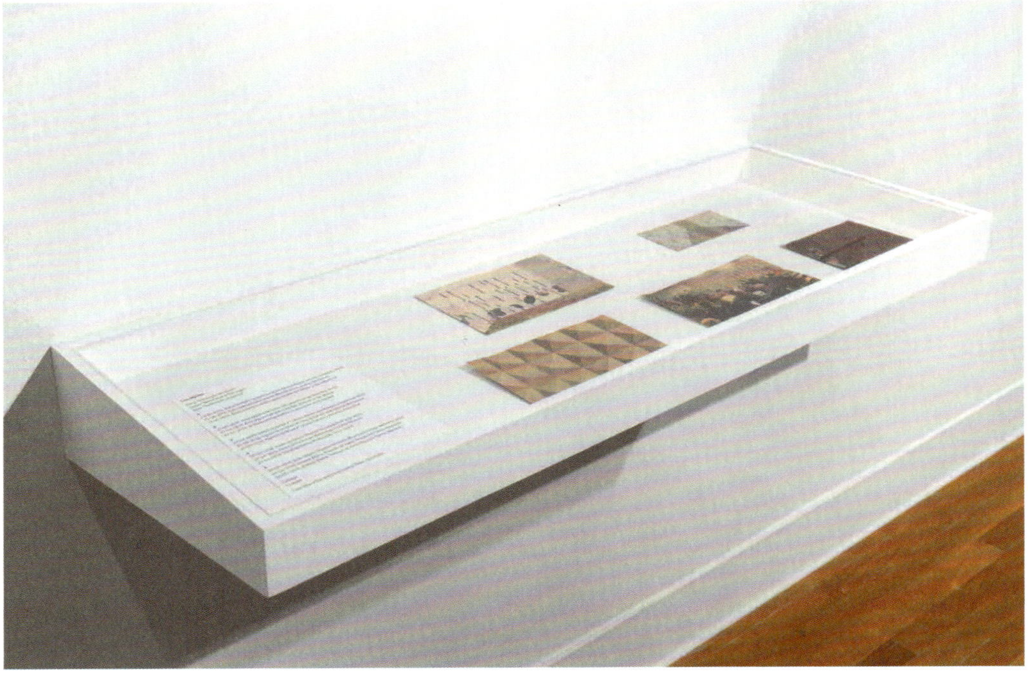

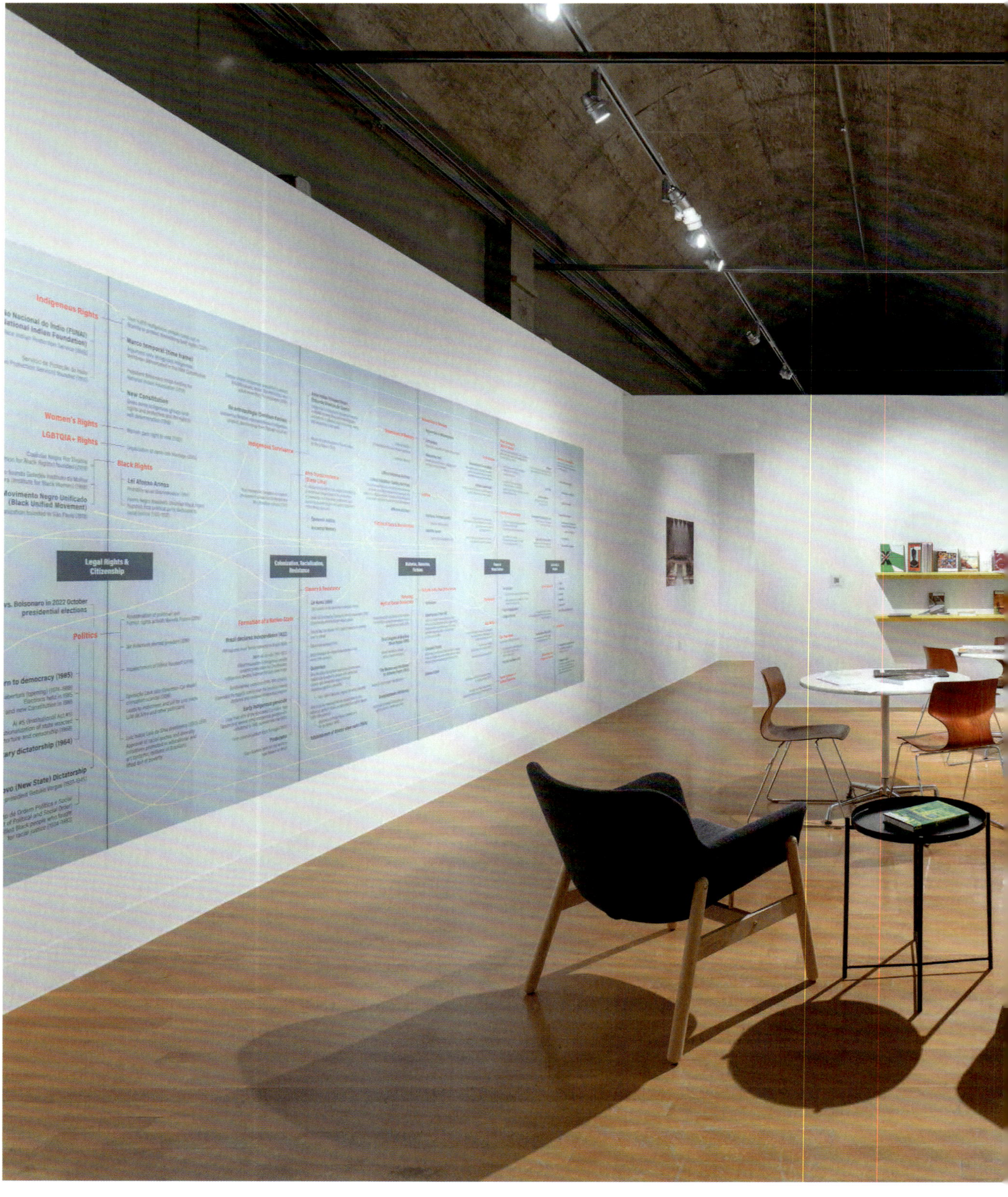
Indigenous Rights
Marco temporal (time frame)
New Constitution
Women's Rights
LGBTQIA+ Rights
Black Rights
Lei Afonso Arinos
Legal Rights & Citizenship
Politics
Formation of a Nation-State

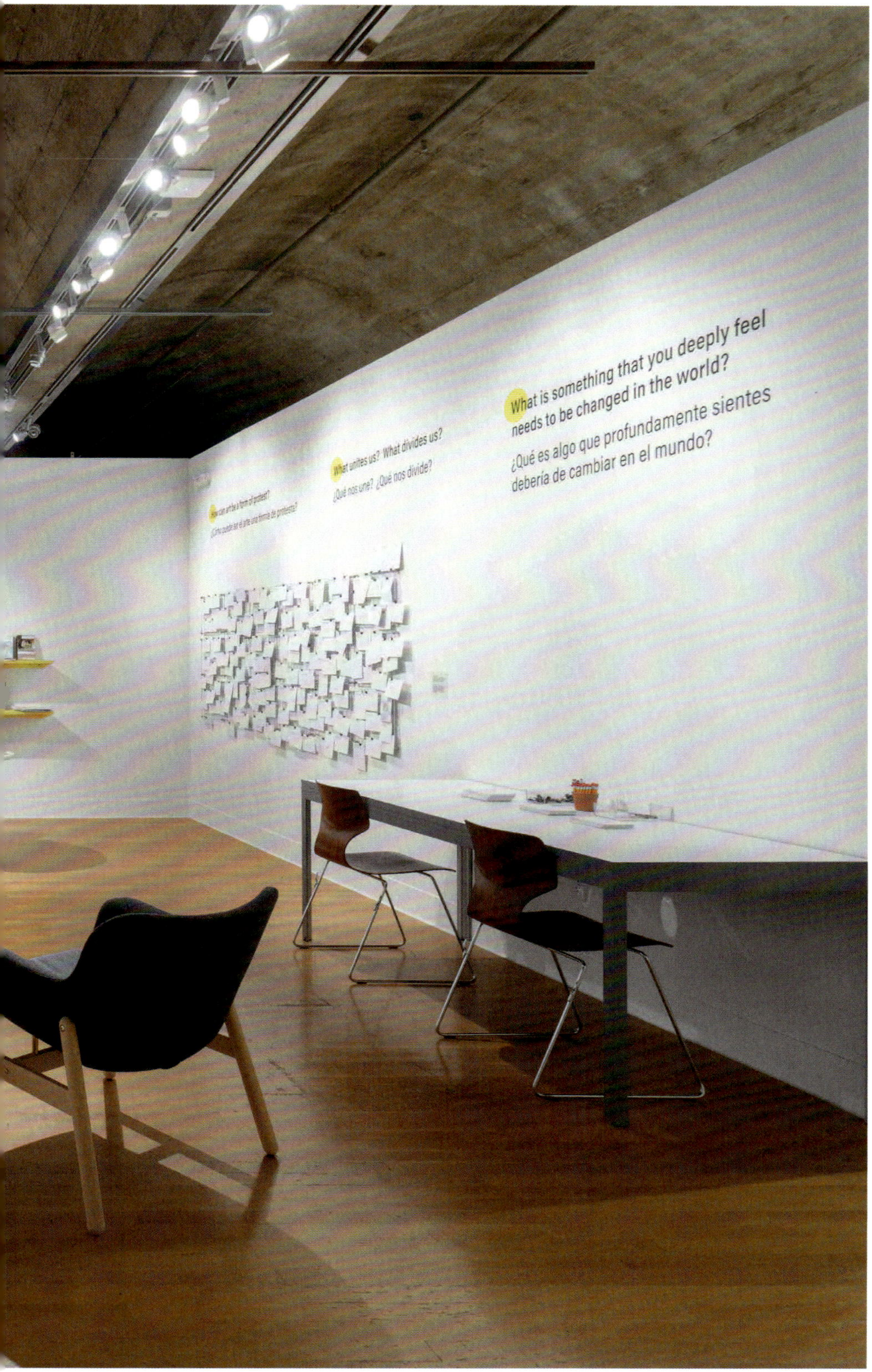
What is something that you deeply feel needs to be changed in the world?
¿Qué es algo que profundamente sientes debería de cambiar en el mundo?
What unites us? What divides us?
¿Qué nos une? ¿Qué nos divide?

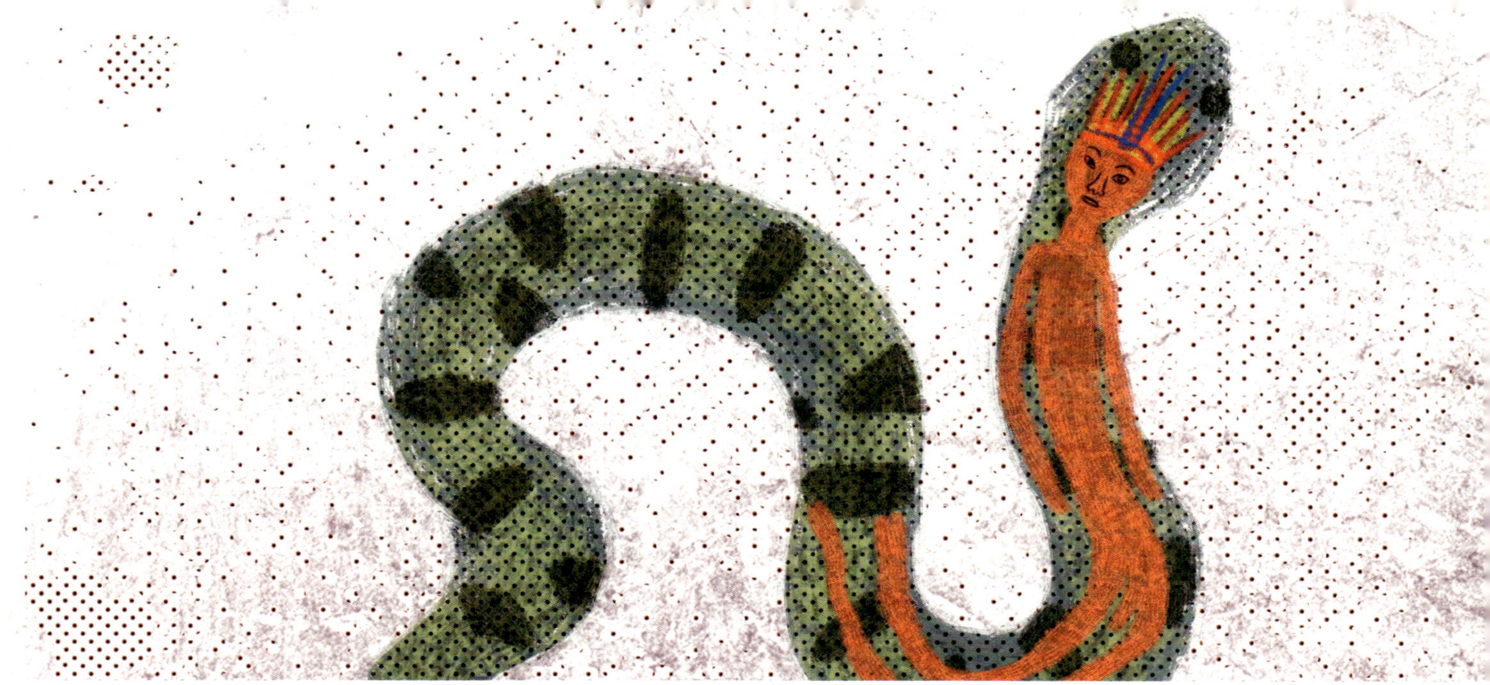

Denilson Baniwa, *Sukuryu-tapuya*, da série *Perspectivismo ameríndio* (*Sukuryu-tapuya*, from the series Amerindian Perspectivism), 2019 (detail).

Denilson Baniwa

Thiago Ferreira

Born in the Darí village in the upper Rio Negro region in the Amazon, Denilson Baniwa currently lives in Niterói, Rio de Janeiro.[1] He is a visual artist, activist, curator, and graphic designer who composes works that oppose the visual language of the European canon with those of his people. In so doing, he addresses the impact of continued colonial structures on Indigenous peoples and speaks to the crystallized and idyllic position reserved for them within the Brazilian cultural imaginary.[2] Baniwa's practice is intrinsically linked to Indigenous activist movements. He contributed to the use of satellite systems in one of the first applications of such a system for the protection of Indigenous territories in the Amazon at the center for Indigenous training he helped found in 2004.[3] In 2013, he and others started Rádio Yandê, the first Indigenous web radio in Brazil, which is broadcast in seventy countries and fosters communication between Indigenous peoples around the world.

Baniwa's activism converges with his interest in technologies and science fiction in the work *Carta aos indígenas do planeta Marte com códigos de reconhecimento do planeta Terra* (Letter to the Indigenous Peoples of the Planet Mars with Recognition Codes of the Planet Earth, 2020) (see plate 6). The artist describes a not-so-distant dystopian future in which there will be "nothing left on this planet" due to the actions of unreliable earthlings. This posture, which emphasizes the different perspectives between "us" and "them," is present in the other works by the artist in *Social Fabric: Art and Activism in Contemporary Brazil*. The images from the series *Perspectivismo ameríndio* (Amerindian Perspectivism, 2019) portray beings as doubles, animal-people spirits, which demonstrate the radical torsion of Amerindian thought, drawing attention to other species' expressive viewpoints (see plates 3 and 4).[4] The artist points to the fact that the naturalization of human superiority over other species does not exist in itself as an "objective" sphere but rather as an effect of a historical construct that asserted a univocal point of view.

Zoo terra indígena (Indigenous Land Zoo, 2018) and *Voyeurs* (2019) incorporate nineteenth-century touristic and ethnographic scenes in which overly romanticized representations of Indigenous people are layered with groups of contemporary non-Indigenous onlookers (see plates 1 and 5). The works stress the colonizers' gaze toward Indigenous people that recognizes Indigeneity only as an unchangeable and fossilized attribute tied to the past. Lúcia Sá and Felipe Milanez Pereira argue that Baniwa celebrates Indigeneity as a present-day reality in these and other works where he portrays Indigenous people with the traits traditionally associated with them (straight dark hair, traditional attire, and body painting and decoration) at ease navigating contemporary technological devices.[5]

Often refusing and challenging contemporary art frameworks, Baniwa claims that there is a collaborative attitude among Indigenous artists, whose work centers the occupation of spaces and social spheres.[6] According to Renata Marquez, Baniwa's work occupies the hegemonic places of art while preserving something out of place, even incommunicable. She writes that the artist proceeds "without nullifying differences, but, on the contrary, manifesting them as an invitation to an epistemic relationship that can transform that place."[7] Baniwa forges new ways of navigating contemporary art discourses, and his processes are interventions in larger historical and social dynamics—resignifying the very idea of art and its function and putting different cosmologies into circulation. His project constitutes an important act of resistance—but even more, of reinvention.

NOTES

1 The Baniwa are a group of Arawak-speaking peoples who live in the northwest of the Amazon between the borders of Brazil, Colombia, and Venezuela and form a cultural complex of twenty-three peoples with an estimated population of twelve thousand. The artist adopted the surname Baniwa for representation in non-Indigenous contexts. The Walipere clan, to which he belongs, means "the grandchildren of the five stars."

2 Clarissa Diniz, "Street fight, vingança e guerra: Artistas indígenas para além do 'produzir ou morrer,'" *Espaço Ameríndio* 14, no. 1 (January–July 2020): 74.

3 Baniwa describes his work with projects for the protection of the Indigenous territories of Rio Negro in Elisa Vieira Queiroz and Débora Caroline Viana Almeida, "Entre vistas, mundos e rios: Arte e tecnologia digital na pussanga de Denilson Baniwa," *Palíndromo* 13, no. 29 (January–April 2021): 250–67.

4 For an in-depth study of Amerindian perspectivism, see Eduardo Viveiros de Castro, *A inconstância da alma selvagem e outros ensaios de antropologia* (São Paulo: Cosac Naify, 2002).

5 Lúcia Sá and Felipe Milanez Pereira, "Painting Racism: Protest Art by Contemporary Indigenous Artists," in *Living (Il)legalities in Brazil: Practices, Narratives and Institutions in a Country on the Edge*, ed. Sara Brandellero, Derek Pardue, and Georg Wink (New York: Routledge, 2020), 160–78.

6 Queiroz and Almeida, "Entre vistas, mundos e rios," 261–65. Also see Baniwa's *Pajé-Onça Hackeando a 33a Bienal de São Paulo* of 2018. Video available at https://www.youtube.com/watch?v=MGFU7aG8kgI.

7 Renata Marquez, "A língua das onças e das lontras," *Arte e ensaios* 26, no. 40 (July–December 2020): 362.

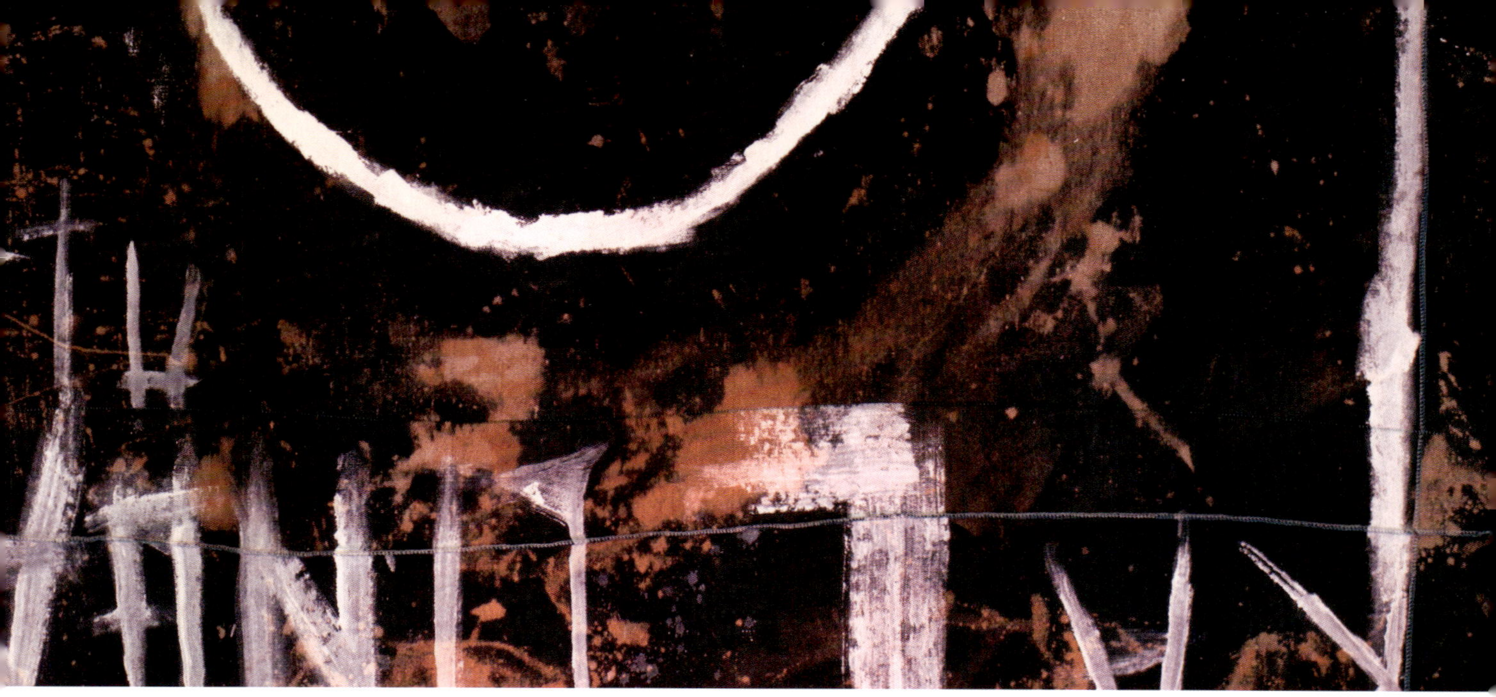

Castiel Vitorino Brasileiro, Flag VI from the series *Prosperity is Memories and Choices*, 2022 (detail).

Castiel Vitorino Brasileiro

Maysa Martins

Grounded in the knowledge and technologies of African Bantu and Black diasporic spiritual traditions, Castiel Vitorino Brasileiro's artistic practice poses expansive ontological and metaphysical questions. Her multidisciplinary body of work challenges ingrained modern colonial notions, such as the linearity of time, material limits of space, and subject-object dualism, pointing instead toward hybridisms, crossings, transmutations, and spiral temporalities as paths to the (temporary) healing of the wounds of coloniality. As a visual artist, writer, and psychologist born into a Bantu Brazilian family lineage, Brasileiro moves across different forms of knowledge to outline original concepts that frame her own work.[1] At the center of her thought and practice are the limits posed by modern racialized identities and the political struggles rooted in them. Without ignoring Blackness in its historical materiality, Brasileiro refuses the constraints of racialization and its fixed origin in the transatlantic slave trade. She instead finds—in the knowledge of the *benzedeiras*, *Umbanda* ritual practices, and Bantu Kongo cosmology as well as in the ancestral and contemporary knowledge of geology and astrophysics—the memory of transfigured ancestry.[2] She thereby traces the origins of dark-skinned bodies to earthly and outer-space ecologies.

As the result of Brasileiro's artistic residency at the Visual Arts Center and presented as part of the exhibition *Social Fabric: Art and Activism in Contemporary Brazil*, the work *Jupiter is Here. Celestial is Everything.* (2022) makes use of local natural materials as its building blocks and *Umbanda's pontos-riscados* as the architectural lines of a temple dedicated to the living memory of transmuted bodies (see plate 7).[3] Within the white walls of the art gallery, surrounded by a carpet of limestone rocks, some white and others painted red, a black path connected to black earth forms a trident—the cosmogram of the orisha Eshu—and leads the viewer into the center of the installation. There, enclosed within a semicircle of compressed earth blocks, a spiral-shaped marine fossil (a reminiscence of when the land now called Texas was at the bottom of an ocean) and various glass vessels filled with water forming a spiral around it invite the viewer to contemplate. Big limestone rocks and slices of mesquite trees engraved with fire are placed around the path. On the right side, a hand-painted cloth hangs from the ceiling on which, among other words and symbols, one can read the word *Kalunga* written upside down.

It is in the symbolic function and cosmological significance of Eshu and *Kalunga* that one can find the driving force of this work. Eshu, the orisha that is simultaneously the prototypical son and the ancestral father, is in charge of redistributing life force between the spiritual and the material realms.[4] *Kalunga*, the infinite water between the visible and the invisible worlds, is the source and origin of all there is in the universe.[5] Together they act in the work to help us see in the water, in the rocks, and in outer space our future and origin in a continuous spiral in which death is only "the memory of transfiguration."[6] Made present through the *pontos-riscados*, the spiral shapes, and the water and earth elements, the force of Eshu and *Kalunga* create what Brasileiro has called "perishable spaces of freedom," places that allow for the temporary withdrawing of Black bodies from the modern colonial geography and chronology and for their restitution into the infinity of time and the immensity of the universe.[7]

The impermanence of freedom, of life, and of the state of any matter is assured by the very ephemerality of the work, which fulfills its cycle by returning all materials to nature. The dismantling of the work reminds us that *Kalunga*, the "principal god of change" and movement, never fails to carry out its purpose.[8] Brasileiro's work does not let us forget that Texas will one day be at the bottom of an ocean again: we have all been stardust once and will one day return to it; Jupiter is here, celestial is everything.

NOTES

1 For Brasileiro on her Bantu heritage, see Maria Emilia Fernandez, "Quotidian Transmutations: Interview with Castiel Vitorino Brasileiro," in this volume.

2 *Benzedeiras* are women who combine the knowledge of plants, minerals, and prayer in ritual healing practices. The knowledge of the *benzedeiras* has been passed on orally through the centuries in Brazil.

3 According to Robert Farris Thompson, *pontos-riscados*, like the Haitian *veves* and the Cuban *firmas*, are cosmograms used ritually throughout the Black diaspora and deriving mainly from the Kongo cosmology. Robert Farris Thompson and Joseph Cornet, *The Four Moments of the Sun: Kongo Art in Two Worlds* (Washington, DC: National Gallery of Art, 1981), 28. Also note the original language of Brasileiro's title is in English; my understanding of Brasileiro's work was enriched by conversations with her in September 2022 and her public conversation with Christen Smith at the University of Texas at Austin on September 26, 2022.

4 Juana Elbein dos Santos, *Os Nàgô e a morte: Pàde, Àsèsè e o culto Égun na Bahia* (Petrópolis: Vozes, 1993).

5 Kimbwandènde Kia Bunseki Fu-Kiau, *African Cosmology of the Bântu-Kôngo: Tying the Spiritual Knot, Principles of Life & Living* (Brooklyn: Athelia Henrietta Press, 2001).

6 Castiel Vitorino Brasileiro, *Quando o sol aqui não mais brilhar: A falência da negritude* (São Paulo: N-1 edições, 2001), 60. Unless otherwise noted, translations are by the author.

7 Brasileiro, *Quando o sol aqui não mais brilhar*, 27.

8 Fu-Kiau, *African Cosmology of the Bântu-Kôngo*, 21.

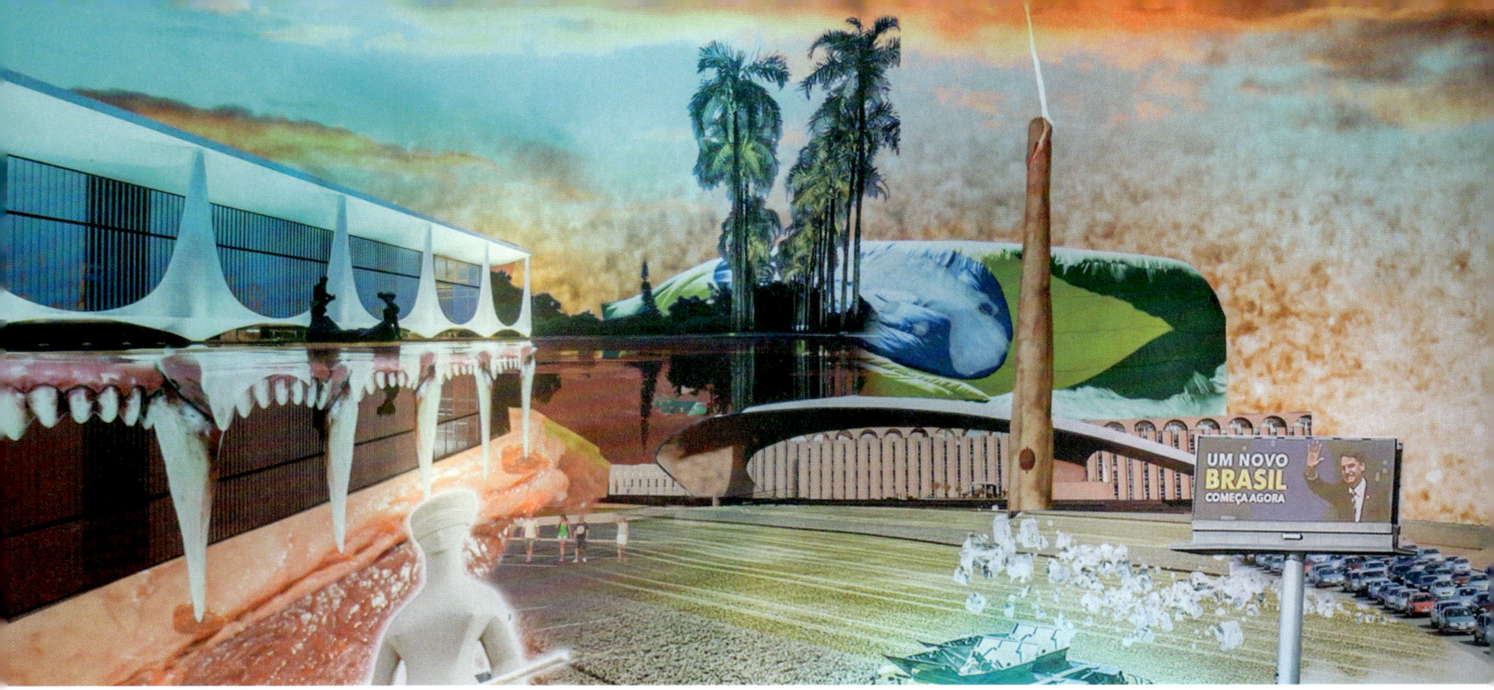

Guerreiro do Divino Amor, *Trilogia cristalizada de Brasília: Formação, cristalização e desabrochar de uma nova Alvorada* (Crystallized Trilogy of Brasília: Formation, Crystallization, and Breaking of a New Dawn), 2022 (detail).

Guerreiro do Divino Amor Jana La Brasca

"My work seeks to address the complexity of the apocalypse," says the Swiss-born, Rio de Janeiro–based artist who goes by the chosen name Guerreiro do Divino Amor.[1] *Guerreiro* (warrior) is part of the artist's surname, while *do Divino Amor* (of divine love) became a nickname as a teenager, in ironic reference to one of his father's girlfriends who was an evangelical pastor. Originally intending to use it as his nom de guerre in an aborted metal/gospel band, the moniker stuck, and its satiric, pseudomillenarian tone matches the critical attitude of Divino Amor's art, which takes form in videos, installations, tabloid-size publications, and glowing sculptural objects.

Divino Amor began his longest-running artistic project, the *Atlas superficcional mundial* (Superfictional World Atlas), in 2005 while dually enrolled in master's programs in architecture at the École Nationale Supérieure d'Architecture in Grenoble, France, and in contemporary urban conditions at the École Nationale Supérieure des Arts Visuels de La Cambre in Brussels, Belgium. Leveraging techniques of urban spatial analysis and cultural geography along with the Euro-Brazilian hybridity of his upbringing, Divino Amor's atlas charts a network of pernicious "Superfictions," interlocking metanarratives that shore up cultural imaginaries of colonialism, white supremacy, religious fundamentalism, and extractivist industry. According to the artist, the Superfictions of the Supernation Brazil rise from a toxic Supervoid generated through "the erasure of any life existing outside the colonialist narrative."[2] The Superpast and Superfuture fuel Superfictions disseminated through the Supermedia, which are complicit with both Superpale ideologies of Superempire and Superdivine mythologies of SuperGod.

So far, the Atlas has six chapters that map the artist's transnational peregrinations: *The Battle of Brussels* (2005), *SuperRio superficções* (SuperRio Superfictions, on Rio de Janeiro, 2006–2016), *Supercomplexo metropolitano expandido* (Expanded Metropolitan Supercomplex, on São Paulo, 2018), *A cristalização de Brasília* (Crystallization of Brasília, 2019), *O mundo mineral* (The Mineral World, on Minas Gerais, 2019), and *The Miracle of Helvetia* (on Switzerland, 2022) (see, for example, plates 8 and 9).

Through extensive research and a method described by curator Clarissa Diniz as "digital archaeology," in which he draws from promotional tourist materials, television, pop culture, print media, and the internet, Divino Amor collages sound and music, archival material, animation, and original elements to generate a signature supersaturated, hyperreal visual language reminiscent of the contemporary memescape.[3] Divino Amor trades in deeply specific references to intertwine Brazilian and European histories, but he filters them through a globalizing language of postmodern critical theory, citing such thinkers as Pierre Bourdieu, Naomi Klein, Roland Barthes, Guy Debord, Georges Bataille, and others among the "Superpeople" he acknowledges as supporters of the publication that accompanies *SuperRio superficções*.[4]

Social Fabric: Art and Activism in Contemporary Brazil features the fourth and fifth chapters of the *Atlas superficcional mundial* projected onto large-scale abutting screens. The screens are flanked by two light-box triptychs, each resting on the reflective surface of a custom pedestal (see plates 10 and 11). Resembling beauty vanities, technodevotional altars, or glowing arcade games, the pedestal bases reference the bays of the iconic facade of the presidential residence, Palácio do Alvorada, in Brasília. The shape, however, is inverted, echoing a memorable sequence in *A cristalização de Brasília* in which the columns turn upside down and morph into rows of bared fangs, which sink into a ground that dissolves into a river of bubbling, red-hot magma. Whether or not the viewer is aware of the stark economic inequality in the area around the capital, the labor and human rights abuses that occurred during its construction, or the recent turmoil of the Brazilian presidency, the message is clear: the vampiric fangs of national mythology sink deep into the nation's political, historical, and geological core.

Divino Amor describes *O mundo mineral* as an "allegorical portrait."[5] As Craig Owens notes, allegory has the "capacity to rescue from historical oblivion that which threatens to disappear."[6] In a play of visually seductive, highly artificial surfaces, Divino Amor reveals the hard truths of Superfiction, exposing insidious forms of whitewashing domination so omnipresent as to be almost invisible.

NOTES

1 Luiz Camillo Osorio, "Conversation with Guerreiro do Divino Amor," August 30, 2019, PIPA Prize: The Window Into Brazilian Contemporary Art, https://www.pipaprize.com/wp-content/uploads/2019/03/ENG-Guerreiro-do-Divino-Amor.docx.pdf. Divino Amor is a dual citizen of both countries; one parent is Swiss, and one is Brazilian.

2 Guerreiro do Divino Amor, wall text for his work *A cristalização de Brasília* (2019) for the *Social Fabric* exhibition.

3 Clarissa Diniz, "Superfictions by Guerreiro do Divino Amor—Whiteness, Superhibernation and Supermessianism," in *PIPA Prize 2019* (Rio de Janeiro: Instituto PIPA, 2019), 92. Full catalog available for download at https://www.pipaprize.com/wp-content/uploads/2020/01/catalogo-pipa_SITE_2019-1_compressed-4.pdf.

4 Guerreiro do Divino Amor, *SuperRio superficções*, 2018. Publication available at https://pt.calameo.com/read/004177604641l142d92d3. For a summary of artist Peter Hill's idea of superfiction, see the sociogram in this volume (see insert after page 104).

5 Guerreiro do Divino Amor, wall text for *O mundo mineral* (2019) for the *Social Fabric* exhibition.

6 Craig Owens, building on Walter Benjamin, in "The Allegorical Impulse: Toward a Theory of Postmodernism," *October* 12 (1980): 68.

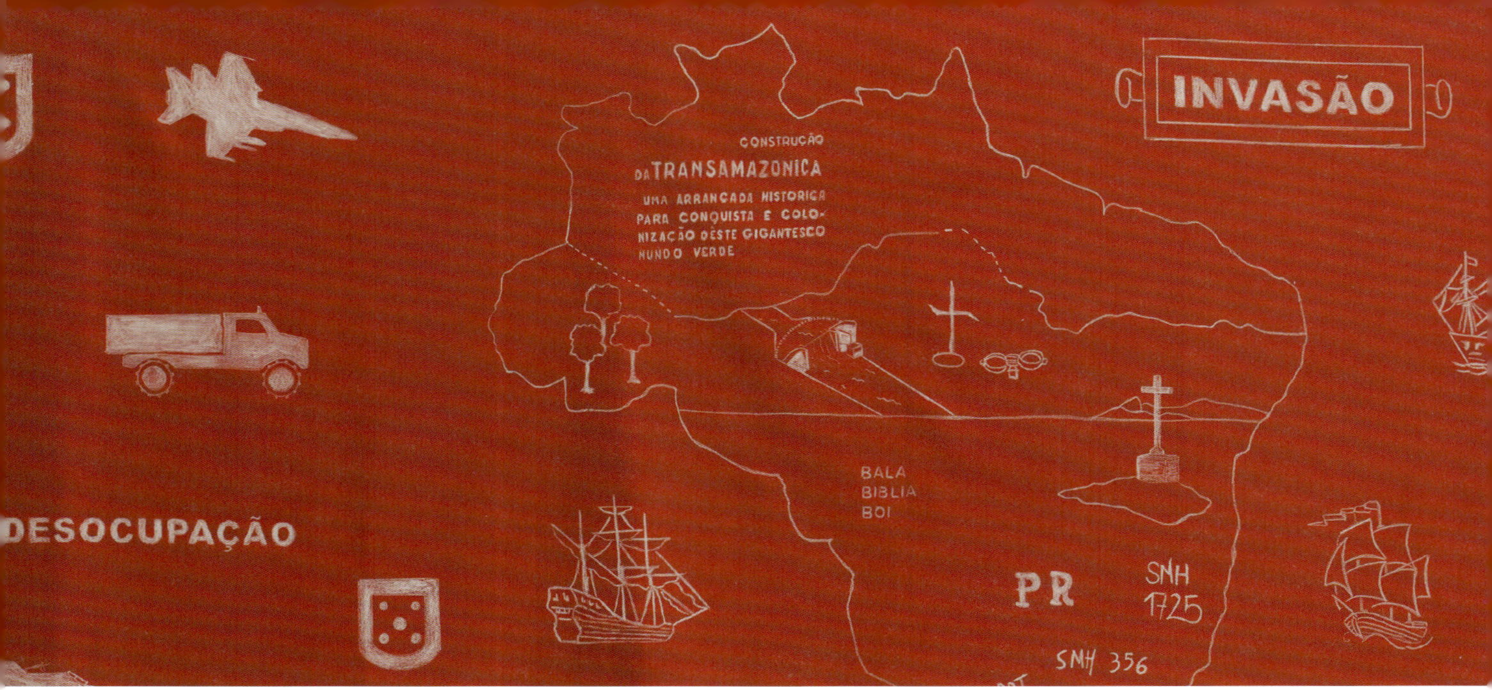

Jaime Lauriano, *Invasão* (Invasion), 2017 (detail).

Jaime Lauriano Lucy Quezada

The work of São Paulo artist Jaime Lauriano is focused on historical markers that have ongoing and profound impacts on Brazilian contemporary society: colonialism, military dictatorship, and slavery. For Lauriano, who was trained as a visual artist at the Centro Universitário Belas Artes in São Paulo, the use of archives is fundamental in addressing these issues that are embedded in the national identity and continually reimagined in present-day Brazil.[1]

Invasão (Invasion, 2017), *America meridionalis: invenção, epistemicídio, contrato racial e genocídio* (America meridionalis: invention, epistemicide, racial contract, and genocide, 2019), and *Bandeirante #1* and *#2* (2019) are the works by Lauriano in *Social Fabric: Art and Activism in Contemporary Brazil* (see plates 12–15). Together these pieces present different layers of meaning to aid in understanding the Brazilian past and present. *America meridionalis* and *Invasão* are part of a series of works in which Lauriano re-creates maps, using the historical nautical charts made by the colonizers of Latin America as a point of departure, imbuing them with significant changes. In contrast to the symbols that the colonizers assigned to these lands, he portrays objects and writes specific words to note how the violence of colonization and slavery is a contemporary reality.

America meridionalis, made with white *pemba*, a type of chalk used in rituals of Umbanda and other Afro-Brazilian religions, is a map of South America following the structure created in 1630 by the Flemish and Dutch engraver and cartographer Jodocus Hondius (fig. 1; see plate 13). This physical map was transformed by Lauriano from its original form, saturated with geographical information, to a flat white surface, in which he chooses to maintain the words *Brasilia* and *America meridionalis*. The inclusion of these terms is an important intervention that points to the violent processes of colonization (*epistemicídio*, *genocídio*) and displays how neocolonialism is embedded in the Brazilian national identity (*contrato racial*, *invenção*). In the original map, the lower left corner portrays an image of the Inca city of Cusco, in Peru. In its place, Lauriano chooses to position three small strips of gold adhesive tape.

Invasão follows the structure of a colonial map, here displaying only the Brazilian territory (see plate 12). Instead of the monsters that sometimes populate the ocean in the original versions of these maps, Lauriano depicts a series of police and military vehicles, such as tanks, trucks, and helicopters. These contemporary monstrosities are framed by the words *invasão* (invasion), *desocupação* (eviction), and *reintegração* (reintegration) as a litany of concepts to trace the different stages of colonization and contemporary racial issues in Brazil. These words and the red color of the flag allude to the Movimento dos Trabalhadores Rurais sem Terra (Landless Workers' Movement, MST), a sociopolitical activist organization formed in the early 1970s to oppose the inequitable agrarian reform of the military dictatorship.[2] Still active, MST organizes thousands of people and promotes the redistribution of unproductive land. *Reintegração* also resonates as the fiction of a unitary nation in which slavery and the resulting structural racism are never confronted as a societal trauma. Instead, cruel police violence, coming from the state, and violent extractivism prevail. Among the many symbols inside

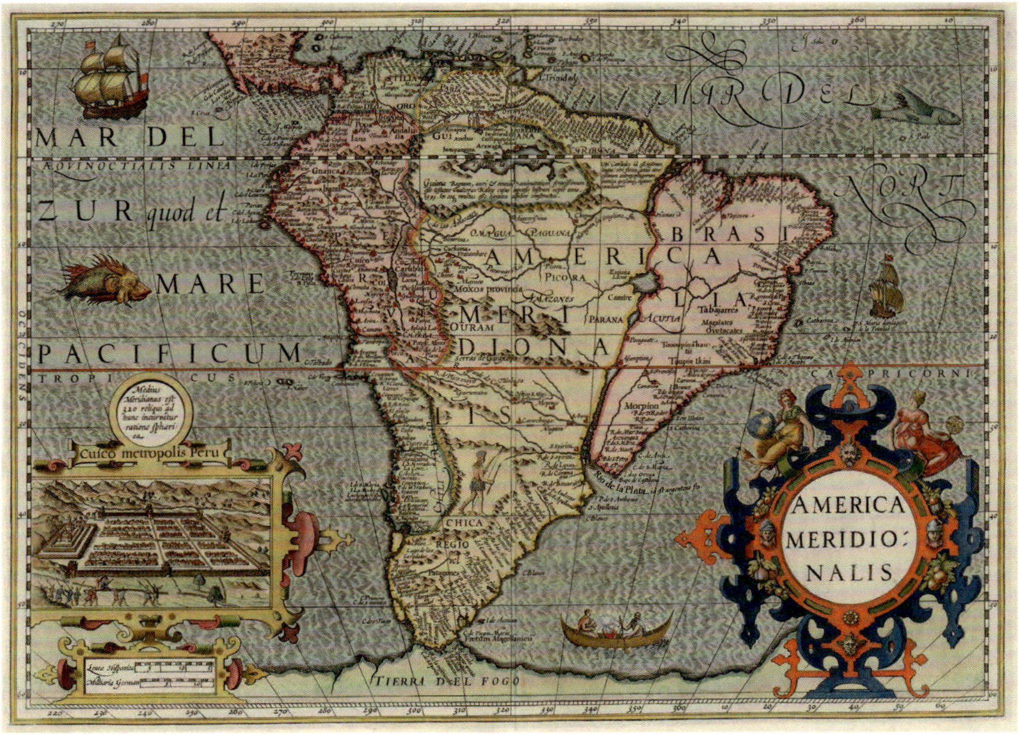

Figure 1. Hendrik Hondius, Jodocus Hondius, and Gerhard Mercator. *America Meridionalis.* Inset: *Cusco metropolis Peru plan*, 1623 edition. Copper engraving, hand colored. David Rumsey Map Collection, David Rumsey Map Center, Stanford Libraries.

the country's contours, one is particularly prominent: the reference to the Trans-Amazonian Highway, a project that involved environmental violence and dispossession of land in the construction of the major highway of Brazil during the military government of Emílio Garrastazu Médici (1969–1974). Lauriano thus not only connects the distant colonial past to current oppression but also notes the persistent afterlives of the military dictatorship in the present.

Bandeirante #1 and *Bandeirante #2* are small sculptures of men who were in charge of colonial expeditions to search for gold and treasure in the interior of Brazil beginning in the sixteenth century (see plates 14 and 15). These expeditions, or *bandeiras*, named for the flags they carried, were also a form of colonial control—*bandeirantes* captured fugitive slaves and massacred Indigenous people.[3] Lauriano reveals how these apparently virtuous figures, often praised as national heroes, are part of a bigger apparatus of historical violence that dates back to the very foundation of the nation. The artist uses brass and spent ammunition cartridges, like those used by the Brazilian military police and armed forces, to construct these figures. Thus, these little men stand in for exercises of violence from different moments of Brazilian history, representing the orchestration of genocide against Black and Indigenous people from the earliest moments of the colonized territories to the police brutality of today—a continuously colonial and racist dynamic.

NOTES

1 My understanding of Lauriano's process and work was enriched by the seminar and artist talk he gave at the University of Texas at Austin on March 11 and March 12, 2020. On the artist's use of archives, see "Luiz Camillo Osorio in Conversation with Jaime Lauriano," PIPA Prize: The Window into Brazilian Contemporary Art, August 23, 2019, https://www.pipaprize.com/2019/08/luiz-camillo-osorio-in-conversation-with-jaime-lauriano/.

2 For this insight I thank Eugenio Y. Arima, who detailed the connection of *Invasão* to the terms and imagery of MST in a conversation with Maria Emilia Fernandez on February 25, 2023. For discussion of terms and tactics of land occupation and change, see Stephen P. Aldrich et al., "Agronomic or Contentious Land Change? A Longitudinal Analysis from the Eastern Brazilian Amazon," *PLOS One* 15, no. 1 (2020): e0227378. https://doi.org/10.1371/journal.pone.0227378.

3 On São Paulo's self-image as the *bandeirante* state, see Barbara Weinstein, *The Color of Modernity: São Paulo and the Making of Race and Nation in Brazil* (Durham, NC: Duke University Press, 2015).

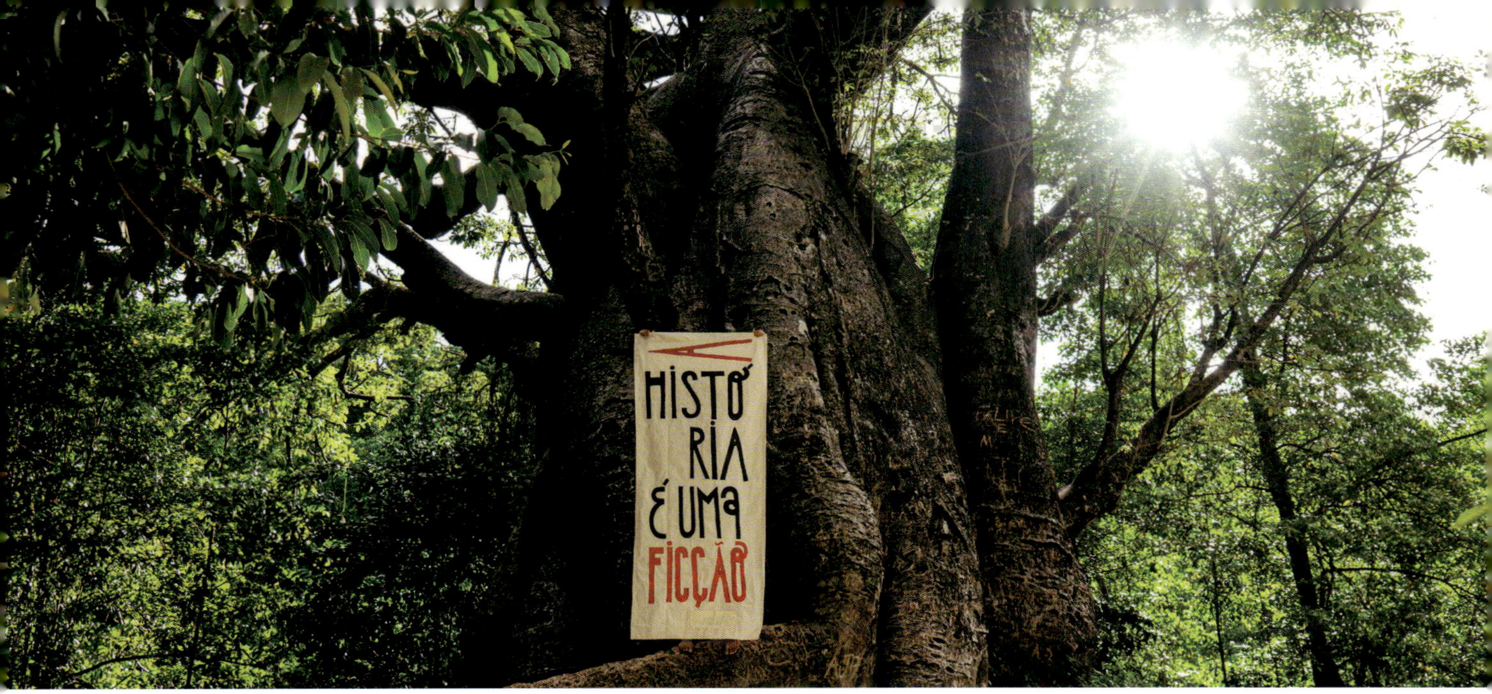

Maré de Matos, *História* (History), 2019–present (detail).

Maré de Matos

Chasitie Brown

Maré de Matos's artistic practice centers poetry as an expressive vehicle to imagine decolonial futures. Linking word, image, sound, and body, Matos creates affective narratives that speak from the perspective of the marginalized Black subject through diverse mediums: photography, textile, and multimedia installations. Her artistic concerns reflect her upbringing and formal education. Born in a predominantly white environment in Minas Gerais, Matos earned her BA in visual arts at the Universidade do Estado de Minas Gerais (2009) and her MA in literary theory from the Universidade Federal do Pernambuco (2019). She is currently based in São Paulo, where she is completing her doctoral studies at the Universidade de São Paulo.

Matos's multimedia installation *Fundamento* (Foundation, 2019) visualizes her poem bearing the same title (see plate 16). Here, Matos dreams of worlds before the violent grip of colonialism took hold in Brazil. The artist experiments with form and typography, inscribing the words of the text in different fonts of her own design on diverse media, including fabric, wooden blocks, bricks, and framed acrylic canvases. As viewers, we are encouraged to slow down our reading and consider the weight of each word. Accompanying the text is a video monitor that depicts Léo Castilho, an art educator and sign language interpreter, performing the poem in sign language while Matos reads it in Portuguese. Interspersed throughout the installation are iPads streaming looped short excerpts of the same performance. Matos implores us to consider the relationship between performance, orality, and language as we read the poetry of a nation whose colonial ambitions of *pátria* (motherland) produced a *lingua* (language) and strategic violence, seen, heard, and felt.[1]

Like *Fundamento,* Matos utilizes the affect of language to give voice to the silent histories of Brazil in her photographic works *História* (History) and *Racismo* (Racism), which she describes as "photo performances" and are part of the ongoing series *Anti-bandeirante* (see plates 17 and 18). In these works, begun in 2019, Matos explores the relationship between space and historical memory through the medium of photography and the body. In *História,* Matos stands firmly rooted on a tree trunk holding a white banner that covers her body, save for her feet and hands. Cast in black and red paint are the words "História é uma ficção" (History is a fiction). Here, Matos questions the construction of national histories that bring violence both to bodies and to the natural environment.[2] Likewise, in *Racismo,* Matos calls attention to structural anti-Black racism. Holding a white banner inscribed with "Racismo é uma tradição" (Racism is a tradition), Matos stands outside the Academia Pernambucana de Letras, one of the earliest elite literary societies established in Brazil. As a silent yet powerful protest, the artist's gesture demands that the state acknowledge its culpability in the tradition, and inscription, of racism.

Finally, in *Mais nascimento que morte* (More Birth than Death, 2021–2022), Matos employs the visual poetics of abstraction to explore the politics of life and death (see plate 19). Two swaths of fabric—one white, the other black—are hung side by side. The white banner is woven with colorful rectangular forms and signifies life, while the black cloth, interlaced with white pieces of fabric, represents death. Here, the white of life becomes usurped by the darkness of death, a haunting reminder of how the Brazilian state exercises necropolitical control through structural policies that determine who lives and who dies.[3]

Language and text serve as the architectural foundation of Matos's artistic practice, functioning as a means through which to criticize the exclusionary practices of Brazilian racial politics. By incorporating performance, photography, and the visual language of abstraction within her works, Matos draws out the affective registers of language, reminding us of the humanity of feeling emotions. Creating intimate spaces for reflection, Matos's work invites us to mourn, love, and feel.

NOTES

1 For an excellent discussion on the relationship between performance and orality as it relates to artistic production in the hemispheric Americas, see Diana Taylor, *The Archive and the Repertoire: Performing Cultural Memory in the Americas* (Durham, NC: Duke University Press, 2003).

2 Matos's commentary on the fictive nature of history is also reminiscent of Haitian historian Michel-Rolph Trouillot's constructions of national histories and the silences within the archives. See Trouillot, *Silencing the Past: Power and the Production of History* (Boston: Beacon Press, 1995). For an analysis on the museum's institutional practices of marginalization and its relationship to exclusionary historical narratives, see Adriano Pedrosa, "History, Histórias," in *Histórias afro-atlânticas*, ed. Adriano Pedrosa and Tomás Toledo (São Paulo: Museu de Arte de São Paulo, 2018), 32–33.

3 See Achille Mbembe, *Necropolitics* (Durham, NC: Duke University Press, 2019); Christen A. Smith, *Afro-Paradise: Blackness, Violence, and Performance in Brazil* (Urbana: University of Illinois Press, 2016); and Denise Ferreira da Silva, "Ninguém: Direito, racialidade, e violência," *Metrium* 9, no. 1 (2014): 67–117.

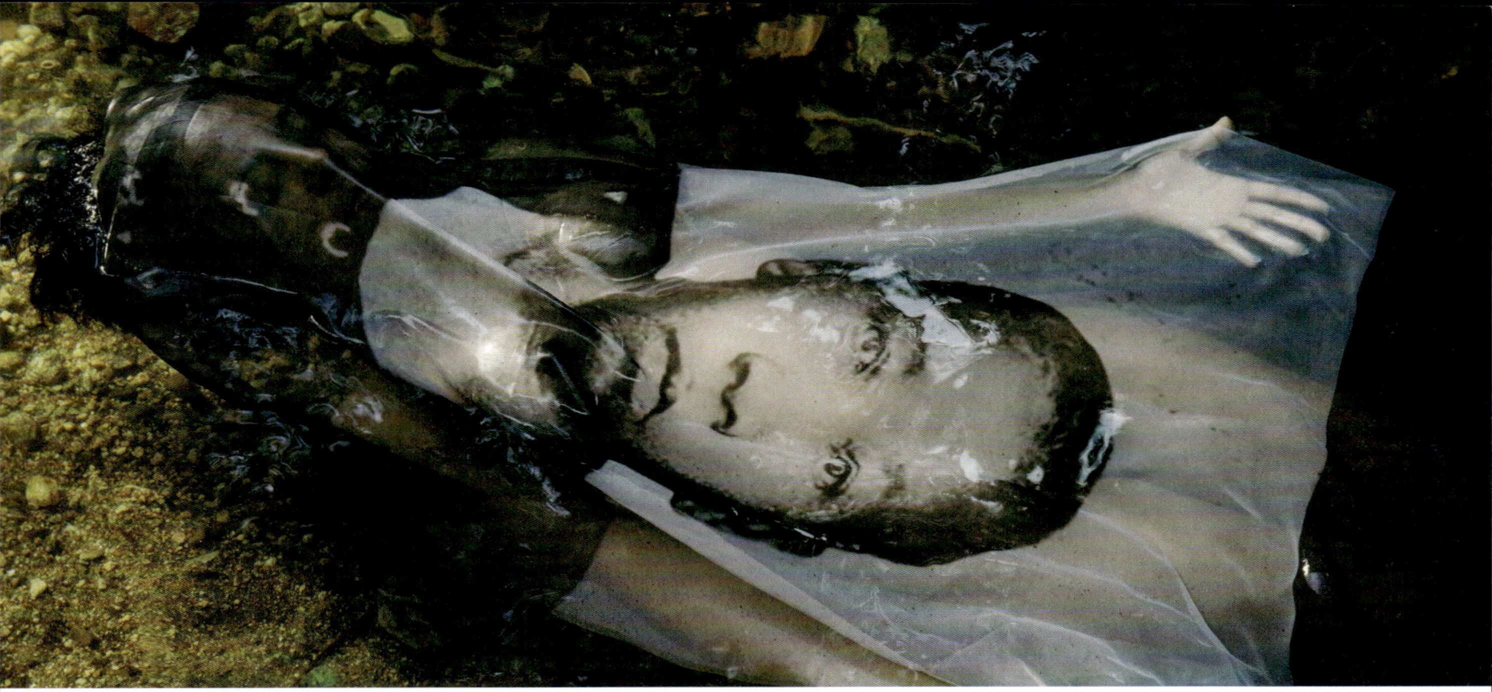

Aline Motta, *Se o mar tivesse varandas #4* (If the Sea Had Balconies #4), 2017 (detail).

Aline Motta Jennifer Sales

The creative practice of Brazilian artist Aline Motta combats the loss and fragmentation of Afro-Atlantic narratives as the result of slavery and colonialism. Read through writer Saidiya Hartman's concept of "critical fabulation," Motta mobilizes narrative strategies to fight against absence and violence in the archive.[1] In literature, photography, video, and installation, the artist speculates on her own matrilineal past in order to invert entrenched social hierarchies within Brazilian society.

Born in Niteroi, Rio de Janeiro, Motta studied communication at the Universidade Federal do Rio de Janeiro and later studied film production at the New School in New York. She worked in the commercial film industry before winning the Rumos Itaú Cultural grant (2015–2016) that launched her artistic career. Motta synthesizes a multitude of audiovisual languages to, as she puts it, "arrive at forms"—identifying how best to compose a cinematic frame for maximum impact.[2] Thus, she carefully layers photography, narration, and performance into a "vehicle for embodiment" to affirm the presence of her ancestors across time and space.[3] The culmination of meticulous archival research, site visits, and oral histories emerges in a series of videos that bring the viewer along on a journey to Brazil, Portugal, and the African continent.

For *Social Fabric: Art and Activism in Contemporary Brazil*, Motta presents the six-channel video installation and accompanying photographic series *Trilogia* (Trilogy, 2017–2019), consisting of *Pontes sobre abismos* (Bridges over the Abyss, 2017), *Se o mar tivesse varandas* (If the Sea Had Balconies, 2017), and *(Outros) Fundamentos* ([Other] Foundations, 2017–2019) (see plates 20–28). *Pontes sobre abismos* follows the familial secret of the abuse and abandonment of her great-grandmother, Mariana, who bore the grandchild of the elite white Pereira de Souza family—her grandmother, Doralice. Scenes flicker between an animated fable, findings from the society columns of newspapers, and the carrying of enlarged printed photographs of her maternal ancestors into the natural environment. These women's photographs reverberate, activated by earth, water, wind, and light, to assert their existence and resilience—a potent gesture against erasure. *Se o mar tivesse varandas* and *(Outros) Fundamentos* further trace the artist's genealogical thread in search of acknowledgment and kinship between Brazil and Africa.[4] Specifically, Motta's narration acts as a form of call and response in hopes of connecting with ancestral origins. Waters, mirrors, and bridges appear to establish an affinity between disparate people and places, not only genealogically but also through shared experiences.[5]

Inside the immersive installation of the trilogy, each video is followed by an interlude of the undulating sea: a repository of memory, a teller and keeper of time. Much like the theme of her first solo exhibition, *Aline Motta: Memória, viagem e água* (Aline Motta: Memory, Travel, and Water) (2020–2021) at Museu de Arte do Rio, Motta centers the *Kalunga*, the aquatic boundary between the living and the dead, from Central African and Afro-Brazilian cosmologies, evoking cyclicality, transmutation, and the possibility of return.[6] Likewise, her book, *A água é uma máquina do tempo* (Water Is a Time Machine) (2022), flows between memoir and documentation—pairing maps, photographs, and archival materials—to relate traumatic histories of her mother and her family in postabolition Rio and collective events in the present day.[7] Ultimately, Motta's interdisciplinary fabulations remain open-ended, ready for the viewer or reader to weave together the fragments to generate their own affiliations and interpretations. Through a process of excavation, accumulation, and creation, Motta's offers a "critical reimagining of the archive," as Kênia Freitas has argued, never filling in the gaps but articulating loss and the possibility of healing as a sociopolitical method for an alternative future.[8]

NOTES

1 Kênia Freitas connects Motta's work to Hartman; Motta subsequently stated that Freitas's proposal was a revelation and a connection that she had not made previously. See Saidiya Hartman, "Venus in Two Acts," *Small Axe* 12, no. 2 (2008): 1–14; Kênia Freitas, "Afro-fabulações e opacidade: As estratégias de criação do documentário negro brasileiro contemporâneo," in *Pensar o documentário, textos para um debate*, ed. Laecio Ricardo (Recife: Editora UFPE, 2020), 2; and Aline Motta, "Aline Motta—Sobre Pontes," October 2020, in *No programa de hoje*, podcast, https://open.spotify.com/episode/4EClhlITSfVaruuJseMp4a?si=6dd9450c9ba74738.

2 Motta uses the phrase "Chegar a formas." Aline Motta, "#3–Aline Motta," August 2020, in *Fotoforma*, podcast, https://open.spotify.com/episode/1dfoKYcogkCiw7gFlKVQc4?si=eb1eb96f34df4f50. Unless otherwise noted, translations are by the author.

3 Maria Emilia Fernandez, "Reimagined Family Ties: Redressing Memory through Photography in Aline Motta's *Pontes sobre abismos* and *Filha Natural*," *Mistral: Journal of Latin American Women's Intellectual & Cultural History* 2, no. 1 (2022): 2. https://doi.org/10.21827/mistral.1.39899.

4 The title *Se o mar tivesse varandas* originates from a well-known line in a traditional Portuguese poetic form called a *quadra* (quatrain). Reciters or singers would then improvise to complete a four-line verse using the same motif, in this case, "if the sea had balconies." On Motta's improvisation and subversion of this verse, see Lorena Galery

Batista, "A casa enquanto paisagem na obra de artistas brasileiras: Rosana Paulino, Conceição Evaristo e Aline Motta," *Palíndromo* 12, no. 28 (September–December 2020): 43–45. https://doi.org/10.5965/2175234612282020035.

5 Fernandez, "Reimagined Family Ties," 1–2.

6 The 2020 Rio exhibition is the second time Motta has shown *Trilogia*. The six-part video installation made its debut in *Em três tempos: Memória, viagem e água* curated by Alexandre Araujo Bispo at the Centro Cultural TCU in Brasília in 2019.

7 Aline Motta, *A água é uma máquina do tempo* (São Paulo: Fósforo Editora/Luna Parque Edições, 2022).

8 Freitas, "Afro-fabulações e opacidade," 4.

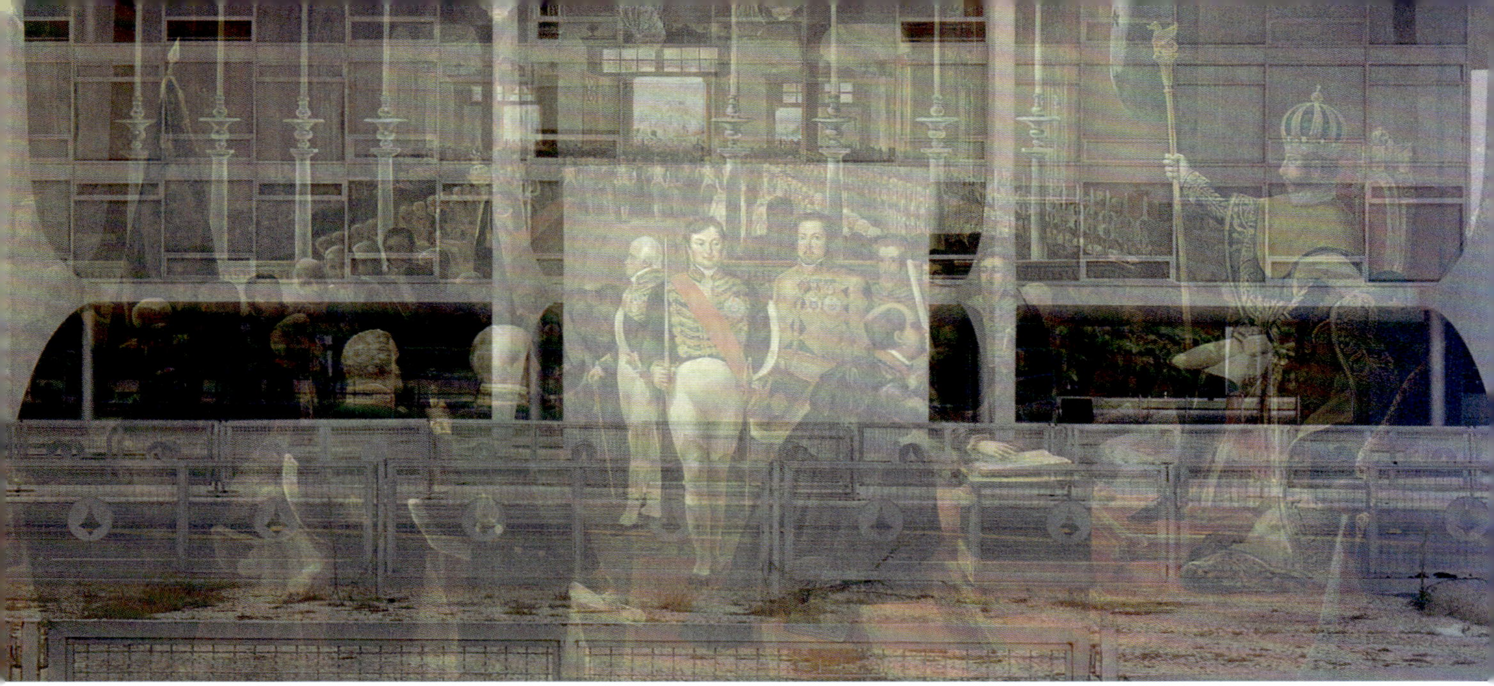

Lais Myrrha, *Dupla exposição (cena #2)* (Double Exposure [scene #2]), 2022 (detail).

Lais Myrrha Pilar Dirickson Garrett

Through a multivalent practice traversing sculpture, printmaking, collage, photography, and video, Lais Myrrha explores the parallel and the paradoxical, offering alternative entry points into Brazilian history in order to subvert the images and narratives canonized in Brazil's national collective consciousness as hegemonic truth.[1] As an artist and social critic, Myrrha is primarily concerned with mechanisms of narrativization and the ways in which frameworks of knowledge are communicated by the spaces we occupy and the images we see. Her earlier works engage transfigurations of maps, flags, newspapers, and television news broadcasts in order to provoke reflections on history-making and the production of shared cultural imaginaries. Many of her recent projects turn explicitly to interrogations of architecture and the built environment, primarily as a means of teasing out the nuances of Brazilian modernism and laying bare the degree to which modern architecture—as an apparatus of the state—translated colonial matrices of power into the twentieth century.

In the series *Dupla exposição* (Double Exposure, 2022) and *Reparação de danos* (Reparation of Damages, 2016), on view in *Social Fabric: Art and Activism in Contemporary Brazil,* Myrrha collapses spatial and temporal fields to reveal the persistent threads of coloniality that haunt Brazil's temples of modernity and spaces of government (see plates 30–38, 40–43).[2] In *Dupla exposição (cena #2)*, scene #2 of her photographic series, the observant viewer is confronted with an external view of the Palácio do Planalto—the president's official workplace designed by Oscar Niemeyer in 1958—juxtaposed with Jean-Baptiste Debret's *The Coronation of Dom Pedro I* (1828), a painting that hangs in the neighboring Itamaraty (Ministry of Foreign Affairs) and refers specifically to the start of Brazil's imperial period (see plate 40). Here, a monumental symbol of Brazilian modernism becomes visually entangled with a painted representation of a highly racialized and Euromimetic regime. Myrrha's provocatively layered images thus render visible those relationships of power obscured by the hand of history, provoking novel counter-memories as she reveals what might lie beyond Brazil's state-mandated narratives of progress and modernity. Identifying an undercurrent of "institutional confusion," as architectural historian Fernando Luiz Lara has noted, her collages make palpable the dissonance between the utopian aspirations of Brazil's modernist project and the country's contemporary sociopolitical realities.[3]

Grounding her early investigations into material and immaterial signification, Myrrha's video work *Bestiário* (Bestiary, 2005) assembles overlapping images of papal visits, political demonstrations, and prime-time news broadcasts into a chaotic hologram of modern life (see plate 29).[4] As the video progresses, the stack of layered footage grows more frenetic and cacophonous until the composite audiovisual form of a news anchor appears as a unified multitude. Recognizable as a compendium of artifice, *Bestiário* collapses everyday signs and symbols into a narrative of sameness, mimicking the process by which heterogenous parts are distilled into the visual and sonic landscapes that compose a nation-space.

Despite differences in content and materiality, Myrrha's body of work is united by an exacting understanding and precise use of materials.[5] Taken together, her practice reveals the violence that undergirds the history of Brazil's built environment and illuminates the systems of communication that construct, augment, and destroy our perceptions of time and place. But as Myrrha's print *Um futuro construído* (A Future Built, 2018) reminds us, the future is also a built environment: Brazil's myths of modernization, she enjoins us, are ready to be excavated and replaced by narratives that make space for a plurality of pasts, presents, and futures (see plate 39).

NOTES

1 According to a 2019 artist's statement, Myrrha sees in her work the "possibility of throwing [herself] into areas of instability, [where] conventional logic seems to fail, and official history appears as a suspicious, deliberate, incomplete, or partial version." "Portfolio (2019)," Le Cube: independent art room, Rabat. https://lecube-art.com/wp-content/uploads/2018/06/Portfolio-Lais-Myrrha_2019.pdf.

2 For definitions of coloniality, see, for example, Anibal Quijano and Immanuel Wallerstein, "Americanity as a Concept, or the Americas in the Modern World-System," *International Social Science Journal* 44, no. 4 (1992): 549–57.

3 Fernando Luiz Lara in "Fernando Lara entrevista Lais Myrrha" (recorded conversation), October 5, 2022, University of Texas at Austin, School of Architecture. https://www.youtube.com/watch?v=qT_NUcI3XlQ&ab_channel=FernandoLara. I would like to thank Fernando Lara for providing me access to the recording of this conversation.

4 Bestiary is a type of visual taxonomy, often accompanied by a moral prescription, of real or mythical beasts popularized during the medieval period.

5 Notable high-profile works exploring notions of scale, materiality, and space include *Projeto Gameleira 1971* (Gameleira Project 1971), exhibited at Pivô São Paulo (2014), and *Dois pesos, duas medidas* (Double Standard), presented during the thirty-second São Paulo Bienal (2016).

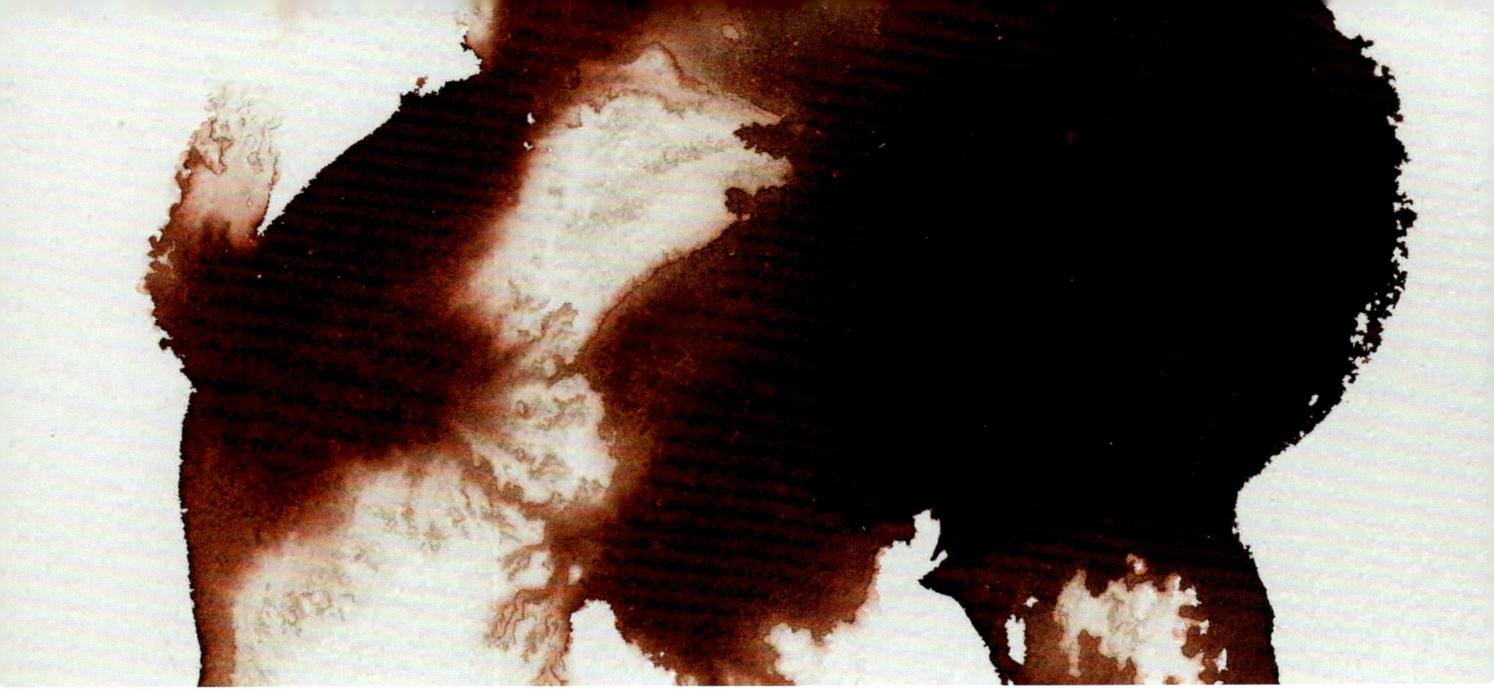

Antonio Obá, *Mãe* (Mother), 2017 (detail).

Antonio Obá Thiago Ferreira

Antonio Obá, born in Ceilândia, a city on the periphery of Brasília, is a visual artist and art educator. Through a varied range of processes, such as drawing, painting, sculpture, photography, engraving, interventions, installation, video, and performance, Obá's practice revolves around the affirmation of the body in an attempt to make the body present. His search culminates in a reflection on identity that oscillates between an intimate memory and a larger social context, where he questions a wide array of ideas, including Blackness, racism, acculturation processes, miscegenation, religious rituals, syncretism, and eroticism, and asks how these issues impact the individual. Obá has expressed the centrality and multivalency of the nexus of ritual and the body as follows: "I have an inclination towards rituals and the relationship they establish with the body, as a representation and transfiguration of it. And their almost erotic relationship with this too. They involve many issues of interdiction and perversion that, in my view, are placed in antithesis, disparate values dialoguing in the same space, in the same body."[1]

Obá was raised in a devout Catholic household, and from the beginning of his production, he addressed the unacknowledged legacy of colonialism and slavery in Catholicism and the broader reproduction of violent social practices. Nicole Smythe-Johnson argues that "his works do not critique or celebrate the tensions inherent in Afro-Catholicism, rather they play out memories of an intense, intimate and complex relationship to a faith that is at once familiar and comforting, like your mother's kitchen, and violently negating."[2]

In 2015, he performed *Atos da transfiguração: Desaparição ou receita para fazer um santo* (Acts of Transfiguration: Disappearance or Recipe to Make a Saint) three times. In these performances, he ground up a plaster statue of the Virgem Aparecida, a Black madonna and the patron saint of Brazil, and poured the white powder over his naked body (fig. 2).[3] Two years later, edited videos of the performance were disseminated on the internet by right-wing groups.[4] The hostile reaction forced Obá into exile from Brazil in 2017. His departure also occurred in the wake of a series of extreme right-wing attacks on cultural manifestations in Brazil to provoke moral panic, culminating in the censorship of the exhibition *Queermuseu*, which was organized by Santander Cultural in the city of Porto Alegre.[5] The sustained polemics against cultural expression arguably strengthened fascist discourse in Brazil.[6] Obá's work included in *Queermuseu—Et verbum* (And the Word, 2011)—was a communion wafer on which he wrote names of parts of the body, such as vulva and tongue.

Although iconoclasm plays an important role in Obá's universe, Roberto Conduru has persuasively proposed that the artist "is more interested in iconophilia, the possibility of survival and reinvention of the image."[7] In six watercolors titled *Mãe* (Mother, 2017) and presented in *Social Fabric: Art and Activism in Contemporary Brazil*, Obá creates fleeting shapes of a female body that are at the same time iconic and reminiscent of a distant appearance, imprecise and organic (see plates 44–49). Part of a larger series, many untitled, in which the subjects are indeterminate, the watercolors were among the works he created while in exile and were traced by his finger in direct contact with the paper.[8] Across the watercolors, he portrays the body on its way to a certain dissolution. Obá has stated that these works address "the idea of a shadow . . . something that is no longer male or female. It was a process of interiorization, a need to reorganize this fragmented body. It is no longer a self-portrait."[9] The exploration of "writings of self" and the mechanisms of racialization remain through lines in his rich multimedia production.[10] The artist studies the resistance of self-images to the representations produced by others, in an endless maneuver between claiming an identity and not being reduced to it.

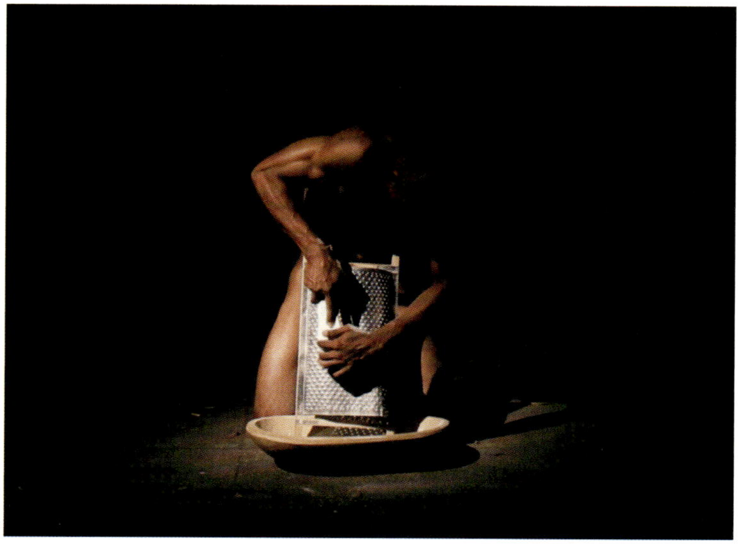

Figure 2. Antonio Obá. *Atos da transfiguração—Desaparição ou receita para fazer um santo* (Acts of Transfiguration—Disappearance or Recipe to Make a Saint), 2015. Still of video documentation of performance. Courtesy of the artist and Mendes Wood DM, São Paulo, Brussels, New York. Copyright of the artist.

NOTES

1 Antonio Obá, quoted in "Antônio Obá," Brasília Memória e Invenção, n.d. https://brasilia.memoriaeinvencao.com/antonio-oba/. Note that the artist's name appears in English as Antonio and in Portuguese as Antônio. Unless otherwise noted, translations are by the author.

2 Nicole Smythe-Johnson, "Amplifying Syncretism: Antonio Obá's Dialectical Conception of Brazil," *MODOS: Journal of Art History* 6, no. 1 (2022): 600.

3 The performances occurred in Brasília at Elefante Centro Cultural and in Rio de Janeiro as part of a solo exhibition. Roberto Conduru, *Antônio Obá: (In)corporações* (Rio de Janeiro: Galerie Cândido Portinari, Universidade Estadual do Rio de Janeiro, 2015). He subsequently performed it at two other venues. See Clauder Lopes Diniz, "Arte Afro-Brasileira e performance: Uma reflexão sobre a obra de Antônio Obá" (master's thesis, Universidade de Brasília, 2018), 38–48.

4 See Oliver Basciano, "Death Threats and Denunciations: The Artists Who Fear Bolsonaro's Brazil," *Guardian*, November 7, 2018, https://www.theguardian.com/artanddesign/2018/nov/07/brazil-artists-death-threats-censorship-intimidation-jair-bolsonaro.

5 *Queermuseu: Cartographies of Difference in Brazilian Art*, curated by Gaudêncio Fidelis, was accused of sacrilege, pedophilia, and zoophilia. Five artworks were particularly targeted: Fernando Baril's *Cruzando Jesus Cristo com deusa Shiva* (Crossing Jesus Christ with Shiva Goddess, 1996); Bia Leite's *Adriano Bafônica and Luiz França She-há* (2013) and *Travesti da lambada e deusa das águas* (Lambada Transvestite and Goddess of the Waters, 2013); Antonio Obá's *Et verbum* (And the Word, 2011); and Adriana Varejão's *Cena interior II* (Interior Scene II, 1994).

6 For reflections on the recent censorship of the Brazilian art world, see Luisa Duarte, ed., *Arte censura liberdade: Reflexões à luz do presente* (Rio de Janeiro: Cobogó, 2018). For press coverage of the censorship of *Queermuseu* as a culture war tactic, see Silas Martí, "Caso da 'Queermuseu' corre o risco de se tornar triste rotina no país," *Folha de São Paulo*, September 12, 2017, https://www1.folha.uol.com.br/ilustrada/2017/09/1917632- caso-da-queermuseu-arrisca-se-tornar-triste-rotina-no-pais.shtml.

7 Roberto Conduru, *Antônio Obá: (In)corporações*, 6.

8 Conversation between MacKenzie Stevens, Matthew Wood, Renato Silva, and Nancy Brown of Mendes Wood DM in New York, December 10, 2021.

9 Antonio Obá, as quoted in Silas Martí, "Exilado após ameaças de religiosos, brasileiro expõe em Nova York," *Folha de São Paulo*, May 29, 2018, https://www1.folha.uol.com.br/ilustrada/2018/05/exilado-apos-ameacas-de-religiosos-brasileiro-expoe-em-nova-york.shtml.

10 Janaína Barros, "Body-Close: Transmutation of Memory and the Performativities of the Sacred in Antonio Obá," in *Mendes Wood DM presents Antonio Obá at Foire internationale d'art contemporain (FIAC) 2019* (São Paulo: Mendes Wood DM, 2019), n.p.

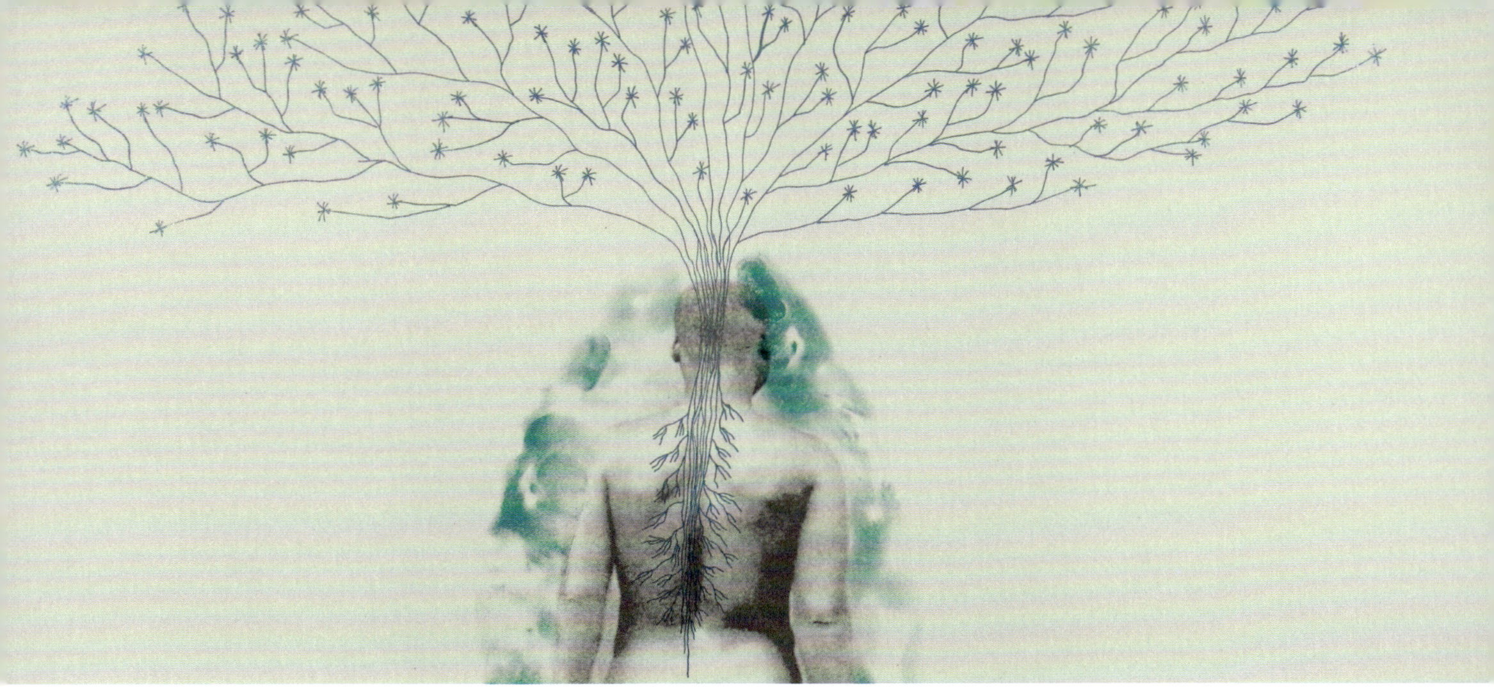

Rosana Paulino, *Assentamento no. 3* (Settlement no. 3), 2012–2013 (detail).

Rosana Paulino Martha Scott Burton

For more than twenty-five years, Rosana Paulino has developed an expansive artistic practice that explores the visual representation and experiences of Black Brazilians, especially Black women, across the country's history of settler colonialism and enslavement and its legacies today. Extensively trained in printmaking, Paulino deploys a wide range of mediums: drawing; collage; varied print processes; sewing and embroidery, which she learned from her mother; installation; sculpture; and video.[1] Her iconography is comparably diverse and bridges, for example, flowing lines of breast milk, menstruation, spider webs, and roots with scientific illustrations, references to the transatlantic slave trade, and more. The body and historical memory are central sites in her work, which she investigates and iterates by exploring archetypes of Black feminine power, plumbing the psychosocial constructions of Black women in the Brazilian social fabric, and renarrativizing nineteenth-century colonial photographs produced toward white supremacist ends.

In several series, Paulino hybridizes the human and the animalistic into symbolic and metaphorical creatures. In *Tecelãs* (Weavers, 2003), Paulino draws on memories of her mother embroidering with other women in silence—"like spiders"—and sculpts terra-cotta women-silkworms that writhe up the wall, partially encased in cotton (see plate 50).[2] Many have rows of breasts, like teats, and thread trailing from their mouths. Grounding the installation are dozens of small, irregular, heavily textured vessels that evoke nests or a beehive. The creatures struggle to emerge from their cocoons, perhaps in a state of evolution and transformation. But if one considers that the standard in the commercial production of silk is to kill silkworms after they have produced this precious luxury resource in order to harvest the highest-quality product, then the work becomes a commentary on the multipronged extraction of Black women's labor and resources.

Probing "archetypes of female wisdom" that draw on Afro-Brazilian, Indigenous, and other cosmologies, Paulino's recent *Jatobá* and *Búfala* women are strengthened by their connection to the natural world and evoke a fecund wholeness.[3] *Jatobá* (2019), a series of watercolors of varying scale, conjures women of color grounded in the earth, legs expanding as trunks and deepening into roots (see plates 59 and 60). They hold bundles of leaves and plant life in their palms, thin tendrils growing upward and cascading downward. These shoots mimic the streams of breast milk, hearkening back to Paulino's *Ama de leite* (Wet Nurse, 2005) series but cast in a more nourishing manner (fig. 3). In the artist book *Búfala e senhora das plantas* (Buffalo and Lady of Plants, 2021), the *Jatobá* are paired with powerful she-buffalos, referencing the orisha Oya or Iansã from the Afro-Brazilian religion Candomblé, a warrior who commands storms, as well as the Hindu goddess Kali, who symbolizes destruction and rebirth (see plate 61). Paulino thinks of the *Búfala* as "liberty, healthy sexuality, and decisiveness" created in an "attempt to use new parameters to think about what it is to be a [black woman] in a country like Brazil."[4]

In *Tecido social* (Social Fabric, 2010), which inspired this exhibition's title, Paulino investigates the social imaginary of Black women as domestic servants, wet nurses, nannies, and

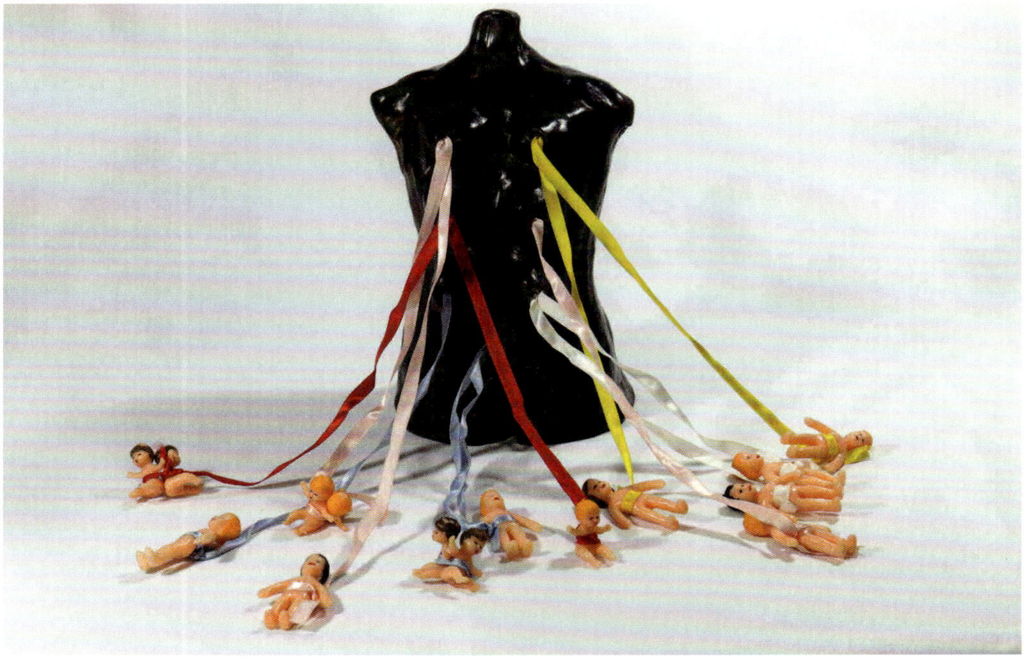

Figure 3. Rosana Paulino. *Ama de leite no. 1* (Wet Nurse no. 1), 2005. Terra-cotta, plastic, and satin ribbons. 12 ⅝ × 6 ⅞ × 3 ¼ in. (32 × 17.5 × 8.2 cm). Private collection. Courtesy of the artist and Mendes Wood DM, São Paulo, Brussels, New York. Photo credit: Isabella Matheus.

objects of sexual pleasure and exploitation—enduring themes in her practice (see plate 51). Monotype prints of guns and mug shots denote high rates of violence—domestic and otherwise—and disproportionate criminalization. A fetus in utero references reproductive exploitation, and a pinup model calls out ongoing oversexualization. Several images hearken the forced labor of nannies, including Jorge Henrique Papf's troubling photograph (circa 1899) of a white child posed astride her Black nanny, who tensely props herself up on all fours. These photographs are produced in silhouette, suggesting anonymization and fungibility as well as refusal. Similarly, Paulino covers several figures' eyes, reminiscent of both censorship and privacy bars—a through line in her practice. Another recurring technique she employs in *Tecido social* is making the printed line material via exposed thread and rough suturing of fabric pieces. She patches the pieces together to wrinkle and strain against the tension of the thread, imaging a fragmented, precarious social fabric and violent integration.

In the 2010s, Paulino committed especially to photography as source material, appropriating and intervening in nineteenth-century so-called forensic and studio portraits of unnamed and often undressed African men and women—some of whom may have been enslaved—that erased the individuality of those pictured and simultaneously spectacularized their bodies.[5] These images, cast as racial "types," constituted a new kind of visual documentation that represented Africans and Afro-descendants as "the other," cemented photography's role in fortifying colonial social control, and contributed to the formulation of racial classifications. While Paulino is concerned specifically with Brazil's past and present, the racialized representation she excavates informs national identity, memory, and amnesia across the Americas.

In the *Assentamento* lithograph series (2012–2013), Paulino deploys challenging photographs by Augusto Stahl, as commissioned by Louis Agassiz, and breaks apart the serial and dehumanizing nature of Stahl's original triptych of a nude woman identified only by the "ethnic" origin, "Mina Bari."[6] In *Assentamento no. 2* (Settlement no. 2), Paulino integrates a fetus in utero flowing from the woman's legs amid an expanding root system; in *Assentamento no. 3* (Settlement no. 3), she draws roots spreading underneath the woman and branches that become stars reaching upward from her spine (see plates 52 and 53).[7] Paulino thus juxtaposes the horrors of enslavement with an assertion of enslaved Africans' formative construction of the Brazilian nation, on the one hand, and a generative reinscribing of individualism and subjectivity onto the woman, on the other.

The collage print series *Paraíso tropical* (Tropical Paradise, 2017) and *A geometria à brasileira chega ao paraíso tropical* (Brazilian-Style Geometry Arrives in Tropical Paradise, 2018) combine Paulino's sustained research on the natural sciences and scientific racism, her critique of Brazil's saleable world image as a "tropical paradise," and the deconstruction of photographic representation deployed toward both ends (see plates 55–58). In the latter series, she layers scientific illustrations of flora and fauna native to Brazil with blocks of color—red, yellow, blue, and green—to reference "this supposed—and still argued for—Brazilian vocation for geometric abstraction," which she identifies as being imported from Europe rather than pulling from African or Indigenous geometry.[8] The photographs of Africans and Indigenous people, meant to naturalize their presence in the landscape for Anglo-European tourists, do not fit within these boxes but, Paulino explains, resist and "break with the moulds."[9]

Paulino deploys these same photographs in *Atlântico vermelho* (Red Atlantic, 2017)—a riff on Paul Gilroy's *Black Atlantic*—to explicitly associate the harsh economics of the slave trade and the diaspora of photographic representation of enslaved Africans (see plate 54). She signals Portugal's driving role and the harsh economics and brutality of the Middle Passage with images of *tumbeiros* (the "floating tombs" that were slave ships) and Portuguese *azulejos* (blue-and-white tiles) interjected with clustered red threads that drip like blood. She uses Stahl's photographs and, twice, a studio photograph by João Goston of a Black woman with a barrel on her head. The photograph was taken in front of a painted backdrop of lush vegetation that frames a coastal view to create, following Krista Thompson's analyses in *An Eye for the Tropics*, an imagined scene of a "picturesque native" in "paradise."[10] One version is manipulated to seem as if from an X-ray—an inversion, in the negative. In the other, Paulino excises the woman's face, leaving an absence and stark emptiness. Again, the work is conjoined via suture; the threads trail at the edges, suggesting that one good tug could pull it all apart.

Juliana Ribeiro da Silva Bevilacqua sensitively encapsulates the "void" in Paulino's work, reading the technique of excision as a "metaphor for the lack of representation and the non-recognition or non-belonging of the black population [that] gave way . . . as a metaphor for self-acknowledgment, even if in the pain caused by the persisting and perverse legacy of slavery."[11] Similarly, Paulino sutures or stamps blindfolds over some figures, gestures the artist has said point to their lack of full citizenship or to their status as "shadows of citizens."[12]

Paulino brings to the foreground what is kept hidden, who is ignored and refused. She approaches these burdened images "in a somewhat homeopathic way," saying that if in the history of visual culture "images were used to mark a position of submission for the black body, more muscle than intellect, then intervening in these photographs and changing their meanings for me brings a sense of healing."[13] Through a process of remaking, inverting, and inventing images of Black women—some mythic, some all too real—she recuperates ancestral memory with an eye toward transformation and freedom.

NOTES

1 Paulino earned her BA and PhD in visual arts with an emphasis on printmaking at the Universidade de São Paulo; she also undertook advanced training at the London Print Studio and held a residency at the Tamarind Institute.

2 Rosana Paulino, "Rosana Paulino Artist Talk," Center for Latin American Visual Studies and the Visual Arts Center, University of Texas at Austin, February 19, 2020. https://www.facebook.com/utxaah/videos/rosana-paulino/176857670278331/.

3 Rosana Paulino, as quoted in Biennale of Sydney, "Rosana Paulino," 2020, https://www.biennaleofsydney.art/participants/rosana-paulino/.

4 Paulino, as quoted in Biennale of Sydney, "Rosana Paulino."

5 For an insightful discussion by Paulino of her views on photography, see Celia Antonacci, "Parede da memória—Rosana Paulino," 2014, video, 2:40–10:47 mins., https://vimeo.com/111885499.

6 For more on Agassiz and his efforts to establish different "racial types" through photographic archives, see Maria Helena P. T. Machado and Sasha Huber, *Rastros e raças de Louis Agassiz: Fotografía, corpo e ciência, ontem e hoje / (T)Races of Louis Agassiz: Photography, Body and Science, Yesterday and Today* (São Paulo: Capacete Entretenimentos, 2010); and Ilisa Barbash, Molly Rogers, and Deborah Willis, eds., *To Make Their Own Way in the World: The Enduring Legacy of the Zealy Daguerreotypes* (Cambridge, MA: Peabody Museum Press, 2020). For more on African

ethnic diversity in Rio de Janeiro and those photographed for Agassiz, see Flávio dos Santos Gomes, "'Pure Race' Africans and Ethnic Diversity in Nineteenth-Century Rio de Janeiro," *The Mirror of Race Project*, May 8, 2012, http://mirrorofrace.org/gomes/.

7 *Assentamento* literally translates as "settlement." It also means "foundation" and in references to Candomblé, the settlement and strength of the *terreiro* (temple). For insightful analyses of Paulino's *Assentamento* works, see Renata Felinto, "A construção da identidade Afrodescendente por meio das artes visuais contemporâneas: Estudos de produções e de poéticas" (PhD diss., Institutos de Artes da Universidade do Estado de São Paulo, 2016), 282–83; Flávia Santos de Araújo, "Rosana Paulino and the Art of Refazimento: Reconfigurations of the Black Female Body in the Land of Racial Democracy," *Brasiliana: Journal for Brazilian Studies* 8, nos. 1–2 (2019): 72–73; and Lorraine Leu, "Settlement: Rosana Paulino and Black Women's Insubordinate Geohistories," in *Black Feminist Constellations: Dialogue and Translation across the Americas*, ed. Lorraine Leu and Christen A. Smith (Austin: University of Texas Press, 2023).

8 Rosana Paulino, as stated in "Rosana Paulino: Inside the Studio," Mendes Wood DM, n.d., https://website-artlogicwebsite0032.artlogic.net/viewing-room/26-rosana-paulino-inside-the-stud io/.

9 Paulino, as stated in "Rosana Paulino: Inside the Studio."

10 Krista Thompson, *An Eye for the Tropics: Tourism, Photography, and Framing the Caribbean Picturesque* (Durham, NC: Duke University Press, 2007).

11 Juliana Ribeiro da Silva Bevilacqua, "The Void in Rosana Paulino's Work," in *Rosana Paulino: A costura da mémoria / Rosana Paulino: The Sewing of Memory*, ed. Valéria Piccoli and Pedro Nery (São Paulo: Pinacoteca de São Paulo, 2018), 154.

12 Rosana Paulino, as stated in Celia Antonacci, "A costura de memória—Rosana Paulino," 2018, video, 26:44 min., https://www.youtube.com/watch?v=uNEIJArBdKw.

13 Rosana Paulino, "In Conversation with Rosana Paulino: The Body Is a Political Issue," interview by Victor da Rosa, translated by Zoë Perry, *Contemporary &: América Latina*, February 21, 2018, https://amlatina.contemporaryand.com/editorial/researcher-and-artist-rosana-paulino/.

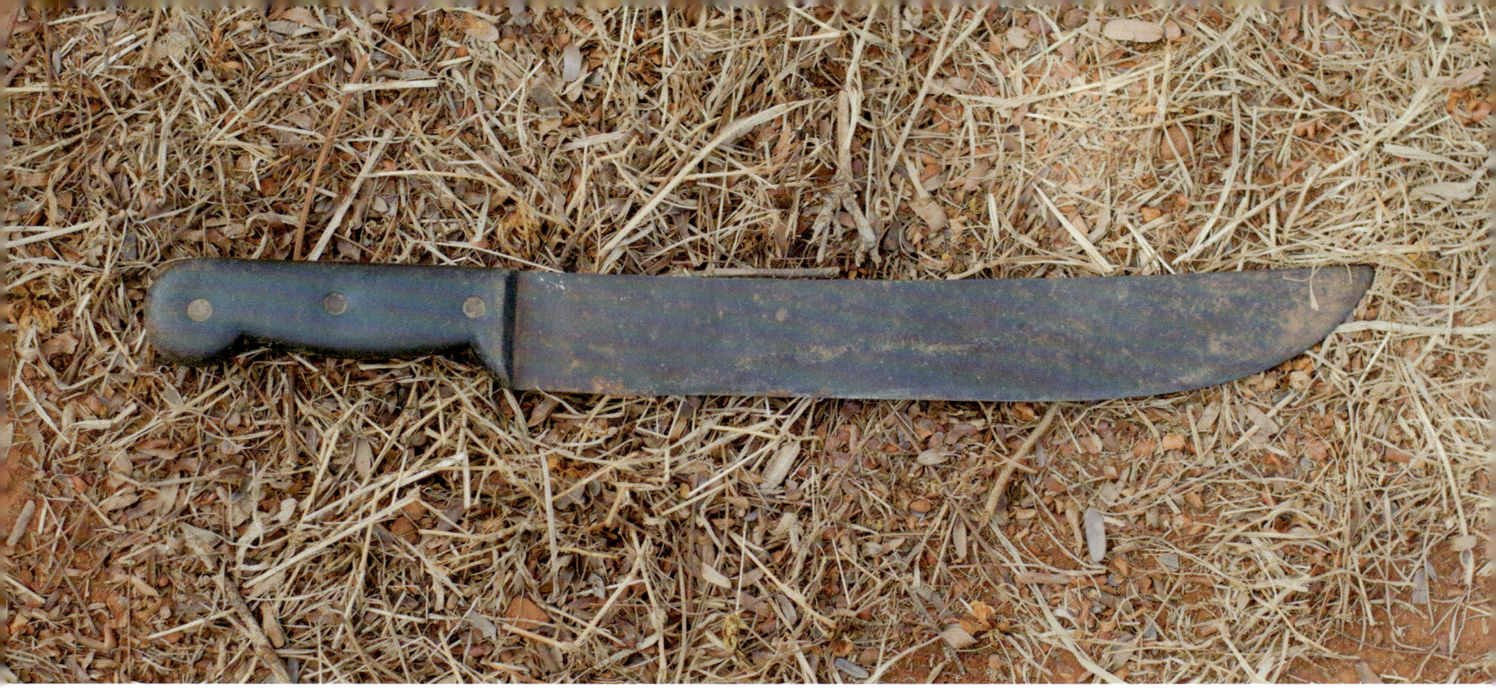

Sallisa Rosa, *Resistência* (Resistance), 2017–present (detail).

Sallisa Rosa Eva Caston

In a multimedia practice that bridges ceramics, sculptures, installations, street actions, drawing, photography, and video, Sallisa Rosa weaves together stories of loss, resistance, and reclamation that refuse the romanticized archetype nonnative audiences expect of Indigenous people. Rosa's often collaborative practice remaps colonial space and visualizes Indigenous futures.[1] She frames her practices as follows: "I keep walking in the dark, but my body glows and lights the way. The path is the writing that nature recounts. My journey is to remember those who had to forget themselves."[2]

Roots are a recurring motif in Rosa's work. Her participatory clay installation *Raízes* (Roots), first realized in 2019, fashion clay local to the area into massive arboreal roots (fig. 4). Visitors add new connections to the existing network, thus connecting themselves to one another through the act of creation. The *Lembranças* series (2021) is a set of drawings of root systems done in pen and ink, five of which are on view in *Social Fabric: Art and Activism in Contemporary Brazil* (see plates 63–67). The roots are meticulously rendered on sheets of colored paper delicately suspended in space and divorced from any environmental context. The complex system of roots and their irregular paths evoke a series of interdependent systems, like rivers and their tributaries or neural pathways. The title *Lembranças*, which translates to "keepsakes," suggests that the drawings are a form of sentimental record-keeping. The familial connotation of the term "roots" and the titular allusion to mementos indicates how the passing down of personal histories of Indigenous people is an act of resistance against the threat of colonial erasure.

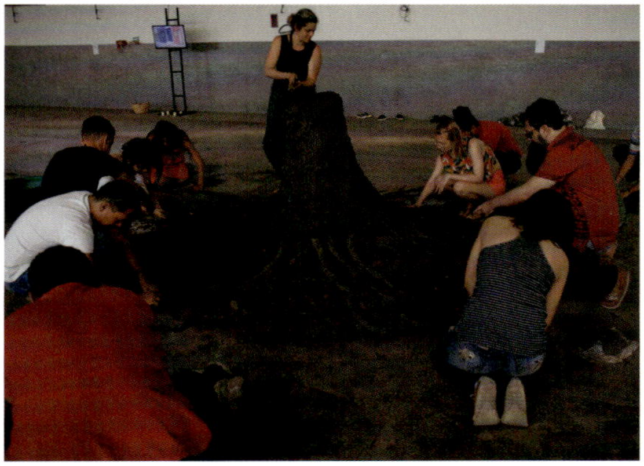

Figure 4. Participants adding to Sallisa Rosa's *Raízes* (Roots), 2019, at the second Bienal do Barro, Caruara, Brazil. Installation in clay, interactive artwork. Courtesy of the artist. Photo credit: Geyson Magno.

In the series *Resistência* (Resistance, 2017–), Rosa shoots photographs of her friends and family's machetes (see plate 62). The photos share a similar composition: the length of the blade bisects the center of the frame with the tip pointing to the right of the photographer/viewer. The backgrounds, however, give us a glimpse of the varied topographies and environments where these machetes are used. The project is closely tied to street-art practices such as *lambe-lambe* (literally, "lick-lick"), a mode of applying posters to street walls to advertise performances as well as political messaging.[3] In the original and in the ongoing iteration of the project, Rosa wheat-pasted the machete series onto walls throughout Rio de Janeiro. In 2019, she created her first version of the project for an art space, tiling the photos into a large grid.

Resistência is also rooted in a social praxis: *lambe-lambe*'s interventions highlight marginalized perspectives in public space. Rosa's choice to make the machete the subject of the photographic series underscores the object's ubiquity for agricultural work in Indigenous and non-Indigenous communities alike. The knife also holds a prominent symbolic role in Indigenous resistance and in the broader struggle for land rights among *povos do campo*, or rural communities, across Brazil.[4] Rosa highlights not only the presence of Indigenous people in urban spaces where they are often invisibilized, but also their active resistance against the encroachment of the state.

NOTES

1 See Sallisa Rosa, "Interview with Sandra Benites," in *América: Da série Supernova / America: From the Supernova Series* (Rio de Janeiro: Museu de Arte Moderna do Rio de Janeiro, 2022), 66. She staged her installation *Oca do Futuro*, which can be translated as *Hut of the Future*, for the landmark show *Dja guata porã: Rio de Janeiro indígena* (Museu de Arte do Rio, 2017), which was co-curated by Sandra Benites, Clarissa Diniz, José Ribamar Bessa, and Pablo LaFuente in collaboration with representatives from Indigenous communities local to the region, namely the Guarani, Puri, and Pataxó.

2 Sallisa Rosa, "Memories Are Omens," in *América: Da série Supernova*, 66.

3 See Hertha Tatiely Silva, "Desvios: Cartaz lambe-lambe, comunicação visual e arte nos espaços de trânsito" (master's thesis, Universidade Federal de Goiás, 2015), https://repositorio.bc.ufg.br/tede/handle/tede/5390. *Lambe-Lambe* also refers to street photographers of the early twentieth century, who stationed themselves in parks and would produce portraits inexpensively. By the 1970s, the profession rapidly declined due to the introduction of cheap cameras like Polaroids. See Museu da Imagem e do Som, "*Lambe-Lambe:* The Street Photographers in São Paulo in 1970s," Google Arts & Culture, n.d., https://artsandculture.google.com/story/lambe-lambe-the-street-photographers-in-são-paulo-in-1970s/KgWhczTDBudLLw.

4 Email correspondence from the artist to MacKenzie Stevens, April 20, 2023.

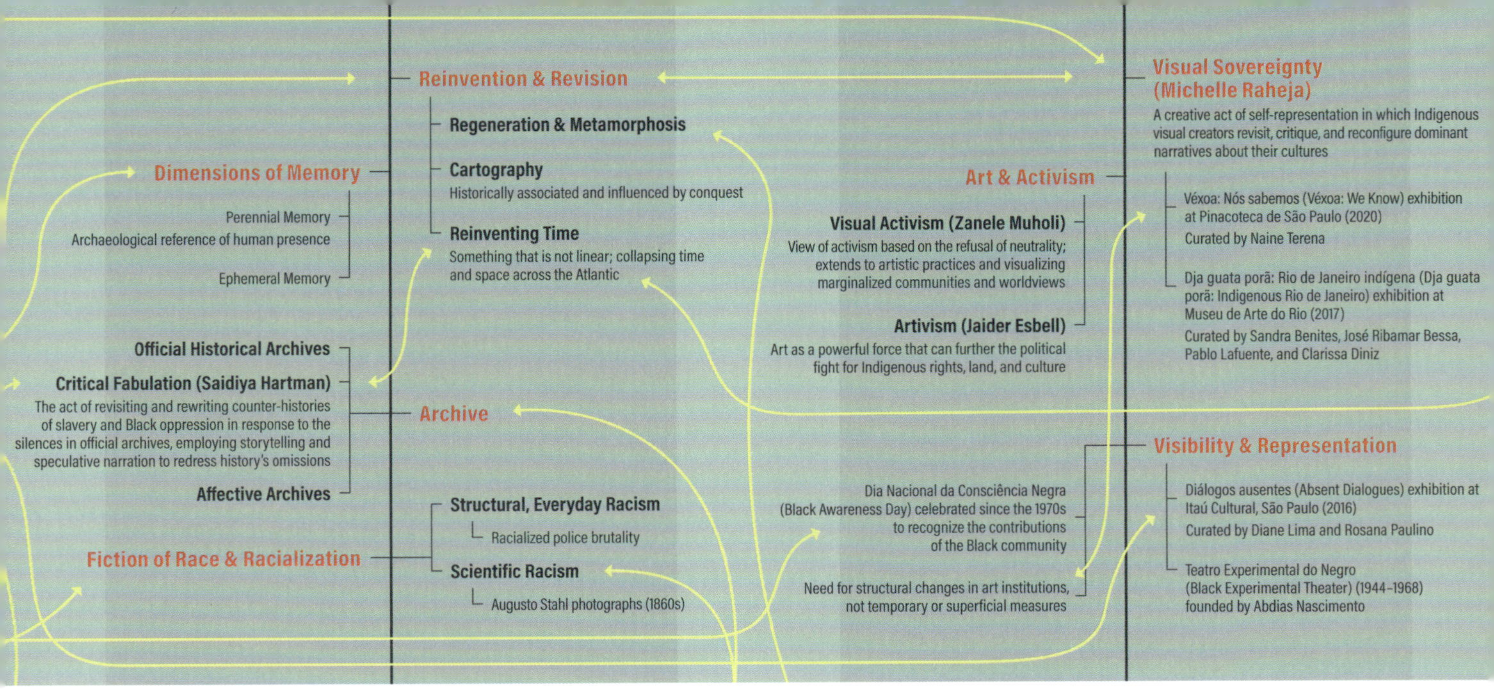

Sociogram, 2022 (detail).

Memories, Histories, and Fictions

THE SOCIOGRAM AS METHOD

Catalina Cherñavvsky Sequeira

Inspired by the title of Rosana Paulino's work *Tecido social* (Social Fabric, 2010), the sociogram is a conceptual map, intertwining moments, people, and geographies of Brazil (see insert after page 104). It is a tapestry of ideas intended to contextualize the themes prevalent throughout the exhibition *Social Fabric: Art and Activism in Contemporary Brazil*. The sociogram does not pretend to be all-encompassing but rather is catalyzed by the sixty-seven artworks exhibited. It is important to consider in the conception of alternative histories that the modern Western understanding of time is not neutral or apolitical. The particular constellation of ideas and events in the sociogram invites visitors to the exhibition and readers of this catalogue to reinterpret temporality and reflect on how traditional history has deliberately erased the realities and cosmologies of Black and Indigenous communities.

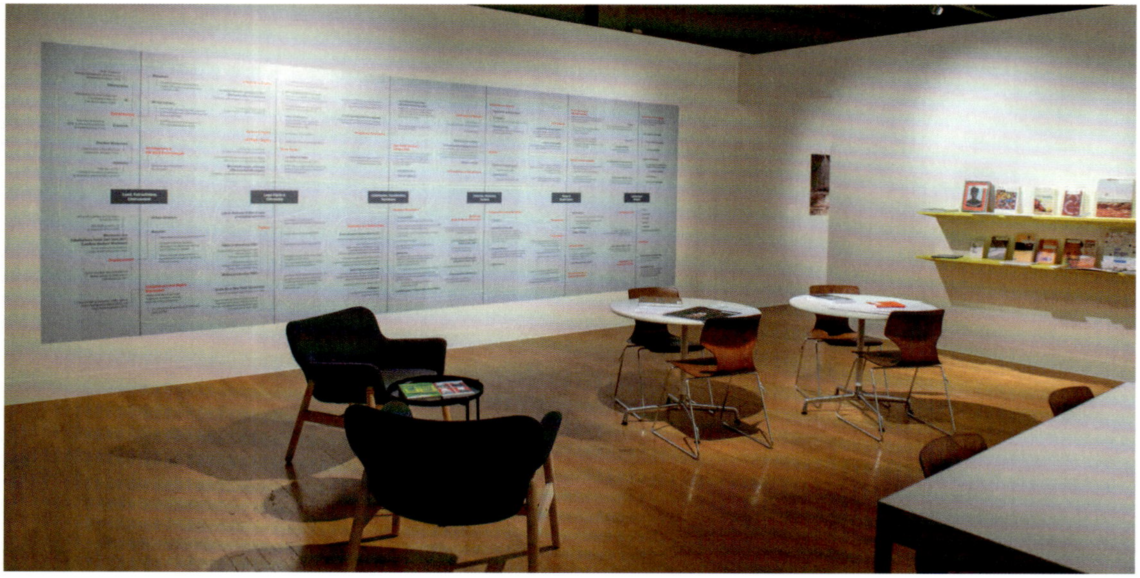

Figure 5. Installation view of sociogram created by Catalina Cherñavvsky Sequeira and Maria Emilia Fernandez with design provided by Hunter Thomas, 2022.

The sociogram is the culmination of research undertaken by students in Adele Nelson's graduate seminars from 2019 to 2022 (see insert after page 104 and fig. 5).[1] These students brought varied research and linguistic specializations: most were MA and PhD students in art history at the University of Texas at Austin, a number were Portuguese speakers or readers with some experience in Brazil, and several were Brazilian or Brazilian American.[2] The majority of students, however, approached the task of creating an alternative time line from the vantage point of outsiders to Brazil. Across three seminars, students considered what information about Brazilian history and society would be necessary for visitors to the exhibition in Austin, which, with the exception of UT's large number of Brazilian studies scholars and notable community of Brazilian graduate students, does not have pronounced ties to the country.

In the first seminar, students debated how to create an illustrated chronology for the exhibition that would not frame the artists and their works in a historicist or reductive manner and would not sever current political and societal events from longer histories, including conquest, slavery, military dictatorship, and their afterlives. The students determined that it would be insufficient to map the last two decades and the recent far-right turn in the country and that the artists' work could be understood only within a wider, more multivalent frame. Two years later, in the 2022 seminar, I expanded upon the work done by prior students, engaged in further research, and developed an initial sketch of the sociogram. In the summer of 2022, Maria Emilia Fernandez and I, in collaboration with designer Hunter Thomas and with feedback from Nelson and former seminar students, created the fully realized version of the sociogram.[3]

Multiple models and dialogues shaped our presentation of time as multidimensional while still being informative to visitors. One influence came from *Perder la forma humana: Una imagen sísmica de los años ochenta en América Latina* (Losing the Human Form: A Seismic Image of the 1980s in Latin America), first exhibited at the Museo Nacional Centro de Arte Reina Sofía in 2012. The curatorial group behind the exhibition, Red Conceptualismos del Sur, aimed to "reverse the flow of the drain of memory" and avoid a totalizing approach to presenting Latin American "conceptualisms."[4] They developed two diagrams to contextualize the exhibition. The first was a conceptual map with key themes from the show illustrated as a network. The second was a linear time line that sought to create transchronological connections through the use of multiple overlapping arrows.

Another point of reference was the exhibition *Vaivém* (To-and-Fro) presented at the Centro Cultural Banco do Brasil in 2019. Curator Raphael Fonseca invited viewers to understand links between different time periods, geographies, and languages by way of the exhibition's focus: iconographies of the hammock, a structure pioneered by Amerindians that moves in a pendular motion.[5] Other crucial influences included Aline Motta's forceful articulation of what is erased by linear, Western time in her work *Trilogia* (Trilogy, 2017–2019); Castiel Vitorino Brasileiro's acknowledgment of the museum space as a colonial one in the conception of her projects as "perishable spaces of freedom"; and Denilson Baniwa's multimedia, nonlinear time line for the exhibition *Dja guata porã: Rio de Janeiro indígena* (*Dja guata porã:* Indigenous Rio de Janeiro) in 2017.[6] Furthermore, discussions in 2021 with artists Christopher Cozier and Rosana Paulino, curator Carla Acevedo-Yates, and archivist Rachel E. Winston illuminated not only the distortions and risks for artists from the Global South in nationally or regionally framed exhibitions in the Global North but also the perils of time lines in exhibitions, which, conceived as didactics, can collapse into colonial devices.[7]

In her text "Performances do tempo espiralar" (Performances of Spiral Time), Leda Maria Martins explains how in ritual performance, the body becomes the site through which time transforms. She states, "The primacy of ancestral movement, the source of inspiration, shades the curves of a spiral temporality, in which the events, undressed from a linear chronology, are in the process of perennial transformation. . . . In the spirals of time, everything goes and everything returns."[8] The artists in *Social Fabric* not only challenge our notion of time but, like Martins, invite us to discover alternative ways of understanding and embodying temporality. The sociogram as a pedagogical tool endeavors to do the same, emphasizing the inextricable and irresolvable links between the past, present, and future.

NOTES

1 The students in the seminars included Chasitie Brown, Laurel Brown, Martha Scott Burton, Sara Carrillo, Eva Caston, Maria Emilia Fernandez, Thiago Ferreira, Devon Gerstenhaber, Jana La Brasca, Izzy Lee, Darren Longman, Victoria McCausland, Sean McPherson, Alexandra Mendez, Aja Edwin Mujinga, Caitlin O'Beirne, Lucy Quezada, Karina Salcido, Jennifer Sales, Marina Schneider, Nicole Smythe-Johnson, Grace Sparapani, Alejandra Valdez Carrasco, André Vechi, and me.

2 Of the seminar participants, two were Brazilian doctoral students who held visiting fellowships at UT (Ferreira and Vechi); one was Brazilian American (Sales); and several had spent extended periods in Brazil and/or spoke or were learning Portuguese (Carrillo, Cherñavvsky Sequeira, Fernandez, Longman, McPherson, and Quezada).

3 Burton, Caston, Ferreira, Gerstenhaber, Quezada, Sales, and Smythe-Johnson generously provided feedback and suggested edits on draft versions, as did Clare Donnelly, former manager of Exhibitions and Programs at the VAC. The sociogram was realized as a wall-scale didactic in the exhibition's final gallery, which functioned as a reading room and learning space (see pp. 102–103). There it was accompanied by a selection of books and articles related to the themes and by or about the artists of the exhibition; an interactive, bilingual English and Spanish pedagogical exercise, developed by Donnelly with collaboration of Fernandez and Hunter Thomas; and a QR code linking to a bibliography compiled by Caston, with Fernandez, Martins, and me, available on the *Social Fabric* exhibition page of the VAC website. For the bibliography and a downloadable illustration of the sociogram, see https://utvac.org/event/social-fabric-art-activism-contemporary-brazil. The interactive exercise was inspired by an art education activity at the Pinacoteca do Estado de São Paulo that Fernandez experienced during a visit in April 2023: a binder composed of questions and placed for visitors to engage in the permanent collection galleries.

4 "Red Conceptualismos del Sur Manifesto," February 2009, as quoted in Manuel Borja-Villel, introduction to *Perder la forma humana: Una imagen sísmica de los años ochenta en América Latina*, ed. Ana Longoni, Miguel A. López, Fernanda Nogueira, André Mesquita, Jaime Vindel, and Fernanda Carvaj (Madrid: Museo Nacional Centro de Arte Reina Sofía, 2012), 9.

5 Raphael Fonseca, ed., *Vaivém / To-and-Fro* (Rio de Janeiro: Centro Cultural Banco do Brasil, 2019).

6 See relevant artist entries and Brasileiro's and Motta's interviews in this volume.

7 The speakers participated in the Afro-Caribbean and Afro-Brazilian Art and Visual Culture Seminar convened by Eddie Chambers, George Flaherty, and Adele Nelson from August 17–19, 2021, at the Center for Latin American Visual Studies, UT Austin.

8 Leda Maria Martins, "Performances do tempo espiralar," in *Performance, exílio, fronteiras: Errâncias territoriais e textuais*, ed. Graciela Ravetti and Márcia Arbex (Belo Horizonte: UFMG, 2002), 84. Translation by the author. Martins subsequently expanded this essay into a book-length study. See Leda Maria Martins, *Performances do tempo espiralar: Poéticas do corpo-tela* (Rio de Janeiro: Editora Cobogó, 2021).

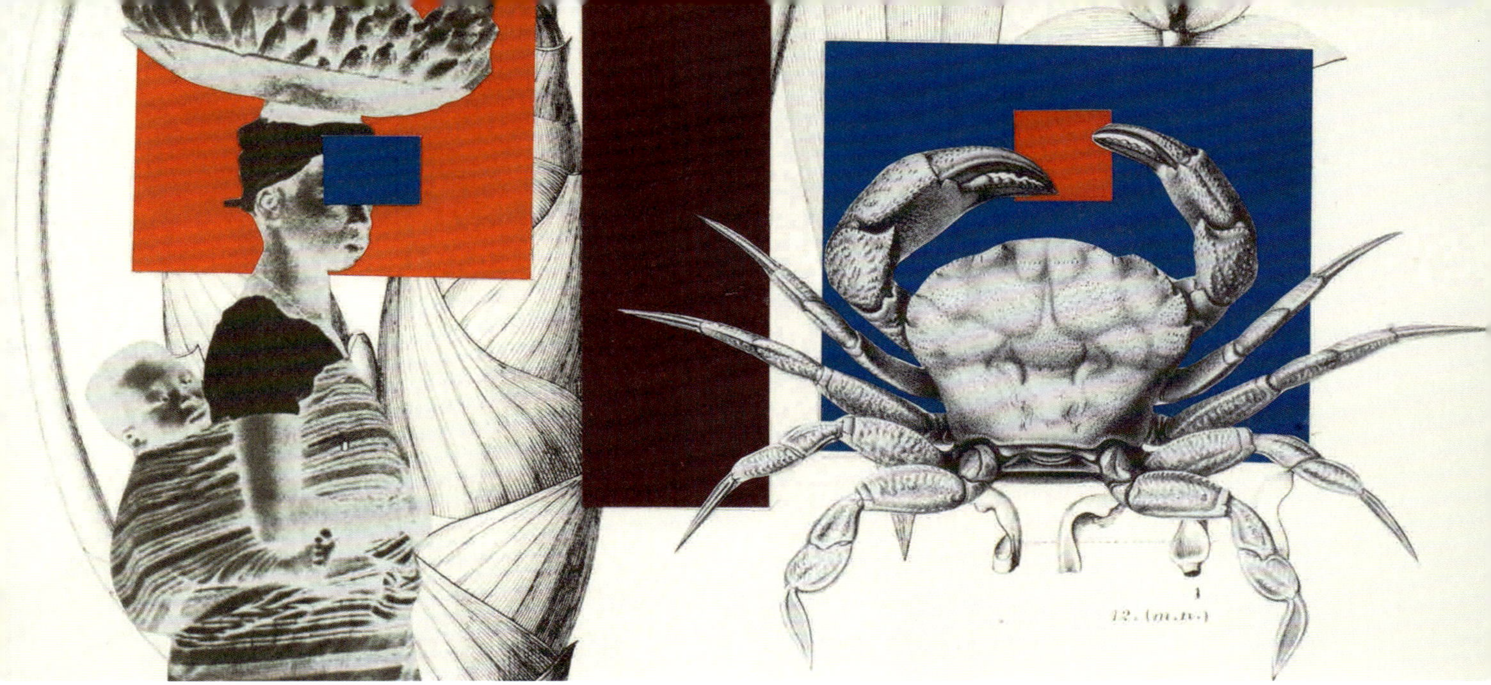

Rosana Paulino, *A geometria à brasileira chega ao paraíso tropical*, 2018 (detail).

Citation, Translation, and Representation

US EXHIBITIONS OF BRAZILIAN ART

Adele Nelson

As a student, I was struck by the different practices of citation encouraged in US and Brazilian graduate art history programs. My classmates and I in the United States were trained to foreground our arguments, buttressed by the work of other scholars but with our contributions differentiated. My Brazilian contemporaries devoted great depth to discussion of the prior study of their subjects and were expected to account not just for national narratives but also those of European, Latin American, and US thinkers. Most striking to me as a young writer was the form these latter citations took: multiple, extended, multilingual block quotations.

What at first was visible to me as rhetorical style—walls of text accompanied by footnotes versus a multivoiced chorus—is of course about much more: different ethics of access and attribution and the extractivist habits of the US academy toward the Global South. Black feminist scholars have productively centered the politics and ethics of citation. Projects like the Cite Black Women campaign, founded in 2017 by Christen A. Smith, make clear the urgency of retraining across the board while Jennifer C. Nash calls for her field's cultivation of "citation as a form of freedom" to not overlook "citation itself as both a site of violence and a logic of property."[1]

And what of art exhibitions and their citation, translation, and representation practices? As Mari Carmen Ramírez argued in 1992,

> Art exhibitions are privileged vehicles for the representation of individual and collective identities, whether they consciously set out to be so or not. By bringing together works produced by artists as individuals or as members of a specific community, they allow insights into the ways those groups visually construct their self-image. This identity-projecting role of exhibitions has been at the heart of controversies surrounding the unprecedented number of shows of Latin American/Latino art organized and funded by U.S. institutions (museums, galleries, alternative spaces) over the last ten years.[2]

This "identity-projecting role" is often scripted by curators who are not part of the communities represented. This is true of the *Social Fabric: Art and Activism in Contemporary Brazil* exhibition, which is organized by two cisgender, heterosexual, white US women with a cisgender, heterosexual Mexican woman. Following Ramírez's analysis, *Social Fabric* participates in the "unprecedented number" of shows focused on Afro-descendant, Indigenous, LGBTQIA+, and women artists—with global, national, regional, and thematic focuses—and funded by Brazilian and US institutions (museums, galleries, art prizes, alternative spaces) over the last ten years.[3] The shows of the mid- to late 2010s and early 2020s respond to the impeachment of Brazil's first woman president in what many view as a veiled coup; the murders of Marielle Franco, Paulo Paulino Guajajara, George Floyd, and other activists and citizens; resurgent Black, Indigenous, LGBTQIA+, and women's rights movements; the necropolitics of the administrations of Jair Bolsonaro and Donald Trump; and, in Brazil, a culture war by the far right that targeted the visual arts.[4]

But the attempt by institutions and curators to highlight the resistance by artists to these oppressive trends is by no means the whole story. As Jota Mombaça wrote in 2020—in dialogue with the ideas of philosopher Denise Ferreira da Silva, musician Baco Exu do Blues, and others, and dedicated to artist Musa Michelle Mattiuzzi—the art world, like other cultural industries, must be understood as a "system of appropriation of Black life," as a "cognitive plantation":

> "*Meus ancestrais todos foram vendidos / Deve ser por isso que meu som vende* (*All my ancestors have been sold / That's probably why my music sells*)." That is probably why this text sells. Or why, according to some institutions, the boom in Black and anticolonial art and thought, that seems to define

> the courses of art and knowledge production on a global scale at the moment, is referred to as a trend, a market tendency. Since the commodification of this perspective—our perspectives—depend directly on a certain continuity between our artistic production and our social-historical place, maybe it makes sense to state that the selling of our music, texts, ideas and images reenacts, as a historical tendency, the regimes of acquisitions of Black bodies that established the predicament of Blackness at the core of the world as we know it.[5]

Thus the current visibility of Black and other artists with marginalized identities in US and Brazilian art worlds cannot be separated from, and even depends on, the violent systems of both societies. Aline Motta asked my collaborators and me this question in our first studio visit: Why not give us, here in Brazil, access to the resources you have at your institution and are assembling for this exhibition project? The question makes evident and indisputable the extractivism of art exhibitions.

In 2023, Diane Lima illuminated for University of Texas at Austin audiences, me included, how artists navigate racial capitalism and "its systems of representation and hypervisibility."[6] While reflecting on the work of Paulo Nazareth, Lima underlined the institutional interventions, refusals, and reclamations by Black artists and curators and articulated an important periodization within the rapid shift in the conditions and critical discussions of Black participation in the art world in the last decade:

> Such questions make me return to the years 2014 and 2015 when we lived in Brazil, a key moment of reclamation regarding our absences and presences in institutional spaces, which consequently led to a fierce debate about visibility regimes. Regimes that, if today are concentrated especially around criticisms of hypervisibility and capture, at that time revolved especially around the problems of institutional erasure and invisibility.[7]

This US exhibition of Brazilian art participates, and should be subject to scrutiny, in the second moment, in the late 2010s and early 2020s, that Lima maps. Critical reflection on the enterprise of *Social Fabric* is indebted to Lima, Mombaça, Motta, Ramírez, the co-editors of this publication, the project's advisory committee, my students, and many others. This also includes, crucially, Rosana Paulino, who has built vital pathways for Black artists and curators while pioneering a multivocal, manifestly multimedia practice that thinks profoundly about the issues of citation, translation, and representation. Paulino intervenes in past and present representations of Black bodies and makes tangible, through reassembly, juxtaposition, and material transformation, the ideological and violent meanings of those representations. Paulino's titles and her works do not pull their punches:

A permanência das estructuras (The Permanence of Structures)
Ainda a lamentar (Still Mourning)

Atlântico vermelho (Red Atlantic; see plate 54)
Tecido social (Social Fabric; see plate 51)[8]

Paulino and the other artists included in *Social Fabric* bring into relief that the colonial systems of the past persist and compose the fabric of contemporary life but with new window dressings—slave ships become armored police vehicles, imperial courts give way to modernist architecture, scientific racism is enacted as tourism, and colonial display morphs into art exhibitions. In acts of profound generosity and what can perhaps be described as practices of critical pedagogy, the artists invite viewers to question official narratives while providing access to the very methods of reorientation, redress, and transmutation.[9]

NOTES

1 Jennifer C. Nash, "Citational Desires: On Black Feminism's Institutional Longings," *Diacritics* 48, no. 3 (2020): 83. On Cite Black Women, see https://citeblackwomencollective.org.

2 Mari Carmen Ramírez, "Beyond 'The Fantastic': Framing Identity in U.S. Exhibitions of Latin American Art," *Art Journal* 51, no. 4 (Winter 1992): 60.

3 The most visible of these was *Histórias Afro-Atlânticas*, held at the Instituto Tomie Ohtake and Museu de Arte de São Paulo (MASP) in 2018 and curated by Ayrson Heráclito, Hélio Menezes, Adriano Pedrosa, Lilia Moritz Schwarcz, and Tomás Toledo, with an extensive US tour from 2021 to 2024. For insightful analysis, see Vivian A. Crockett, "A Place to Call Home: Reflections on Transnational Translations," in *Afro-Atlantic Histories*, ed. Adriano Pedrosa and Tomás Toledo (New York: DelMonico, 2021), 52–62.

4 Other important educational programs and exhibitions, solely organized or coorganized by artists and curators of color, include *AfroTranscendence*, directed by Diane Lima, São Paulo and Munich, 2015–2019; *Diálogos ausentes*, curated by Diane Lima and Rosana Paulino at Itaú Cultural, São Paulo, in 2016; *Dja guata porã: Rio de Janeiro indígena*, curated by Sandra Benites, Clarissa Diniz, José Ribamar Bessa, and Pablo LaFuente at the Museu de Arte do Rio in 2017; and *Vexóa: Nós sabemos*, curated by Naine Terena at the Pinacoteca do Estado de São Paulo in 2020.

5 Jota Mombaça, "The Cognitive Plantation," *Afterall*, June 11, 2020, https://www.afterall.org/article/the-cognitive-plantation. For illustrated Portuguese text, see "A plantação cognitiva," *Arte e descolonização: MASP Afterall*, 2020, https://masp.org.br/arte-e-descolonizacao. The italicized quotation is from Baco Exu do Blues's "Imortais e fatais," released on his 2017 album *Esú*.

6 Diane Lima, "Negros na piscina / Blacks in the Pool: Hypervisibility, Art and Curatorship in Brazil" (lecture, UT Austin, March 1, 2023; lecture in Portuguese, translation by the author). https://utvac.org/event/clavis-permanent-seminar-latin-american-art-diane-lima. Also see her essay in *Paulo Nazareth* (São Paulo: Pivô; Toronto: Power Plant, forthcoming 2023), and her edited volume *Negros na piscina* (Rio de Janeiro: Fósforo Editora/Luna Parque Edições, forthcoming 2023).

7 Lima, "Negros na piscina."

8 For illustrations and insightful analysis of Paulino's production, including works not included in *Social Fabric*, see Valéria Piccoli and Pedro Nery, eds., *Rosana Paulino: A costura da mémoria / Rosana Paulino: The Sewing of Memory* (São Paulo: Pinacoteca de São Paulo, 2018).

9 I am inspired by Anna Arabindan-Kesson's methodology of taking cues from contemporary artists in historical study, of thinking with (rather than just about) artists. Anna Arabindan-Kesson, *Black Bodies, White Gold: Art, Cotton, and Commerce in the Atlantic World* (Durham: Duke University Press, 2021), 6.

Artist Biographies

Denilson Baniwa (b. 1984, Rio Negro, Brazil) lives and works in Niterói, Brazil. He has had solo exhibitions at the Pinacoteca do Estado de São Paulo (2023); Centro Municipal de Arte Hélio Oiticica, Rio de Janeiro (2022); Centro Cultural São Paulo (2019); Museu do Índio, Uberlândia (2019); and Galeria de Arte UFF, Niterói (2019). His work has also been included in group exhibitions at The Getty Center, Los Angeles (2022); Kunsthalle Wien, Vienna (2021); Museu de Língua Portuguesa, São Paulo (2021); Kixpatla, Mexico City (2021); Pivô, São Paulo (2021); Frestas—Trienal de Artes, Sorocaba (2020/2021); ONCA, Brighton (2020); Sesc Santana, São Paulo (2020); Pinacoteca do Estado de São Paulo (2020); Museu de Arte de São Paulo (2020); Museu de Arte do Rio, Rio de Janeiro (2020); Museum of Contemporary Art Metelkova, Ljubljana (2020); Sydney Biennial (2020); and Museu Afro Brasil, São Paulo (2020); among others. In 2019 he won the PIPA Award in the online category, and in 2021 he was selected by jury for the PIPA Award. He was in residence at Corpus Urbis in Oiapoque, Brazil, in 2018.

Castiel Vitorino Brasileiro (b. 1996, Vitória, Brazil) lives and works on planet Earth. She earned her BA in psychology at the Universidade Federal do Espíritu Santo (2019) and an MA in clinical psychology at the Pontifíca Universidade Católica de São Paulo (2021). She has had solo exhibitions at Mendes Wood DM, New York (2022); Hessel Museum of Art, Bard College, New York (2021); and Galeria Homero Massena, Vitória (2019). Her work has also been included in group exhibitions at the Pinacoteca do Estado de São Paulo (2022); Museo de Arte Contemporáneo de Panamá (2022); Museu de Arte Moderna do Rio de Janeiro (2021); Museu de Arte do Rio, Rio de Janeiro (2021); LUX, London (2021); Kunsthalle Wien, Vienna (2021); Centro Cultural São Paulo (2020/2021); Frestas—Trienal de Artes, Sorocaba (2020/2021); Centro Municipal de Arte Hélio Oiticica, Rio de Janeiro (2019); and Museu Capixaba do Negro, Vitória (2019); among others. She is a recipient of the PIPA Prize (2021) and the ZUM/Instituto Moreira Salles Photography Grant (2021). She was in residence at La Becque, Lausanne, in 2022; the Museu de Arte Moderna do Rio de Janeiro in 2021; and the studio of Rosana Paulino in 2018.

Guerreiro do Divino Amor (b. 1983, Geneva, Switzerland) lives and works in Rio de Janeiro, Brazil. He earned his MA in architecture from the École Nationale Supérieure d'Architecture de Grenoble, France, and La Cambre, Brussels (2006). He has had solo exhibitions at the Centre d'Art Contemporain Genève (2022);

Centro de Arte Contemporânea W, Ribeirão Preto (2019); and Paço das Artes at Museu da Imagem e do Som, São Paulo (2018). He has been included in group exhibitions at Frestas—Trienal de Artes, Sorocaba (2020/2021); Instituto Moreira Salles, Rio de Janeiro (2020); Museu de Arte da Pampulha, Belo Horizonte (2019); and Museu de Arte Brasileira da Fundação Armando Alvares Penteado, São Paulo (2019); among others. He is the recipient of the DAAD Artists-in-Berlin Award Grant (2021); the PIPA Prize (2019); and the 24th Salão Anapolino de Arte Prize (2019). He was in residence at DAAD in Berlin between 2021 and 2022 and at Casa da Cultura da América Latina at Universidade de Brasília in 2018. He will represent Switzerland at the Venice Biennale (2024).

Jaime Lauriano (b. 1985, São Paulo, Brazil) lives and works in São Paulo, Brazil. He earned his BA in visual arts from the Centro Universitário Belas Artes de São Paulo (2011). He has had solo exhibitions at Museu de Arte do Rio (2023), Fundação Joaquim Nabuco, Recife (2018); Sesc Santana, São Paulo (2018); and Museu de Arte Contemporânea de Niterói (2018). His work has been included in group exhibitions at the Museu de Arte Moderna de São Paulo (2022); Museu de Arte de São Paulo (2022); National Gallery of Art, Washington, DC (2022); Museum of Fine Arts, Houston (2021); Museu da Língua Portuguesa, São Paulo (2021); NGBK, Berlin (2021); Instituto Moreira Salles, São Paulo (2021); Anya and Andrew Shiva Gallery, New York (2020); Maus Hábitos, Porto (2020); CAIXA Cultural Brasília (2020); CAIXA Cultural Rio de Janeiro (2019); Museu de Arte do Rio, Rio de Janeiro (2018); and Museu de Arte de São Paulo and Instituto Tomie Ohtake, São Paulo (2018); among others. Lauriano was the winner of the O.F.F. Award at the 20th Contemporary Art Festival Sesc Videobrasil (2018) and the FOCO Bradesco ArtRio Award (2016). He was in residence at Q21 Museums Quartier, Vienna (2017); Casa Wabi, Oaxaca (2017); and Hotel Cambridge, São Paulo (2016).

Maré de Matos (b. 1987, Governador Valadares, Brazil) lives and works in São Paulo, Brazil. She earned her BA in visual arts at the Universidade do Estado de Minas Gerais (2009) and an MA in literary theory from the Universidade Federal do Pernambuco (2019); she is currently pursuing her doctorate at the Universidade de São Paulo. She has had solo exhibitions at Galeria Lume, São Paulo (2022); Museu de Arte Moderna Aloisio Magalhães, Recife (2016); and A Casa do Cachorro Preto, Olinda (2016). Her work has been included in group exhibitions at the Museu de Arte Moderna de São Paulo (2022); Museu de Arte do Rio, Rio de Janeiro (2022); Museu de Arte de São Paulo (2022); Museu da Língua Portuguesa, São Paulo (2021); Museu Afro Brasil, São Paulo (2021); Museu Brasileiro de Escultura e Ecologia, São Paulo (2021); Instituto Moreira Salles, São Paulo (2021); Centro Cultural São Paulo (2020); Sesc Pompeia, São Paulo (2020); Museu de Arte Moderna de São Paulo (2019); Museu da Abolição, Recife (2019); and Museu Murilo La Greca, Recife (2018); among others. She was in residence at Koda, New York, in 2022; Veiculo Sur between 2021 and 2022; Pivô Pesquisa, São Paulo in 2021; and AfroTranscendence, São Paulo in 2016.

Aline Motta (b. 1974, Niterói, Brazil) lives and works in São Paulo, Brazil. She earned her BA in communications at the Universidade Federal do Rio de Janeiro (1995) and a film production certificate at The New School, New York (2004). She has had solo exhibitions at Museu de Arte de São Paulo (2022); Sesc Belezinho, São Paulo (2022); New Museum, New York (2021); and Museu de Arte do Rio, Rio de Janeiro (2021); among others. Her work has been included in group exhibitions at the Sharjah Biennial (2023); Museu de Arte Moderna do Rio de Janeiro (2022); Les Rencontres de la Photographie Arles (2021); Centro Cultural Kirchner, Buenos Aires (2021); Museu de Artes do Espírito Santo, Vitória (2021); Bienal do Mercosul, Porto Alegre (2020); Museu de Arte de Santa Catarina, Florianópolis (2020); Goethe-Institut Salvador-Bahia (2020); and Museu de Arte de São Paulo (2019); among others. She received the 7th Indústria Nacional Marcantonio Vilaça Award for the Arts (2019) and the ZUM/Instituto Moreira Salles Photography Grant (2018).

Lais Myrrha (b. 1974, Belo Horizonte, Brazil) lives and works in São Paulo, Brazil. She earned her MA in visual arts (2007) at the Universidade do Estado de Minas Gerais, where she is currently pursuing a PhD in visual arts. She has had solo exhibitions at Galeria Millan, São Paulo (2023); Pinacoteca do Estado de São Paulo (2021); Blanton Museum of Art, Austin, Texas (2017); Galeria Athena Contemporânea, Rio de Janeiro (2017); Broadway 1602, New York (2017); and Sesc Bom Retiro, São Paulo (2017); among others. Her work has been included in group exhibitions at Museu Nacional da República, Brasília (2023); Museu de Arte Moderna de São Paulo (2022); Centro Cultural Maria Antônia—USP, São Paulo (2022); Galleria Ron Manos, Amsterdam (2020); Museu de Arte do Rio, Rio de Janeiro (2020); Bienal de La Habana (2019); Palácio das Artes, Belo Horizonte (2019); Sala de Arte Santander, Madrid (2019); Gwangju Biennale (2018); Museu de Arte de São Paulo (2017); Museu de Arte Contemporânea de Serralves, Porto (2022, 2017); Bienal de São Paulo (2016); Los Angeles Municipal Art Gallery (2017); and Bienal do Mercosul, Porto Alegre (2011); among others. She received the Honor Award for Art and Heritage from Paço Imperial, Rio de Janeiro (2013); Funarte Scholarship to Stimulate Visual Arts Production (2012); and Pampulha Scholarship from the Museu de Arte da Pampulha, Belo Horizonte (2003). She was in residence at IASPIS (International Artist Studio Programme in Stockholm) in 2022.

Antonio Obá (b. 1983, Ceilandia, Brazil) lives and works in Brasília, Brazil. He studied art at the Faculdade de Artes Dulcina de Moraes in Brasília (2010). He has had solo exhibitions at the Oude Kerk, Amsterdam (2022); X Museum, Beijing (2022); Mendes Wood DM, Brussels (2021); and Galeria Cândido Portinari, UERJ, Rio de Janeiro (2016). His work has been included in group exhibitions at the Museum de Fundatie, Zwolle (2023); Museu de Arte de São Paulo (2022); Zeitz Museum of Contemporary Art Africa, Cape Town (2022); Pinacoteca do Estado de São Paulo (2021); Instituto Moreira Salles, São Paulo (2021); Bourse de Commerce–Pinault Collection, Paris (2021); MO.CO, Montpellier (2020); Museu de Arte Moderna de São Paulo (2019); Museu de Arte de São Paulo and Instituto Tomie Ohtake, São Paulo (2018); Museu de Arte do Rio, Rio de Janeiro (2018); Casa da Cultura da América Latina, Brasília (2016); and Museu Nacional da República, Brasília (2015); among others.

Rosana Paulino (b. 1967, São Paulo, Brazil) lives and works in São Paulo, Brazil. She received a BA in visual art from the Universidade de São Paulo (1995), a specialization in engraving from the London Print Studio (1998), her doctorate in visual arts from the School of Communications and Arts at the Universidade de São Paulo (2011), and a residency focused on lithography at the Tamarind Institute, Albuquerque (2022). Paulino has had solo exhibitions at Kunstverein Braunschweig, Braunschweig, Germany (2022); Mendes Wood DM, Brussels (2022); Museu de Arte do Rio, Rio de Janeiro (2019); The Frank Museum of Art, Otterbein University, Westerville, Ohio (2019); Pinacoteca do Estado de São Paulo (2018); Museu de Artes Visuais da Unicamp, Campinas (2018); Senac, São Paulo (2017); and Empresa de Gestão de Equipamentos e Animação Cultural, Lisbon (2017); among others. Her work has been included in group exhibitions at the Museu Nacional da República, Brasília (2023); Centro Cultural São Paulo, São Paulo (2022); Instituto Inhotim, Brumadinho (2022); Sesc Pinheiros, São Paulo (2022); Biennale di Venezia (2022); DePaul Art Museum, Chicago (2022); Museu de Arte de São Paulo, São Paulo (2022); Centro Cultural Banco do Brasil, Rio de Janeiro, São Paulo, Brasília, and Belo Horizonte (2022); Public Art Foundation, New York, Boston, and Chicago (2022); National Gallery of Art, Washington, DC (2022); Museum of Fine Arts, Houston (2021); Museu Judaico de São Paulo (2021); Instituto Moreira Salles, São Paulo (2021); Museu de Arte do Rio, Rio de Janeiro (2020); Sesc Pinheiros, São Paulo (2020); Mana Contemporary, Chicago (2020); Kunstverein Hannover (2020); and Sydney Biennial (2020); among others. She was a Ford Foundation Fellow (2006–2008) and received a CAPES (Coordenação de Aperfeiçoamento de Pessoal de Nível Superior) grant (2008–2011). In 2014, she was the recipient of a Rockefeller Foundation scholarship for a residency at the Bellagio Center in Bellagio, Italy. In 2022, she received the Konex Mercosur Prize for Visual Arts, Argentina.

Sallisa Rosa (b. 1986, Goiânia, Brazil) lives and works in Rio de Janeiro, Brazil. She had her first solo exhibition at Museu de Arte Moderna do Rio de Janeiro in 2021. Her work has been included in group exhibitions at Théâtre de L'Usine, Geneva (2022); Royal Academy of Arts, London (2021); Paço das Artes, São Paulo (2021); Frestas—Trienal de Artes, Sorocaba (2020/2021); Anya and Andrew Shiva Gallery, New York (2020); Museu de Arte do Rio, Rio de Janeiro (2020, 2017); Museu de Arte de São Paulo (2022, 2020, 2019); Banco do Brasil Centro Cultural, Rio de Janeiro (2019); and Barro de Caruaru Bienal (2019); among others. Rosa was nominated for the PIPA prize (2022, 2020) and is a recipient of the Prince Claus Fund Seed Award (2021).

Contributors

Chasitie Brown (b. 1993, Raleigh, North Carolina) is a PhD candidate in the Department of Art and Art History at the University of Texas at Austin, specializing in contemporary Caribbean and Latin American art with a focus on Cuba. Her dissertation examines exhibition practices centered on race in Cuba and its global diaspora in the United States and Spain during the 1990s and early 2000s. She earned her MA at Tulane University and BA at Southern Methodist University.

Martha Scott Burton (b. 1992, Winston-Salem, North Carolina) is an arts and culture worker based in Brooklyn. Currently at the Mellon Foundation, she has held curatorial and research positions at the Whitney Museum of American Art, Morgan Library, and Studio Museum in Harlem and has contributed to a wide range of exhibition catalogues, academic publications, and literary works. She holds an MA from the University of Texas at Austin and a BA (magna cum laude) from Columbia University.

Eva Caston (b. 1998, Washington, DC) is an MA student in art history at the University of Texas at Austin. She graduated with honors from the University of Michigan in 2020 with a BA in the history of art. She has held positions at the University of Michigan Museum of Art, the Cranbrook Museum of Art, and the Dallas Museum of Art. Her thesis examines the early 1970s work of artists Regina Vater and Cecilia Vicuña through an ecocritical lens.

Catalina Cherñavvsky Sequeira (b. 1995, Buenos Aires, Argentina) is a PhD student at the University of Texas at Austin specializing in modern and contemporary Latin American art. Her research is centered around artistic networks, experimental film and video art, materiality, and art production under dictatorship in Argentina and Brazil from the 1960s to the 1980s. She received an MA in art history from the Courtauld Institute of Art and a BA from Yale University, where she double-majored in art history and psychology.

Maria Emilia Fernandez (b. 1990, Mexico City, Mexico) is assistant curator at the Visual Arts Center at the University of Texas at Austin. She earned her MA in art history at the University of Texas at Austin and is an alumna of the Center for Latin American Visual Studies (CLAVIS) there. Prior to pursuing her master's degree, she worked as curatorial assistant at Museo Jumex in Mexico City. She holds a BA in art history from Vassar College.

Thiago Ferreira (b. 1991, São Gotardo, Brazil) is a PhD candidate in social history at the Universidade Federal do Rio de Janeiro, with a focus on the history and theory of modern and contemporary Brazilian art and architecture. Originally trained as an architect, he received an MA in art history, theory, and criticism from the Universidade Federal do Rio de Janeiro, where he was also an assistant instructor of art history from 2018 to 2020. In 2021 he was a visiting student at the Center for Latin American Visual Studies (CLAVIS) at the University of Texas at Austin.

Pilar Dirickson Garrett (b. 1993, São Sebastião, Brazil) is a PhD student in art history at the University of Texas at Austin, where she specializes in modern Latin American art and architecture with a focus on postwar exhibition histories, histories of vernacular art and design, and midcentury political discourse in Brazil. She holds a BA in history from the University of British Columbia and an MA in Latin American studies and museum studies from New York University.

Jana La Brasca (b. 1989, Los Angeles, California) is a doctoral candidate in art history at the University of Texas at Austin and curatorial researcher for the forthcoming exhibition *Groundswell: Women of Land Art* at the Nasher Sculpture Center. Previously she was the co-organizer of *Without Limits: Helen Frankenthaler, Abstraction, and the Language of Print* at the Blanton Museum of Art and the Catalogue Research Fellow at Judd Foundation in Marfa, Texas, and New York.

Lorraine Leu (b. 1969, Trinidad and Tobago) is professor of Latin American cultural studies at the University of Texas at Austin, with a joint appointment in the Teresa Lozano Long Institute for Latin American Studies and the Department of Spanish and Portuguese. Recent book publications include *Defiant Geographies: Race and Urban Space in 1920s Rio de Janeiro* (2020) and the coedited anthologies *Latin American Cultural Studies: A Reader* (2017) and *Black Feminist Constellations: Dialogue and Translation across the Americas* (forthcoming 2023). She has been an editor of the *Journal of Latin American Cultural Studies* since 2000.

Maysa Martins (b. 1989, Londrina, Brazil) is a PhD student in art history at the University of Texas at Austin. She received her MA in art history at the Universidade Federal de São Paulo and her BA in visual arts at the Universidade Estadual Paulista. Her research interests include modern and contemporary art of the Black diaspora in Latin America and the Caribbean and decolonial perspectives toward diasporic spiritualities, collective mourning, and healing practices.

Adele Nelson (b. 1976, Fort Worth, Texas) is associate professor of art history and associate director of the Center for Latin American Visual Studies (CLAVIS) at the University of Texas at Austin. She is the author of *Forming Abstraction: Art and Institutions in Postwar Brazil* (2022), the 2023 Antonio Candido Prize recipient for the best humanities book from the Brazil Section, Latin American Studies Association, and *Jac Leirner in Conversation* (2011; Portuguese edition 2013). Her research has been supported by the American Philosophical Society, the Fulbright US Scholar Program, and the National Endowment for the Humanities.

Lucy Quezada (b. 1990, Talagante, Chile) is a PhD candidate in art history at the University of Texas at Austin, where her studies have been supported by the National Research and Development Agency of Chile and the Fulbright Program. She received her BA and MA from the Universidad de Chile. She has coauthored volumes focused on cultural institutions from the early 1970s in Chile, including the Museo de la Solidaridad (2019) and the Instituto de Arte Latinoamericano (2022).

Jennifer Sales (b. 1988, San Francisco, California) is a PhD candidate in the Department of Art and Art History at the University of Texas at Austin, specializing in modern and contemporary Latin American and Latinx art. Her dissertation examines racial, gender, and queer subjectivities in experimental art production during the Brazilian military dictatorship (1964–1985). She received an MA in art history from the University of Utah and a BA from California State University, Long Beach.

MacKenzie Stevens (b. 1978, Corpus Christi, Texas) is director and curator of the Visual Arts Center at the University of Texas at Austin. She has organized solo exhibitions with Carmen Argote, Nikita Gale, Juan Pablo González, Madeline Hollander, Lisa Lapinski, Kate Newby, Michael Queenland, Luiz Roque, and Kenneth Tam, among others, and is editor of *Miss Swiss* (2023), the first monograph focusing on the work of Lisa Lapinski.

Exhibition Checklist

1 Denilson Baniwa
Zoo terra indígena
Indigenous Land Zoo
2018
Inkjet print on paper
5 15/16 × 5 15/16 in. (15 × 15 cm)
Courtesy of the artist
(This work was realized as a takeaway postcard.)

2 Denilson Baniwa
A Amazônia é *uma invenção*, da série *Todo território é invenção*
The Amazon Is an Invention, from the series Every Territory Is Invention
2019
Pen and ink on paper
11 13/16 × 11 13/16 in. (30 × 30 cm)
Courtesy of the artist

3 Denilson Baniwa
Kwatá-tapuya, da série *Perspectivismo ameríndio*
Kwatá-tapuya, from the series Amerindian Perspectivism
2019
Inkjet print on PhotoTex
27 9/16 × 39 3/8 in. (70 × 100 cm)
Courtesy of the artist

4 Denilson Baniwa
Sukuryu-tapuya, da série *Perspectivismo ameríndio*
Sukuryu-tapuya, from the series Amerindian Perspectivism
2019
Inkjet print on PhotoTex
27 9/16 × 39 3/8 in. (70 × 100 cm)
Courtesy of the artist

5 Denilson Baniwa
Voyeurs
2019
Inkjet print, China ink, and collage on paper
15 3/4 × 20 1/4 in. (40 × 51.5 cm)
Collection of the Pinacoteca do Estado de São Paulo, São Paulo
Donated by Patrons of Contemporary Art of the Pinacoteca do Estado de São Paulo 2019, through the Associação Pinacoteca Arte e Cultura—APAC

6 Denilson Baniwa
Carta aos indígenas do planeta Marte com códigos de reconhecimento do planeta Terra
Letter to the Indigenous Peoples of the Planet Mars with Recognition Codes of the Planet Earth
2020/2022
Acrylic
7 × 10 ft. (219 × 310 cm)
Courtesy of the artist
(This work was realized as a mural, painted by Maggie Exner.)

7 Castiel Vitorino Brasileiro
Jupiter is Here. Celestial is Everything.
2022
Site-specific installation
Soil, limestone, rammed-earth brick wall, acrylic paint, glass, water, *Craginites serratescens* fossil, LED lights; Flag VI from the series *Prosperity is Memories and Choices* (painted fabric); three sculptures from the series *Translate. Learn. Angola. All is about that fear and that love* (burned mesquite wood) (2022–present)
Courtesy of the artist

8 Guerreiro do Divino Amor
A cristalização de Brasília, da série *Atlas superficcional mundial*
Crystallization of Brasília, from the series Superfictional World Atlas
2019
Video, color, sound
9:46 min.
Courtesy of the artist

9 Guerreiro do Divino Amor
O mundo mineral, da série *Atlas superficcional mundial*
The Mineral World, from the series Superfictional World Atlas
2019
Video, color, sound
7:44 min.
Courtesy of the artist

10 Guerreiro do Divino Amor
Trilogia cristalizada de Brasília: Formação, cristalização e desabrochar de uma nova Alvorada
Crystallized Trilogy of Brasília: Formation, Crystallization, and Breaking of a New Dawn
2022
Backlit triptych, wood, inkjet print on acrylic, LED lights, kinetic light mechanism
Image divided in 3 parts, each 39 ⅜ × 26 in. (100 × 66 cm)
Courtesy of the artist

11 Guerreiro do Divino Amor
Trilogia mineral
Mineral Trilogy
2022
Backlit triptych, wood, inkjet print on acrylic, LED lights, kinetic light mechanism
Image divided in 3 parts, each 39 ⅜ × 26 in. (100 × 66 cm)
Courtesy of the artist

12 Jaime Lauriano
Invasão
Invasion
2017
Dermatographic pencil on fabric
63 × 122 1/16 in. (160 × 310 cm)
Collection of the Pinacoteca do Estado de São Paulo, São Paulo
Donated by Collection of Otavio and Gustavo Cutait Abdalla

13 Jaime Lauriano
America meridionalis: invenção, epistemicídio, contrato racial e genocídio
America meridionalis: invention, epistemicide, racial contract, and genocide
2019
Pemba and dermatographic pencil on raw cotton
55 ⅛ × 74 in. (140 × 188 cm)
Courtesy of Galeria Leme, São Paulo

14 Jaime Lauriano
Bandeirante #1
2019
Miniature of monument cast in brass and ammunition cartridges, rammed earth
18 ⅞ × 7 ⅞ × 7 ⅞ in. (48 × 20 × 20 cm) (base)
8 11/16 × 7 ⅞ × 7 ⅞ in. (22 × 20 × 20 cm) (miniature figure)
Collection of Instituto PIPA, Rio de Janeiro

15 Jaime Lauriano
Bandeirante #2
2019
Miniature of monument cast in brass and ammunition cartridges, rammed earth
18 ⅞ × 7 ⅞ × 7 ⅞ in. (48 × 20 × 20 cm) (base)
14 ¾ × 7 ⅞ × 7 ⅞ in. (37.5 × 20 × 20 cm) (miniature figure)
Collection of Instituto PIPA, Rio de Janeiro

16 Maré de Matos
Fundamento
Foundation
2019
Paint on canvas, fabric, clay, wood, acrylic panel, LED sign, video, color, sound
118 ⅛ × 196 ⅞ in. (300 × 500 cm)
Courtesy of the artist

17 Maré de Matos
História
History
2019–present
Inkjet on paper
39 ⅜ × 59 1/16 in. (100 × 150 cm)
Courtesy of the artist

18 Maré de Matos
Racismo
Racism
2019–present
Inkjet on paper
39 3/8 × 59 1/16 in. (100 × 150 cm)
Courtesy of the artist

19 Maré de Matos
Mais nascimento que morte
More Birth than Death
2021–2022
Embroidery on fabric (diptych)
Left: 49 3/16 × 27 15/16 in. (125 × 71 cm)
Right: 68 1/2 × 36 5/8 in. (174 × 93 cm)
Courtesy of the artist

20a Aline Motta
Pontes sobre abismos
Bridges over the Abyss
2017
Three-channel video installation, color, sound
8:28 min.
Courtesy of the artist

20b Aline Motta
Se o mar tivesse varandas
If the Sea Had Balconies
2017
Two-channel video installation, color, sound
9:11 min.
Courtesy of the artist

20c Aline Motta
(Outros) Fundamentos
(Other) Foundations
2017–2019
Single-channel video installation, color, sound
15:48 min.
Courtesy of the artist

(These three works were exhibited as a six-channel video installation and titled *Trilogy*.)

21 Aline Motta
Pontes sobre abismos #2
Bridges over the Abyss #2
2017
Inkjet print on paper
27 9/16 × 49 3/16 in. (70 × 125 cm)
Courtesy of the artist

22 Aline Motta
Pontes sobre abismos #24
Bridges over the Abyss #24
2017
Inkjet print on paper
27 9/16 × 49 3/16 in. (70 × 125 cm)
Courtesy of the artist

23 Aline Motta
Pontes sobre abismos #6
Bridges over the Abyss #6
2017
Inkjet print on paper
27 9/16 × 49 3/16 in. (70 × 125 cm)
Courtesy of the artist

24 Aline Motta
Se o mar tivesse varandas #3
If the Sea Had Balconies #3
2017
Inkjet print on paper
27 9/16 × 49 3/16 in. (70 × 125 cm)
Courtesy of the artist

25 Aline Motta
Se o mar tivesse varandas #4
If the Sea Had Balconies #4
2017
Inkjet print on paper
27 9/16 × 49 3/16 in. (70 × 125 cm)
Courtesy of the artist

26 Aline Motta
(Outros) Fundamentos #2
(Other) Foundations #2
2017–2019
Inkjet print on paper
27 9/16 × 49 3/16 in. (70 × 125 cm)
Courtesy of the artist

27 Aline Motta
(Outros) Fundamentos #3
(Other) Foundations #3
2017–2019
Inkjet print on paper
27 9/16 × 49 3/16 in. (70 × 125 cm)
Courtesy of the artist

28 Aline Motta
(Outros) Fundamentos #4
(Other) Foundations #4
2017–2019
Inkjet print on paper
$27\frac{9}{16} \times 49\frac{3}{16}$ in. (70 × 125 cm)
Courtesy of the artist

29 Lais Myrrha
Bestiário
Bestiary
2005
Video, color, sound
40:35 min.
Collection of the Blanton Museum of Art,
The University of Texas at Austin
Gift of Antonio C. La Pastina and Dale A. Rice,
2016

30 Lais Myrrha
27-04-2016. Articulação (vampiros não aparecem no espelho), da série *Reparação de danos*
27-04-2016. Articulation (Vampires Do Not Appear in the Mirror), from the series Reparation of Damages
2016
Collage with newsprint
$5\frac{11}{16} \times 2\frac{15}{16}$ in. (14.5 × 7.5 cm) unframed
Courtesy of the artist and Galeria Millan,
São Paulo

31 Lais Myrrha
27-04-2016. Painel do futuro (Raimundo Lira and others), da série *Reparação de danos*
27-04-2016. Panel of the Future (Raimundo Lira and Others), from the series Reparation of Damages
2016
Collage with newsprint
$4\frac{15}{16} \times 7\frac{7}{8}$ in. (12.5 × 20 cm) unframed
Courtesy of the artist and Galeria Millan,
São Paulo

32 Lais Myrrha
27-04-2016. Vultos do Brasil #1 (Aécio Neves and Antonio Anastasia), da série *Reparação de danos*
27-04-2016. Figures from Brazil #1 (Aécio Neves and Antonio Anastasia), from the series Reparation of Damages
2016
Collage with newsprint
$4\frac{15}{16} \times 7\frac{7}{8}$ in. (12.5 × 20 cm) unframed
Collection of Fábio Tremonte, São Paulo

33 Lais Myrrha
04-05-2016. Isola! (Maria Thereza de Assis Moura and Gilmar Mendes), da série *Reparação de danos*
04-05-2016. Isolate! (Maria Thereza de Assis Moura and Gilmar Mendes), from the series Reparation of Damages
2016
Collage with newsprint
$4\frac{3}{4} \times 5\frac{9}{16}$ in. (12 × 14.2 cm) unframed
Courtesy of the artist and Galeria Millan,
São Paulo

34 Lais Myrrha
04-05-2016. Vultos do Brasil #2 (Delcidio do Amaral), da série *Reparação de danos*
04-05-2016. Figures from Brazil #2 (Delcidio do Amaral), from the series Reparation of Damages
2016
Collage with newsprint
$4\frac{15}{16} \times 7\frac{7}{8}$ in. (12.5 × 20 cm) framed
Collection of Júlia Rebouças, Belo Horizonte

35 Lais Myrrha
13-05-2016. Ratos (andam baixo mas também fazem sombra) (Michel Temer and his ministers), da série *Reparação de danos*
13-05-2016. Rats (Walk Low but Also Cast Shadows) (Michel Temer and His Ministers), from the series Reparation of Damages
2016
Collage with newsprint
$4\frac{15}{16} \times 7\frac{7}{8}$ in. (12.5 × 20 cm) framed
Collection of Antonio C. La Pastina and
Dale A. Rice, College Station

36 Lais Myrrha
13-05-2016. Ratos (sempre deixam buracos) (Michel Temer and his ministers), da série *Reparação de danos*
13-05-2016. Rats (Always Leave Holes) (Michel Temer and His Ministers), from the series Reparation of Damages
2016
Collage with newsprint
$4\frac{15}{16} \times 7\frac{7}{8}$ in. (12.5 × 20 cm) framed
Courtesy of the artist and Galeria Millan,
São Paulo

37 Lais Myrrha
16-06-2016. Problema de fundo #1 (Michel Temer), da série *Reparação de danos*
16-06-2016. Background Problem #1 (Michel Temer), from the series Reparation of Damages
2016
Collage with newsprint
5 15/16 × 5 11/16 in. (15 × 14.5 cm) framed
Collection of Antonio C. La Pastina and Dale A. Rice, College Station

38 Lais Myrrha
16-06-2016. Tudo azul #2 (Michel Temer), da série *Reparação de danos*
16-06-2016. All Good #2 (Michel Temer), from the series Reparation of Damages
2016
Collage with newsprint
3 1/8 × 3 3/4 in. (8 × 9.5 cm) framed
Collection of Yudi Rafael, Rio de Janeiro

39 Lais Myrrha
Um futuro construído
A Future Built
2018
Engraving, woodcut, lithograph, and serigraph on Rives paper
31 1/2 × 23 5/8 in. (80 × 60 cm) unframed
Collection of Antonio C. La Pastina and Dale A. Rice, College Station

40 Lais Myrrha
Dupla exposição (cena #2). View of Palácio do Planalto and Internal View of Itamaraty with Jean-Baptiste Debret's Painting The Coronation of Dom Pedro I
Double Exposure (scene #2). View of Palácio do Planalto and Internal View of Itamaraty with Jean-Baptiste Debret's Painting *The Coronation of Dom Pedro I*
2022
Facsimile of inkjet print on PhotoTex
31 5/16 × 40 3/4 in. (79.5 × 103.5 cm)
Courtesy of the artist and Galeria Millan, São Paulo

41 Lais Myrrha
Dupla exposição (cena #3). View of Palácio do Planalto and View of the National Congress
Double Exposure (scene #3). View of Palácio do Planalto and View of the National Congress
2022
Facsimile of inkjet print on PhotoTex
31 5/16 × 40 3/4 in. (79.5 × 103.5 cm)
Courtesy of the artist and Galeria Millan, São Paulo

42 Lais Myrrha
Dupla exposição (cena #5). The Three Plenaries (Senate, Deputy Chamber, and Federal Supreme Court)
Double Exposure (scene #5). The Three Plenaries (Senate, Deputy Chamber, and Federal Supreme Court)
2022
Facsimile of inkjet print on PhotoTex
31 5/16 × 47 1/16 in. (79.5 × 119.5 cm)
Courtesy of the artist and Galeria Millan, São Paulo

43 Lais Myrrha
Dupla exposição (cena #7). View of Palácio do Planalto and Internal View of the Brasília Cathedral
Double Exposure (scene #7). View of Palácio do Planalto and Internal View of the Brasília Cathedral
2022
Facsimile of inkjet print on PhotoTex
31 5/16 × 47 1/16 in. (79.5 × 119.5 cm)
Courtesy of the artist and Galeria Millan, São Paulo

44 Antonio Obá
Mãe
Mother
2017
Watercolor on paper
15 9/16 × 11 5/16 in. (39.5 × 28.8 cm) framed
Courtesy of Mendes Wood DM, São Paulo, Brussels, New York

45 Antonio Obá
Mãe
Mother
2017
Watercolor on paper
15 9/16 × 11 5/16 in. (39.5 × 28.8 cm) framed
Courtesy of Mendes Wood DM, São Paulo, Brussels, New York

46 Antonio Obá
Mãe
Mother
2017
Watercolor on paper
15 9/16 × 11 5/16 in. (39.5 × 28.8 cm) framed
Courtesy of Mendes Wood DM, São Paulo, Brussels, New York

47 Antonio Obá
Mãe
Mother
2017
Watercolor on paper
15 9/16 × 11 5/16 in. (39.5 × 28.8 cm) framed
Courtesy of Mendes Wood DM, São Paulo, Brussels, New York

48 Antonio Obá
Mãe
Mother
2017
Watercolor on paper
15 9/16 × 11 5/16 in. (39.5 × 28.8 cm) framed
Courtesy of Mendes Wood DM, São Paulo, Brussels, New York

49 Antonio Obá
Mãe
Mother
2017
Watercolor on paper
15 9/16 × 11 5/16 in. (39.5 × 28.8 cm) framed
Courtesy of Mendes Wood DM, São Paulo, Brussels, New York

50 Rosana Paulino
Tecelãs
Weavers
2003
Faience, terra-cotta, cotton, and synthetic thread
Dimensions variable
Collection of Inhotim Institute, Minas Gerais

51 Rosana Paulino
Tecido social
Social Fabric
2010
Monotype and sewn thread on fabric
90 9/16 × 114 15/16 in. (230 cm × 292 cm)
Courtesy of Mendes Wood DM, São Paulo, Brussels, New York

52 Rosana Paulino
Assentamento no. 2
Settlement no. 2
2012–2013
Color lithograph on paper
30 × 22 1/4 in. (76.2 × 56.5 cm) unframed
Collection of Professor Lorraine Leu, Austin

53 Rosana Paulino
Assentamento no. 3
Settlement no. 3
2012–2013
Color lithograph on paper
30 × 22 1/4 in. (76.2 × 56.5 cm) unframed
Private collection, Austin

54 Rosana Paulino
Atlântico vermelho
Red Atlantic
2017
Inkjet print, sewn thread, and collage on fabric
50 × 43 5/16 in. (127 × 110 cm) unframed
Collection of the Pinacoteca do Estado de São Paulo
Donated by Collection of Fernando Assad Abdalla

55 Rosana Paulino
Paraíso tropical
Tropical Paradise
2017
Inkjet print, collage, and linoleum block print on paper
18 7/8 × 13 in. (48 × 33 cm) unframed
Courtesy of Mendes Wood DM, São Paulo, Brussels, New York

56 Rosana Paulino
Paraíso tropical
Tropical Paradise
2017
Inkjet print, collage, and linoleum block print on paper
18 7/8 × 13 in. (48 × 33 cm) unframed
Courtesy of Mendes Wood DM, São Paulo, Brussels, New York

57 Rosana Paulino
A geometria à brasileira chega ao paraíso tropical
Brazilian-Style Geometry Arrives in
Tropical Paradise
2018
Inkjet print, collage, and monotype on paper
18 ⅞ × 13 in. (48 × 33 cm) unframed
Courtesy of Mendes Wood DM, São Paulo,
Brussels, New York

58 Rosana Paulino
A geometria à brasileira chega ao paraíso tropical
Brazilian-Style Geometry Arrives in
Tropical Paradise
2018
Inkjet print, collage, and monotype on paper
18 ⅞ × 13 in. (48 × 33 cm) unframed
Courtesy of Mendes Wood DM, São Paulo,
Brussels, New York

59 Rosana Paulino
Sem título, da série *Jatobá*
Untitled, from the series Jatobá
2019
Watercolor and graphite on paper
25 9/16 × 19 11/16 in. (65 × 50 cm) framed
Collection of Fairfax Dorn, New York

60 Rosana Paulino
Sem título, da série *Jatobá*
Untitled, from the series Jatobá
2019
Watercolor and graphite on paper
25 9/16 × 19 11/16 in. (65 × 50 cm) framed
Collection of Fairfax Dorn, New York

61 Rosana Paulino
Búfala e senhora das plantas
Buffalo and Lady of Plants
2021
Offset artist book
11 ¼ × 8 ⅞ × ⅜ in. (28.6 × 22.5 × 0.9 cm)
Benson Latin American Collection,
The University of Texas at Austin

62 Sallisa Rosa
Resistência
Resistance
2017–present
Inkjet prints on paper, wheat paste
Dimensions variable
Courtesy of the artist

63 Sallisa Rosa
Sem título, da série *Lembranças*
Untitled, from the series Keepsakes
2021
Ink on paper
11 11/16 × 8 ¼ in. (29.7 × 21 cm)
Courtesy of the artist

64 Sallisa Rosa
Sem título, da série *Lembranças*
Untitled, from the series Keepsakes
2021
Ink on paper
11 11/16 × 8 ¼ in. (29.7 × 21 cm)
Courtesy of the artist

65 Sallisa Rosa
Sem título, da série *Lembranças*
Untitled, from the series Keepsakes
2021
Ink on paper
11 11/16 × 8 ¼ in. (29.7 × 21 cm)
Courtesy of the artist

66 Sallisa Rosa
Sem título, da série *Lembranças*
Untitled, from the series Keepsakes
2021
Ink on paper
11 11/16 × 8 ¼ in. (29.7 × 21 cm)
Collection of Antonio C. La Pastina and
Dale A. Rice, College Station

67 Sallisa Rosa
Sem título, da série *Lembranças*
Untitled, from the series Keepsakes
2021
Ink on paper
11 11/16 × 8 ¼ in. (29.7 × 21 cm)
Collection of Antonio C. La Pastina and
Dale E. Rice, College Station

Acknowledgments

This project owes its existence to the assistance and collaboration of many individuals and institutions. First, we are indebted to each of the artists in the exhibition, whose contributions to global and local conversations about art and activism are still beginning to be understood. Denilson Baniwa, Castiel Vitorino Brasileiro, Guerreiro do Divino Amor, Jaime Lauriano, Maré de Matos, Aline Motta, Lais Myrrha, Antonio Obá, Rosana Paulino, and Sallisa Rosa, we are deeply grateful for your trust, care, time, commitment to your work and the work of others, and collaboration at every step of this multilayered endeavor, made all the more remarkable because the exhibition's research and planning occurred during the COVID-19 pandemic.

Museums and individuals made essential loans. At the Pinacoteca do Estado de São Paulo, we are profoundly grateful to Jochen Volz, Valéria Piccoli, Fernanda Pitta, Teodora Carneiro, Gabriela Pessoa de Oliveira, Rafael Guarda Laterza, Priscila Alegre, and Tatiana Russo dos Reis, as well as their colleagues at the Unidade de Preservação do Patrimônio Museológico and the Secretaria de Cultura e Economia Criativa do Estado de São Paulo, for their tremendous collegiality, expertise, and determination in making possible three major loans from their institution's landmark collection. Very special thanks for key loans are due to Julieta González, Bruna Oliveira, Paulo Rodrigues, and André Chaves at the Instituto Inhotim, Brumadinho, Minas Gerais; Luiz Camillo Osorio and Patrícia Bello at the Instituto PIPA, Rio de Janeiro; Simone Wicha, Vanessa K. Davidson, Cassandra Smith, and Meredith Sutton at the Blanton Museum of Art, University of Texas at Austin; and Lisa Boucher, Non-vertebrate Paleontology Lab, Jackson School Museum of Earth History, UT Austin.

We warmly thank Francisco Cestero, Fairfax Dorn, Antonio C. La Pastina and Dale A. Rice, Lorraine Leu, Yudi Rafael, Júlia Rebouças, and Fábio Tremonte for parting with beloved works, with special gratitude to Antonio and Dale for welcoming us to your home, preparing such a delicious meal, and above all for the pioneering support you have given contemporary art, of Brazil and beyond, in Central Texas—the art scene and stories that art institutions can tell here would not be the same without your vision and generosity. Essential loans were made possible by the leadership and staff of galleries: Eduardo Leme and Tathiane Oberleitner at Galeria Leme, São Paulo; Hena Lee and Thalyssa Araújo at Galeria Millan, São Paulo; and Matthew Wood, Renato Silva, Nancy Natalia Brown, Stephanie Lucchese, Melissa Ganaha, Rafaella Tamm, Taciana Birman, and Viviana Bejarano at Mendes Wood DM, São Paulo, Brussels, and New York. The opportunity to study artworks at Mendes Wood DM in New York when travel to Brazil was prohibited because of the COVID-19 pandemic was fundamental to our research.

Rosana Paulino was a touchstone for us from the very inception of this project, and we thank her and her entire studio, including Caio Carpinelli and Irana Gaia, for their essential collaboration and guidance along the way. Likewise, we would like to thank Rafaela Campos in Denilson Baniwa's studio for her dedicated support and Giulia Bravo for her collaboration in the design of Castiel Vitorino Brasileiro's installation. We also express gratitude to other individuals who provided essential assistance with loans and other matters: Stephanie Alvarado, Letícia Becker Savastano, Jonathan Mergele, and Molly Rindfuss.

We gratefully acknowledge Ana Gonçalves Magalhães and her colleagues, including Ana Maria Antunes Farinha, at the Museu de Arte Contemporânea da Universidade de São Paulo. Although financial constraints ultimately prevented the exhibition from traveling to MAC-USP, we appreciate their collaboration and collegiality: the exhibition and its catalogue benefited from our dialogue.

Specialists and scholars at UT Austin and beyond gave generously of their time, expertise, and encouragement. We give our sincere thanks to Beverly Adams, Ana Avelar, Paul Bonin-Rodriguez, Roberto Conduru, Vivian A. Crockett, Vanessa K. Davidson, Patience Epps, Seth Garfield, James N. Green, Wendy Hunter, Abigail Lapin Dardashti, Lorraine Leu, Diane Lima, D Ryan Lynch, Luiz Camillo Osorio, Sônia Roncador, Lúcia Sá, Igor Simões, and Christen A. Smith.

The advice of these scholars, including Camillo's incisive guidance at the project's early stage, as well as group and individual discussions with them were essential to the conceptualization, planning, and execution of the exhibition and its catalogue and programs. Several scholars shared their expertise with UT and Austin audiences in public programs; these included Vivian and Abigail virtually, and Roberto, Diane, Camillo, and Christen in person.

For their generous sponsorship of the exhibition, we are tremendously grateful to Rachel Bers and James Bewley at the Andy Warhol Foundation for the Visual Arts; Diane and Bruce Halle, Kim Miller, and Jared Leslie at the Diane and Bruce Halle Foundation; Shannon and Mark Hart and Janet Evans; Khib Kugler at the Jedel Family Foundation; Geoffrey Raynor, Bethany Cale, and Spencer Meeks at Once Upon a Time . . . ; Judy and Charles Tate; Deborah Dupré and Richard Rothberg; Kathleen Irvin Loughlin and Chris Loughlin; and the VAC Circle. Special thanks are due to Daniel Guilarducci Lopes, diplomat with the Brazilian Ministry of Foreign Affairs, and Ambassador Maria Izabel Vieira of the Brazilian Consulate in Houston for the assistance and encouragement they provided in obtaining funding for this publication from the Instituto Guimarães Rosa. This publication would not have been possible without the support of the Andy Warhol Foundation for the Visual Arts; the Instituto Guimarães Rosa; Mendes Wood DM in São Paulo, Brussels, and New York; Nara Roesler in New York, Rio de Janeiro, and São Paulo; and Allison and David Ayers; and we extend our deep gratitude to them, to Renato Silva at Mendes Wood DM, and to Daniel Roesler, Luis Pérez-Oramas, and Camila Bechelany with Nara Roesler. Tracy Mann envisioned a wonderful closing event for Brazilians attending SXSW 2023 and secured the support of Invest SP. At UT Austin, we gratefully acknowledge the support of the exhibition and its publication from the Center for Latin American Visual Studies (CLAVIS), the Center for Women's and Gender Studies (CWGS), Jackson School of Geosciences, the LLILAS Brazil Center, the Meredith and Cornelia Long Chair in Art and Art History, the Office of the Dean, College of Fine Arts (COFA), the Office of the Vice President for Research, Scholarship, and Creative Endeavors, and Texas Global. We also thank Sonia Feigenbaum, senior vice provost for global engagement; Dan Jaffe, vice president for research, and Jennifer Lyon Gardner, deputy vice president for research; Ramón H. Rivera-Servera, dean, and Raquel Monroe, associate dean of graduate education and academic affairs of COFA; David Mohrig, associate dean for research, Jackson School of Geosciences; Susan Rather, chair of the Department of Art and Art History; George Flaherty, director of CLAVIS; Marcelo Paixão, director of the Brazil Center; and Christen A. Smith, director of CWGS.

The preparation of the exhibition, its public programming, and its publication has drawn on the resources of many units at UT Austin. Our foremost thanks go to Ramón H. Rivera-Servera, dean of the College of Fine Arts, who, despite the pressures of a demanding schedule in a new role, provided unflagging support from the moment he joined UT Austin in 2021. Linda Shaunessy, business contracts administrator; Cynthia O. Akatugba, assistant vice president for legal affairs; their colleagues; the Office of the President at UT Austin; and the Board of Regents and Office of the Chancellor of the University of Texas System were instrumental in facilitating the loans from the Pinacoteca. Kayla Dryden, research development officer for Arts and Humanities, and Bob McGarrett, program director in the Office of the Vice President for Research, Scholarship, and Creative Endeavors have been essential advocates and crucial to the accomplishment of this exhibition. Alex Christiansen and Sean Redmond in Foundation Relations, Laura Caloudas and Lena Suk at Texas Global, Leslie Martinez in the Office of Sponsored Projects, and Erik Cabrera, Karli Capps, Murphy Crain, Kevin Crook, Lauren Cunningham, Alicia Dietrich, Gina Hollis, Joseph Jernejcic, Sondra Lomax, Trey Mitchell, Raquel Monroe, Alex Scull, Richard Stimpert, Jackie Tamayo, and Cami Yates in the College of Fine Arts have extended key and often extraordinary support. We also warmly thank Douglas Dempster, former dean of the College of Fine Arts, for his support at this project's inception.

We have counted on the steadfast and creative cooperation of many individuals at archives, institutes, libraries, and museums across UT Austin. Carla O. Alvarez, Liz Garza, Melissa Guy, Adrian Johnson, D Ryan Lynch, and Rachel E. Winston at the Benson Latin American Collection, and Paloma Diaz, Seth Garfield, Marcelo Paixão, Adela Pineda Franco, Sônia Roncador, and Susanna Sharpe at the Lozano Long Institute of Latin American Studies (LLILAS) and its Brazil Center were indispensable partners in this project's planning, research, and public programming. This exhibition would not have been possible without the exceptional intellectual community fostered by LLILAS Benson Latin American Studies and Collections; the thriving nexus of scholars, specialists, and students focused on Brazilian Studies; a Mellon Faculty Research Grant from LLILAS to Adele Nelson at a crucial moment; and Brazil Center support for the exhibition's programs. Cherise Smith and Phillip Townsend at Art Galleries at Black Studies; Lorraine Leu, Rachel E. Winston, and the Archiving Black América initiative at LLILAS Benson; and Christen A. Smith of the Center for Women's and Gender Studies were not only creative partners in the public programming of the exhibition but also intellectual interlocutors whose thinking and leadership in Black Studies at UT Austin crucially shaped this project. Luis E. Cárcamo-Huechante of the Program in Native American and Indigenous Studies (NAIS) helped us shape programming featuring Indigenous artist Denilson Baniwa; his guidance, and the curricular innovation of the NAIS program, also importantly shaped this endeavor. Neville Hoad at the Rapoport Center for Human Rights and Justice, Fernando Luiz Lara in the School of Architecture, Samantha Pinto and Pauline Strong at the Humanities Institute, and Jeff Chipps Smith at the Art History Lecture Series in the Department of Art and Art History were key partners in public programming. We give our appreciation to individuals at these and other units that provided vital assistance: Ashley Berry, Melissa Biggs, Anna Gallio, Caroline Hahn, Patricia Heisler, Josette Lehman, Joy Scanlon, Mallary Tenore, and Jill Velez.

Tracy Bonfitto and Rachel Mochon at the Harry Ransom Center generously shared their insights on technical questions regarding works on paper. Cassandra Smith at the Blanton Museum of Art shared her unparalleled expertise on international loans, and discussions with Florencia Bazzano, Holly Borham, Vanessa K. Davidson, Claire Howard, and Veronica Roberts and study of works in their collection enriched and sustained our thinking as this project developed.

The exhibition was activated during its six-month run at the VAC thanks to many across campus. We give our profound thanks to the UT instructors who brought their classes to the exhibition while on view and from whom we learned a tremendous amount. They are too numerous to list, but in particular let us thank Eugenio Y. Arima, Pam Arnold, Alexander Birchler, Paul Bonin-Rodriguez, Denise Braz, Michael Charlesworth, Erin Cunningham, Patricia Epps, Enrique Figueredo, Scherezade García, Julia Guernsey, Donalyn Heise, Teresa Hubbard, Lindsey Jamieson, Yuliya Lanina, Janice Leoshko, Lorraine Leu, Eric McMaster, Marcelo Paixão, Margo Sawyer, Jeff Williams, Jennifer Wilson, and Pilar Zazueta. We also thank Pam Arnold, Christina Bain, Donalyn Heise, Pam Reyes, Dawn Stienecker, and Art Education undergraduate and graduate students for the innovative Family Day they conceived and helped to realize at the VAC during the exhibition. *Social Fabric* has been enriched beyond those already named by conversations with artists, scholars, and specialists, including Carla Acevedo-Yates, Nicole Awai, Allison Ayers, Eddie Chambers, C. Ondine Chavoya, Laura Copelin, Christopher Crozier, Aglaíze Damasceno, Esther Gabara, Gris García, Verónica Gerber Bicecci, Fabiola Iza, Dária Jaremtchuk, Jennifer Josten, Harper Montgomery, Daisy Nam, Cassandra Nollmann, Ann Reynolds, Matthew H. Robb, Roxanne Schroeder-Arce, Rob Storr, and Edward Sullivan.

We relied on the expertise and skills of numerous individuals to realize this exhibition. First is Jacqueline Cabrera, who served as the unflappable and deeply knowledgeable project registrar and guided the project with resourcefulness and good judgment. Antonio Madrid and Jim Hallock of Native Earth Block expertly realized the brick structure in Castiel Vitorino Brasileiro's installation and the rammed-earth pedestals for Jaime Lauriano's sculptures. We are indebted to Ty Kasey and his team at UT Landscape Services for providing expertise on and many of the materials for Castiel's installation. We also wish to thank framers Laura Caffrey and Jody Arthur Mercado (Fine Arts Services) and Ryan Huseman (East Side Picture Framing); mount maker John Maisano; and fine art printer Kat Paez (Miller Imaging and Digital Solutions). Additionally, event planner Anoush Crane; caterer Zach Knight (Tivity); and interpreters Steven Mines, Annette Candanedo, and Corrie Ault (Interpret Language Services) as well as Art Quality, Compu Signs, Eriksen Translations, Holland Photo Imaging, Masterpiece, and McCarthy Print went above and beyond in making the exhibition and its events and programs possible.

This catalogue would not have been possible without the excellent guidance and stewardship of Gretchen Otto at Motto Publishing Services and the enthusiasm of Robert Kimzey at the University of Texas Press. We also warmly thank M.Wright for the lovely design, Alison Rainey for detailed copyediting, Christine Gever for sharp proofreading, and Kerry Webb at UT Press for her early interest in the project. Libby Hruska shared her expert and sensitive feedback on drafts of the introduction and Adele's essay.

We are greatly indebted to the authors who contributed to this catalogue, including Lorraine Leu and Rosana Paulino, who allowed us to reprint their insightful conversation; Castiel Vitorino Brasileiro and Aline Motta, who shared their time and insights in the beautiful interviews with Maria Emilia Fernandez; Denilson Baniwa, Castiel, and Maré de Matos, who worked with us to realize trilingual translations of their texts for the exhibition; and the current and former graduate students who wrote new, rigorous, and thoughtful texts on each artist and the sociogram.

For research and translation assistance at various stages of the project and the realization of its pedagogical components online and in the exhibition, Adele and MacKenzie warmly thank Kendall Ayers, Regina Balmaceda, Taylor Bradley, Eva Caston, Catalina Cherñavvsky Sequeira, Isabella (Bella) Ditzler, Maria Emilia Fernandez, Thiago Ferreira, Devon Gerstenhaber, Maysa Martins, Sean McPherson, and Nicole Smythe-Johnson. We are thankful for the participation of the students who contributed their research and insights in Adele's seminars in 2019, 2020, and 2022, including Chasitie Brown, Laurel Brown, Martha Scott Burton, Sara Carrillo, Eva Caston, Catalina Cherñavvsky Sequeira, Thiago Ferreira, Devon Gerstenhaber, Jana La Brasca, Izzy Lee, Darren Longman, Victoria McCausland, Sean McPherson, Alexandra Mendez, Aja Edwin Mujinga, Caitlin O'Beirne, Lucy Quezada, Karina Salcido, Jennifer Sales, Marina Schneider, Nicole Smythe-Johnson, Grace Sparapani, Alejandra Valdez Carrasco, and André Vechi.

The main burden of this project has fallen on the Department of Art and Art History and on the VAC. We gratefully acknowledge the leadership of department chair Susan Rather, who provided wise counsel at myriad moments, including when problems inevitably arose, and very generously supported this publication. We give our heartfelt thanks to Anita Bennett, Brittny Johnson, and Theron Smith as well as to former colleagues Michelle Harper, Amy Hauft, Lauren MacKnight, Jack Risley, Clare Thoman, and most especially Jill Velez, who facilitated the appointment of Adele's research assistants and was instrumental in the ambitious public programs during the research and on-view stages of the exhibition and whose administrative acumen and collegiality cannot be overstated. Designer Hunter Thomas, whose responsibilities span the department and the VAC, was a true partner in the realization of this exhibition, from creatively collaborating in the design of the sociogram and its realization as a wall-scale didactic and illustration in this publication to producing a banner, a rear projection, and myriad posters and printed matter and patiently fine-tuning the presentation of multilingual labels and takeaways. Public affairs coordinator Jennifer Irving joined UT Austin just as we were about to the install the exhibition and quickly became a trusted partner in the promotion of *Social Fabric*. Clare Donnelly, former manager of Exhibitions and Programs, expertly managed loan agreements and reams of correspondence while developing a thoughtful pedagogical exercise that was an essential interactive component of the exhibition. Kate Joly, whose good humor is matched only by her administrative savvy, managed with aplomb the complex processes of UT Austin and an international loan exhibition.

Chief preparator Marc Silva took on this at times logistically challenging exhibition involving numerous international and domestic loans, multiple new commissions, and every possible media with a quiet determination, laser-sharp and vast skill sets, and uncompromising commitment to craftsmanship. Os nossos mais sinceros agradecimentos. Adrian Aguilera, assistant preparator, supported every aspect of the installation and lent his expertise to Guerreiro do Divino Amor; Rachael Starbuck, preparator and gallery coordinator, was a joyful, dedicated collaborator; and Zoe Berg brought her exceptional knowledge of video to the installation's planning and execution. We profoundly thank them, Mark Kovitya, Kerry Maguire, Kaya Halil Sümer, and Ariel Wood for their beautiful work.

Neither the exhibition nor its catalogue would have existed if not for Maria Emilia Fernandez, who joined the project when she was pursuing a master's degree in art history and moved from research assistant to the exhibition's assistant curator and, after earning her degree, to assistant curator of the VAC. Her intellectual curiosity, extraordinary intelligence and foresight, linguistic abilities, and coolheaded yet always kind and organized approach to each facet of the project were a marvel to witness.

MacKenzie is indebted to Adele and to Maria Emilia for being such incredibly thoughtful and insightful collaborators. Over the long runway of this project, I have learned so much from both of them, especially from their commitment to scholarship, to learning, and to artists. I am in awe of their generosity and the care they give to their work. My husband, Gavin Stevens, encouraged me every step of the way and is loving, patient, and supportive. And my children, Eleanor and Aden Stevens, always ask the hard questions, and for that I am grateful.

Adele would like to wholeheartedly thank MacKenzie and Maria Emilia for embarking on the adventure of this exhibition with her—it has been a wild, learning-filled, nail-biting, and joyful ride. My friends and family, including Amanda Ellis, Aubrey Ellman, Sophie Gibson, Jennifer Kane, Nan Nelson, and Perry Nelson, provided support and wise perspective. Scott Campbell has been, as always, a compassionate and giving spouse and coparent as I took on yet another out-over-my-skis professional project. Thank you, and the magical Arthur and Evelyn, for your patience with my long hours—you have all my love.

Maria Emilia would like to thank the co-curators of this exhibition for the opportunity to work and learn alongside them and for their mentorship, trust, and generosity in all aspects, both personal and professional. She is also thankful for the unwavering support of her family, to Jose Enrique Fernandez, Juan Pablo Fernandez, and Maria Eugenia Nadurille, who often play the role of thinking partners, editors, and first readers. And to Patrick Stephens, for his love and kind understanding.

Social Fabric: Art and Activism in Contemporary Brazil is made possible by a grant from The Andy Warhol Foundation for the Visual Arts. Lead support is also provided by The Diane & Bruce Halle Foundation; Shannon and Mark Hart; The Jedel Family Foundation; Once Upon a Time . . . ; and Judy and Charles Tate. Additional support provided by the Center for Latin American Visual Studies (CLAVIS); Deborah Dupré and Richard Rothberg; the Irvin–Loughlin Family Fund; the Marsh Family Foundation; Texas Global; and the VAC Circle.

This publication is made possible by a grant from The Andy Warhol Foundation for the Visual Arts. Lead support also provided by the Instituto Guimarães Rosa of the Ministry of Foreign Affairs of Brazil through the Consulate General of Brazil in Houston; Mendes Wood DM, São Paulo, Brussels, New York; and Nara Roesler, New York, Rio de Janeiro, and São Paulo. Additional support provided by Allison and David Ayers and the Center for Latin American Visual Studies (CLAVIS); the Center for Women's and Gender Studies; the Jackson School of Geosciences; the LLILAS Brazil Center; the Meredith and Cornelia Long Chair in Art and Art History; the Office of the Dean, College of Fine Arts; and the Office of the Vice President for Research, Scholarship, and Creative Endeavors at the University of Texas at Austin.

Operations and programs at the Visual Arts Center are made possible by support from the Curtis R. and Carol O. Kayem Endowment for the Visual Arts Center; the Visual Arts Center Endowment; the VAC Artist-in-Residence Endowed Fund; the Department of Art and Art History; and the Office of the Dean, College of Fine Arts, UT Austin.

Visual Arts Center

The Andy Warhol Foundation for the Visual Arts

IGR
Instituto Guimarães Rosa

CONSULATE GENERAL OF
BRAZIL
HOUSTON

PHOTOGRAPHY

All installation images from *Social Fabric: Art and Activism in Contemporary Brazil*, Visual Arts Center, UT Austin. Unless otherwise noted, images courtesy of the artist.

Blanton Museum of Art: plate 29.

© Alexander Boeschenstein: cover image; pages 80, 82–83, 84 (top), 85–92, 93 (top), 94–95, 97, 99–103; plates 2, 5, 10–11, 16, 19, 34–35, 37–38, 50–51, 61.

© Sandy Carson: pages ii, 10, 84 (bottom), 93 (bottom), 96, 98, 107, 134; plates 7, 62.

Galeria Leme: plate 13, photo: Filipe Berndt.

© Geyson Magno: page 131.

Instituto PIPA, Rio de Janeiro, Brazil: plates 14–15.

Mendes Wood DM, São Paulo, Brussels, New York: pages 5, 122–123, 125, 126: photo Isabella Matheus, 137; plates 44–49, 52–53, 55–60.

Pinacoteca do Estado de São Paulo, São Paulo: pages 6, 112; plates 12, 54, photo: Isabella Matheus.

Stanford Libraries, David Rumsey Map Center: page 113.

Hunter Thomas: page 133, foldout insert after page 104.

COLLEGE OF FINE ARTS

Ramón H. Rivera-Servera
Dean and Professor in the College of Fine Arts,
Effie Marie Cain Regents Chair in Fine Arts

DEPARTMENT OF ART AND ART HISTORY

Anita Bennett
Executive Assistant

Jennifer Irving
Public Affairs Coordinator,
Department of Art and Art History and Visual Arts Center

Brittny Johnson
Accounting Lead

Tawnya Palmquist
Administrative Associate

Susan Rather
Department Chair and Professor of Art History,
Cornelia and Meredith Long Chair in Art and Art History

Theron Smith
Assistant Operations Manager

Hunter Thomas
Senior Graphic Designer,
Department of Art and Art History and Visual Arts Center

VISUAL ARTS CENTER

Adrian Aguilera
Assistant Preparator

Maria Emilia Fernandez
Assistant Curator

Kate Joly
Administrative Associate

Marc Silva
Chief Preparator

Rachael Starbuck
Gallery Coordinator

MacKenzie Stevens
Director and Curator

Project Preparators
Zoe Berg
Mark Kovitya
Kerry Maguire
Kaya Halil Sümer
Ariel Wood

Project Registrar
Jacqueline Cabrera

Project Research Assistants
Eva Caston
Catalina Cherñavvsky Sequeira
Maria Emilia Fernandez
Thiago Ferreira
Maysa Martins

Curatorial Fellows
Taylor Bradley (2018–2019)
Devon Gerstenhaber (2021–2022)
Nicole Smythe-Johnson (2022–2023)

Curatorial Interns
Kendall Ayers (2021)
Regina Balmaceda (2021–2022)
Isabella Ditzler (2022–2023)

Gallery Attendants (2022–2023)
Antje Idsellis Arthur
Gabriel Casanova
Ethany Castillo
Ye Ji (Jinnie) Jung
Grace Lee
Mathew McIntyre

VAC Founding Donors
Curtis R. and Carol O. Kayem
Ollabelle and Gary Hall
Anne Scott Ebert
Charlene Cline Marsh
Ann S. Butler
Robin and Trey Hancock
Alma C. Madden
Allison and David Ayers
Carla and Kelly Thompson
Sara and Robert Hallam
Margaret Wilson Reckling
Mary Crouch

VAC Circle
Allison Ayers
Deborah Dupre
Andee Friedrich
Amanda Kadinov
Sarah Kitchen
Kathleen Irvin Loughlin
C. C. Marsh
Lynsey Provost
Robyn Siegel
Charlie Tames
Anna Wulfe
Mary Frances Young